A World
Abandoned by God

A World Abandoned by God

Narrative and Secularism

Susanna Lee

Lewisburg
Bucknell University Press

Associated University Presses
2010 Eastpark Boulevard
Cranbury, NJ 08512

The paper used in this publication meets the requirements of the American National Standard for Permanence of Paper for Printed Library Materials. Z39.48-1984.

Library of Congress Cataloging-in-Publication Data

Lee, Susanna, 1970–
  A world abandoned by God : narrative and secularism / Susanna Lee.
      p.   cm.
  Navigating the secular world — Flaubert's superior joke — Faith in realism — The joy of mystification — The narrator who knew too much.
  Includes bibliographical references and index.
  ISBN 0-8387-5609-3 (alk. paper)
  1. French fiction—19th century—History and criticism.   2. Russian fiction—19th century—History and criticism.   3. Secularism in literature.   4. Religion and literature.   I. Title.
PQ653.L44   2006
843'.709382—dc22   2005012254

Contents

5

Acknowledgments

I AM GRATEFUL TO MANY FRIENDS AND COLLEAGUES FOR THE SUPPORT AND guidance they gave me during this project.

The following people read all or portions of the manuscript and offered superb advice and encouragement: Susann Cokal, Florence Dore, Edwin Duval, Svetlana Grenier, Philipe Hamon, Robert Louis Jackson, Patrick Laude, Olga Meerson, Barbara Mujica, Gerald Prince, Debarati Sanyal. Thanks to Penny Burt, who provided crucial help with Russian translations, to John McKay for pointing me in the direction of *Demons* in the summer of 2001, and to Robert Louis Jackson, whose excellent graduate course on Turgenev led both directly and indirectly to the present work. I am particularly grateful to Marianna Lee, whose ministrations helped the prose of this book immensely, and to Jared Stark, whose thoughtful suggestions have long (and especially recently) been enormously valuable. Last but not least, my heartfelt thanks to Peter Brooks, whose guidance and support have been crucially important over the years.

Georgetown University's generosity, in the form of two consecutive summer grants and a junior research leave, was instrumental in enabling me to complete this book. I am grateful also to the following people at Bucknell University Press and AUP: Greg Clingham, Christine Retz, and, for her attentive copyediting, Cathy Slovensky.

I could not have completed this project without the encouragement of my friends and family. Masha Belenky, Jeremy Billetdeaux, Susann Cokal, Roger Donahue, Angie Graham, Cynthia Hobbs, Marie-Chantal Killeen, Peter Kok, Betsy Konrad, Sandra Lee, Elizabeth Letcher, Katie MacKaye, Brian Pope, Kirsten Singleton, Andrew Sobanet, and Georges Steiner cheered me on in all weather. Chapter 5 unquestionably owes its existence to the generosity and hospitality of Michele and Lily Von Stein. Many thanks to them. And my deepest gratitude to Denis Crean, for his optimism and his love.

And finally, for their inspiration, love, and support, I thank my parents: Marianna Lee, Edward Lee, and Kathryn Shevelow. This book is dedicated to them.

A World
Abandoned by God

Introduction

> The novel is the epic of a world that has been abandoned by God.
>
> —Georg Lukács, *The Theory of the Novel*

> There is something about narrative that puts the world in doubt.
>
> —James Wood, *The Broken Estate*

THE IDEA OF A GOD, IN ONE FORM OR ANOTHER, IS A FUNDAMENTAL PART of human experience—a given, almost. And yet, for over one hundred and fifty years, we have lived in a world that has become increasingly secular. The goal of this book is to reconcile these facts, or rather to examine their interaction and, in so doing, to understand the idea and the experience of secularism.

The book does not offer a broad history of secularization or secular culture, nor does it analyze exhaustively the particular social, economic, and political systems that have been associated with secularism. Rather, it examines secularism as an idea and an impression and, what is more, as an idea especially clearly articulated through the novel form. Georg Lukács's assertion that the novel is the epic of a world abandoned by God does not mean that God abandoned the world, leaving human beings to recount that abandonment through the novel. Instead, God's abandonment is built into and out of the very structure of the novel. Rather than a secular culture producing the novel form, or the novel form initiating the idea of a secular culture, the two stand in a synergistic relation to one another. Thus the departure of God becomes the formal substance and undertone of the novel, and the novel in turn informs our understanding of secularism and its crises, uncertainties, and potentials.

Especially in nineteenth-century Europe, secularism was an idea in motion, formed, disseminated, and received both with bursts of creativity and with gloom. It was seen as a code for intellectual clarity and for spiritual emptiness, sometimes for both at once. It was also

11

considered as a philosophical condition, a view of a world in need
of, or open to, a different narrative. European literary criticism of
that century generally reads secularism as a condition of absence or
loss—the emotional equivalent, as it were, of postmodern antifoun-
dationalism. As J. Hillis Miller writes in the introduction to *The Disappearance of God,* "The lines of connection between us and God
have broken down, or God himself has slipped away from the places
where he used to be. He no longer inheres in the world as the force
binding together all men and all things. Only if God would return
or if we could somehow reach him might our broken world be uni-
fied again. But this has not yet happened. God keeps himself hidden. There seems to be no way to re-establish connection."[1]

In this formulation, the departure of God from the landscape
means the departure of a spiritual force and a spiritual cement: a
force to which (or to whom) we connect and that connects us to one
another. In narrative terms, this God is author and embodiment of
coherence and of meaning: the power that engenders incidents and
connects them. Given the absence of such a power, it is not surprising that the secular world would stand in need of the mourning
function of poetry (Miller) and the distinctly reparative function of
narrative (Lukács, Brooks, and others).[2]

Despite critical assessments such as these, however, secularism is
not a random spiritual disaster, not a cosmic accident, but a human
creation. There was no single morning when the world woke up,
sensed a curious absence, and understood that God had departed.
Instead, secularism developed as an impression and an idea—an
idea that was introduced and absorbed into European culture for
numerous reasons. If the secular world were nothing but a series of
abandonments, nothing but the vale of tears described by Miller,
then it could not have taken root. The notion of a secular world became so thoroughly incorporated into modern thought because it
held considerable attraction, and here we come to a point that is
crucial for narrative and other acts of human ingenuity: the elimination of God from master narratives—indeed, the elimination of master narratives entirely—constitutes not simply a menace but also a
significant series of opportunities. The notion of a God who controls
the entire world, who inscribes all people and all moments in a narrative of divine providence or of divine punishment and reward,
leaves no space for human manipulation and no room for individual
accomplishment as we have come to understand it in the modern
era. Secularism and attendant philosophies such as capitalism prom-

ise a way to be exceptional—to expand the boundaries and indeed the very quality and volume of self.

Although this book does not propose a complete philosophical analysis of secular modernity, any examination of secularism as narrative structure, or secularism as idea, demands some mention of the idea and ideologies of modernity. Fredric Jameson, in the recent *A Singular Modernity*, writes, "Modernity is not a concept, philosophical or otherwise, but a narrative category."[3] It is also a narrative impulse, or a ground on which narrative can be deployed. François Lyotard writes in *The Postmodern Condition*: "A collectivity that takes narrative as its key form of competence has no need to remember its past. It finds the raw material for its social bond not only in the meaning of the narratives it recounts, but also in the act of reciting them. The narratives' reference may seem to belong to the past, but in reality it is always contemporaneous with the act of recitation."[4] If modernity constitutes and legitimates itself through the recitation of narrative, meta or not, secularism is both the moment of emptiness that precedes that recitation and the consciousness that lends it authority. Indeed, in this sense, secularism, the sense of a present more practiced and at the same time more jaded than the past by narrative formulations, aligns with postmodernism. Lyotard of course described postmodernism as "incredulity toward metanarratives."[5] Secularism resides in that space between pleasure in narrative and distrust in narrative, between a vision of narrative as legitimating, and narrative as manipulative and retrograde. In this book, I am concerned with secularism—the idea of the absence of a supreme structuring power—as a cornerstone both of modern epistemological models and of social and political power relations; in this sense, I would propose a secular unconscious as corollary to the "political unconscious" described by Jameson.[6] This study thus comes in line with those critics who envisioned fundamentally theological or spiritual stakes of modernity, and who saw the novel both as arena for and chronicle of them. Mikhail Bakhtin, one such critic, saw in the dialogism of the novel a departure from the (absolutist) ideologies of monologism.[7] Walter Benjamin (in contrast to Lyotard) sees the novel as connected to the "secular productive forces of history" and to the decline of storytelling and the human interaction it represents,[8] while for Paul Ricoeur, "What is ultimately at stake in the case of the structural identity of the narrative function as well as in that of the truth claim of every narrative work, is the temporal character of human experience."[9]

The desire to live in an ordered world and the desire to determine the order of that world clash explosively and thus guarantee the paradoxical nature of what we understand as secularism. Tension between these desires brings out the extremes of human behavior, fantasy, narrative, and political production.[10] These extremes, these crises, can be best read through narrative and, more particularly, through the narrator-character relationship. Through that relationship, we see how individuals view the world around them, how they see their role in their own destinies, as well as how they treat each other, and on the basis of what spiritual axioms. We also observe individual fantasies about God and supreme power, whether those are fantasies of replacement and incarnation or fantasies of being cared and provided for. We see too how those various fantasies can be used or exploited: that is, how the name of God or the possibility of spiritual solace is wielded as a discursive instrument, in narrative production and in political manipulation. The narrator-character relationship, in other words, reveals fundamental ideological structures that subtend modern power systems and ideas about spiritual connection.

In considering secularism as a narrative structure, even a narrative strategy, I will also explore the role of secularism in political manipulation. I want to propose that there is much to be gained in authorial power by declaring not only the advent of the secular world but, even more, by declaring that advent to be a problem for humankind. There is also much to be gained in political and personal power by declaring the imminence of such a world, and it is just this junction of the authorial and the political that is central to this book.

The more disorder is present and dangerous, the easier it is for the reparative hand of the author to peddle his product. James Wood writes: "Fiction was always fictional, it was not in the same order of truth as the Gospel narratives. During the nineteenth century, these two positions began to soften and merge."[11] Much as the dissolution of Gospel truths made possible the elevated status of narrative, it is the imminence of disorder that necessitates the reparative hand of the politician. Generations of monarchs and tsars used the same discursive principle as the novelists: in a world abandoned by God, or more precisely in a world about to be abandoned by God, the leader who perceives and promises to impede that abandonment cuts an irresistible figure. The menace of secularism is thus an important component of narrative and political "emplotment" as

Hayden White describes it.[12] It enables both leader and author to profit by the threat of a looming disorder to create a sense of emptiness and need; indeed, the absence of God has proven as versatile an instrument of manipulation and political control as the presence of God had been.[13]

Both aspects of secularism—as menace and as open door—demand that the idea of it remain in a state of becoming. Throughout the transition to a nonreligious culture, some sense of the divine must remain intact. There must be some familiarity with transcendent order so that the author or politician can claim the power and the value that derive from spiritual connection. If not, the fundamental theoretical binarisms on which political dominance is based (the one who knows versus the one who does not, the one with total power versus the one with limited power, great versus small, true versus false) lose their reason for being. Some remnant of structure must be in place for the politician to come across as a spiritual leader rather than a loose cannon in a chaotic world—and for there to be some recognizable order for the leader to maintain, some truth for the philosopher to access.

The novel's special role in the study of literature is both intriguing and worthwhile because of its disclosure of fundamental ideas, desires, and modes of conduct that the world outside literature has numerous reasons for, and numerous means of, concealing. A politician who claims that the nation needs to focus on God and traditional religious values, for instance, can hardly announce that the very specter of secular disorder that he claims to despise is simultaneously his ace in the hole, the "problem" that justifies his presence. Similarly, and somewhat paradoxically, a politician who warns his people of another nation's religious fanaticism can hardly proclaim that such a fanaticism, curiously portrayed as a sort of godlessness, is the perfect foil for his own purported spiritual exemplarity. The novel form, by contrast, implies the evolution of secularism through its various and subtle permutations as an idea, as an experience, and as a political instrument. Layering its worlds of action, novelistic construction gives us a framework for reading problems political and philosophical. Indeed, this layering can be rendered and in some sense created only in narrative, be that narrative philosophical, historical, psychological, religious, or fictional. Gary Morson wrote that narrative problems are theological in nature, but it is also true that theological and philosophical problems are narrative, and narratological, in nature.[14] Narratology, in other words, provides a language and a framework for analyzing issues of freedom and spirituality, for which the nineteenth century, in medias res, had no such clear vocabulary.[15] As the basic discourse for modern understandings of self, history, and social relations, narrative is crucial to our conception of both God and individual freedom. For that purpose, as the richest and most varied source of narrative production, the modern novel embodies the most fruitful repertory of ideas about God, meaning, and individual agency. The vocabulary and conceptual structures of narrative criticism, furthermore, can offer invaluable insight into personal and political power structures.

This study examines a number of features distinctive to fictional narrative, such as the narrator's vision of and distance from the characters, the tension between what he or she perceives and what the characters see, the function of chance, logical inconsistency, multiple narrative strands, closure or its absence, the discourses of sacred or scientific order, as well as the narrator's qualms, disclaimers, superstitions, and audacities to the extent they are distinctively expressive of the uncertainties (and opportunities) that emerge in a world without God. These features, the building blocks of narrative theory, provide the vocabulary and the forms with which to illuminate the evolution of ideas that subtend modern sociopolitical climates. Throughout this study, I concentrate primarily on the relationship between character and narrator, or between character and situation. In five novels by French and Russian authors, the characters have a particular vision of the role of sacred order in the world, whether they celebrate it, deny it, or try to circumvent or align themselves with it. And in each, the narrator's vision of the place of sacred order in the world is often different or distinct from that of the characters. These disparities or similarities enact (in a most theatrical sense) the very tensions, disillusions, fantasies, fabrications, political injustices, superstitions, and grandiosities that were benchmarks on the road of secular culture. Through this study, I do not propose that a secular culture produced the novel form, or that the novel form initiated the idea of a secular culture. Rather, much as the evolutions of "modernity" and the novel form fed into and shaped one another, so here do I propose a synergy of secularism and the novel.

The book is divided into five chapters, each of which reads one novel of the nineteenth century as a chronicle or portrait of the transition to a secular culture. The authors and their novels are major representatives both of national novelistic tradition and of the spiritual problematic. The first chapter, "Navigating the Secular World," focuses on Stendhal's *The Red and the Black*. Written in 1830, this novel is the most profoundly skeptical about the ultimate livability of a world without God. Julien Sorel's determination is consistently subverted by the intrusion of other agencies, any of which might represent the epic supernatural, the force of biological destiny, or the random hand of coincidence. Thus the hero inhabits a sort of semisecular limbo, unable either to disengage himself from these intrusions or to engage with them in a way that would give his life spiritual, narrative, ontological coherence. In conveying this limbo, the novel poses two foundational questions about secularism: If we lose hold of the idea of God, what can take its place? And what is at risk and what to be gained? Also at issue is the idea that secularism is a series of conceptual aporia fabricated in the service of narrative production. Secularism in this novel, emanating from an amalgam of disingenuousness and skepticism, opens the door to numerous narratives, including the novel itself. And yet what looms in the doorway epitomizes the arbitrariness and ultimate insufficiency of *all* stories, articulating a substantial ambivalence about first causes, last words, and the very enterprise of narrative production.

The second chapter, "Flaubert's Superior Joke," reads Flaubert's *Madame Bovary* (1857) as a nightmarish enactment of the transition to a secular world. Emma Bovary's dreams of celestial intervention encounter only the ironic, elusive, and rigorously secular hand of the narrator at every turn. The narrator has the last word, but instead of lucidity, he offers a landscape hopeless and dismal. The reader, like Emma, is also to be demoralized, at best confronted with a malicious and vaporous God. But here, God's absence or distance is more than a metaphor for a narrative mode. A distant and contemptuous God, of a world in which secularism ambushes and disillusions and in which dispassionate human authority dominates, is Flaubert's principal thematic and formal concern and, to a large extent, that of French realism in its entirety. When religion is represented as obtuse and secularism as a vacuous hopelessness, the elimination of God from human experience provides a bottomless dramatic source of authorial Schadenfreude.

The third chapter, "Faith in Realism," concentrates on Turgenev's *A Nest of Gentry* (1858), which traces the distinctions and intersections between narrative production as instrument of ideological and political manipulation and as defense mechanism and articulation of faith. Throughout, disingenuous manipulators arbitrarily determine the plot, while the principal characters insist on humble acceptance and faith-driven reconciliation. The narrator isn't sure whether to celebrate or to pity those who continue to dignify the machinations of others in the name of God's will. As he deliberates, he employs a series of tentative narrative gestures that indicate on the one hand a reluctance to wield authorial power and on the other hand a desire to demonstrate, by example, the snares of excessive submissiveness and self-restraint. In some sense, there can be no fools in the hands of a narrator who echoes his characters and refuses recourse to authorial "objectivity." And yet, when affirmation of belief means embracing the most unsacred of deceptions and audacities, religion can become a hindrance, an anachronism unsuited to the modern world.

The fourth chapter, "The Joy of Mystification," returns to France, to Barbey d'Aurevilly's *Bewitched* (1851). The novel paints the transition to a nonreligious culture as spiritual disaster, as cultural and social calamity, even as public health menace. The narrator subverts every component of worldly modern thought. His scientific "elucidations" so reproduce the discourse of possession, magic, and the supernatural that they become almost parodic and useless; the discourse of science, ostensibly a vehicle of nascent secular elucidation, functions as a Trojan horse re-enveloping the modern world with shades of mystery. And yet, in the end, the drama of narrative production becomes the principal focus of the novel, placing human pomposity above religious principle and demonstrating the often disingenuous motives behind the desire to incarnate spiritual understanding. The narrator who laments secularism because it has dismantled a particular social order sometimes discloses more about his own self-importance than about the disorder of the world around him. Such a narrator treads a seductive but ultimately untenable conceptual border: the border between desire for personal grandeur and the desire to have that grandeur enabled and validated through his association with God.

The final chapter, "The Narrator Who Knew Too Much," analyzes Dostoevsky's *Demons*—sometimes translated as *The Possessed* (1872). Here, inconsistencies in narrative distance and situation, sometimes perceived as signs of authorial carelessness, in fact parody human pretense to wield or even understand the hand of God. The chronicler's alternation between reckless authorial machination and scrupulous hesitation embodies both the Westernist political scandal of arbitrary manipulation and power and the literary scandal of false modesty and gratuitous self-reference, implying that the person who proclaims his humble limitations may be as disingenuous and self-serving as the person who strides with enthusiasm into the place of God. In its narrative construction, then, *Demons* represents problems of the intersection between finite and infinite that are fundamental to the political and philosophical substance of the novel. In so doing, it elucidates the crises produced on national and international levels when a mortal proclaims a fusion with God.

Because I am interested in secularism as an impression and an experience rather than in a genealogy of secularism as historical phenomenon, I have chosen novels that articulate a diverse series of responses to that experience. Other nineteenth-century novels could also have performed that function, such as Tolstoy's *War and Peace*, Flaubert's *L'Education sentimentale*, Zola's *La faute de l'abbé Mouret*, or Balzac's *La peau de chagrin*, among others. As the novels considered here are representative without being exhaustive or definitive, so too are the national literatures selected. France and Russia represent two strains of responses to secularism. England, Germany, and Italy could also serve as examples, as could countries outside the Western tradition; the way of reading used here, because it relies on tight correlations between cultural circumstance and narrative construction, is valid for other national literatures and other eras. I have chosen to focus on France and Russia for a number of reasons; these countries anchor the European continent at both ends and were the sites of its most important revolutions. They have rich nineteenth-century realist novelistic traditions and numerous literary, political, social, and artistic connections between them. And yet these cultures remain in stark contrast in their ideas about God, sacred order, fate, and the force of the individual: in its political structures and its philosophical foundations, France welcomed a secular culture much earlier than Russia. The rise of industrialization and discoveries in science, liberalism, Marxism, and anticlericalism, as well as the dismantling of monarchic regimes went hand in hand with a diminishing absolute authority and a corollary loss of a master voice. Nineteenth-century French narrative is inextricably, even enthusiastically, intertwined with this loss. Like the scientist and the philosopher, the novelist *is* one of a multitude of voices that come to stand as replacements for a vanished religious order.

In nineteenth-century Russia, such a substitution, with its accompanying dissolution of master narratives and eventual dominance of the individual voice, elicited a much greater cultural ambivalence.

In Russia, whose respect for, even awe of, an abiding superior force lasted well into the twentieth century and whose serfs were not emancipated until 1861, the authorial voice was never the welcome emblem of individual power that it was in France. Rather, the disappearance of God was an occasion for uneasiness and resistance; the authorial voice sounded an alarm, a warning about individual dominance and its perils. (Even those cultures (or individuals) that renounce the idea of secularism, as it turns out, must contend with it.[16])

As for the historical frame of reference, arguably, the narrative logic of secularism described here is already at work in earlier centuries, in the works of Defoe, Cervantes, and others.[17] The logic of secularism is also at work in the novels of the twentieth century. I have chosen to focus on nineteenth-century Europe because it was then—and there—that the gradual elimination of God from narratives of reason and explanation most demonstrably dovetailed with a momentous alteration in the spiritual, philosophical, and political landscape. With the rearrangement of governments, progress in the realm of science, the advent of the Industrial Revolution, the evolution of capitalist economic systems, loss of ecclesiastical power, an emerging bourgeoisie, the development of cities, and the end of the feudal system, secularism in the nineteenth century is the closest it ever comes to being an actual historical process. And inherent in Nietzsche's "God is Dead" of 1882 is the specter of secularism as a circumstance or situation rather than an epistemological foundation.[18] In fiction of the nineteenth century, secularism emerges as a thematic as well as structural concern; the result is an interaction of form and content that enriches the examination of secularism as experience, idea, crisis, opportunity, and narrative instrument.[19]

Finally, a word about the decision to focus on the novel form. Other forms of representation such as photography, film, and music could also claim a connection with secular culture (indeed, Walter Benjamin posits just such a connection in "The Work of Art in the Age of Mechanical Reproduction" in *Illuminations*). Analyses of these forms as generators/interpreters of secular culture are certainly worthwhile. The decision to concentrate on the novel rather than on other forms of narrative is an attempt to reconcile and restructure other primarily literary analyses of the move toward a secular culture. These studies also accord a particular value and status to the novel as theater, if not blueprint, for the manifestations of social and political power. At the same time, the claims made here regarding novelistic construction are equally valid for other forms of narrative, particularly political addresses, religious sermons, and written histories, for the precise reason that arguments for the political or theological resonance of novelistic construction can only underscore the novelistic resonance of political and theological discourse. While this is a literary study, it is also a study of those discourses and of the many stories we tell ourselves.

The elimination of God from the modern landscape constitutes one of the momentous conceptual metamorphoses in history and stands as a testament to the symbiosis between ideas and experience. In this book, I intend above all to offer an innovative way of reading and of using narratological analysis that can better enable us to understand that metamorphosis—and to read not only the nineteenth-century political scene, but our own as well.

1

Navigating the Secular World

IN 1830, THE QUESTION OF WHAT SORT OF EXPLANATORY NARRATIVES WERE viable or believable was much at the fore of French cultural consciousness. For one, political posturing since the Revolution had compromised the notion of an absolute truth, of a definitive version of how the world is and how it should be. The ideological rationales of the ancien régime gave way to those of the Revolution, were then revived, and then phased out once more. Within the Restoration period, laws were introduced and then abandoned, then introduced again.[1] The multiplicity of confessions, allowed by the Revolution's nominal separation of church and state, was compromised in 1814 and resuscitated in 1830. These continuous mutations, and the various justifications mounted to sustain them, put in question the entire notion of a final truth or formula. Meanwhile, in the philosophical-spiritual domain, secular modes of understanding were coming increasingly to dominate religious modes. Positivist philosophies moved to replace religion as a means of explanation, to replace sacred forces with social forces, God with science, fate with biological determinism. Given these substitutions and the political and legal turbulence of the Restoration, God as a means of explanation began to seem both archaic and somewhat disingenuous. In the midst of these evolutions was published Stendhal's *The Red and the Black* (*Le rouge et le noir*).

The historical particulars of 1830, recounted in *Le rouge*, are emblematic of the tensions intrinsic to the idea of secularism. *Le rouge et le noir*, like a world without a master plot, both embodies and inspires a number of explanatory narratives. But it also underscores the arbitrariness and ultimate insufficiency of all these narratives—at a historical moment when, for reasons political, economic, and philosophical, organization is most desired. It undermines even those modes of narrative production that do not seem to be "productions" at all, such as science, psychology, the logical discernment

22

of cause and effect, intuition, as well as biblical narratives and the idea of destiny. In an environment in which problems of who or what (if anything) structures the world had a particular philosophical as well as political import, this novel, in the name of realism, carefully undermines the viability of all explanatory narratives. In an ironic subversion suitable to the historical moment, it radically undermines the theoretical bases of secular culture as well as the convictions of the ecclesiastics, and, in so doing, questions the nature and function of narrative.

The transition to secularism poses the problem of where meaning is to be situated: in the outside world, within the domain of the mind, or somewhere in between. This is the problem to which Hegel (among others) responded when he tried to reconcile freedom and the "demands of union with cosmic spirit," or the opposition between mind and world as the source of meaning. As Charles Taylor writes, "A disenchanted world is correlative to a self-defining subject, and the winning through to a self-defining identity was accompanied by a sense of exhilaration and power, that the subject need no longer define his perfection or vice, his equilibrium or disharmony, in relation to an external order. With the forging of this modern subjectivity there comes a new notion of freedom, and a newly central role attributed to freedom, which seems to have proved itself definitive and irreversible."[2]

The question of what drives Julien Sorel's ascent and descent stands at the base of *Le rouge* plot criticism. Critics generally recognize that Julien does not ascend the social scale on his own steam but rather on a tide of outside forces. For Miller, Brombert, Blin, and others, those outside forces mean the social machine, the vicissitudes of Restoration culture, and the sentimental caprices of others.[3] It is Madame de Rênal's love and not Julien's strategies that produces his amorous success. It is Chélan who puts Julien in Besançon, the marquis via Pirard who brings him to Paris, this marquis' boredom that invents the blue suit, and Mathilde's unplanned pregnancy that turns him into the chevalier de La Vernaye. The "outside forces" that decide Julien's existence can also be read as forces of the unconscious (Felman, Crouzet) or, should Julien in fact be the son of an aristocrat, of some biological determinism. But these outside forces, it is worth noting, have in common an element that embodies both the pursuit and the subversion of explanatory apparatuses. This is the force of chance.

When Julien is with the Rênals, he is chosen to ride at the head of the king's parade. It constitutes a moment of great pride for Julien, particularly at the instant when he barely escapes falling into the mud: "His joy exceeded all measure when, as they passed by the old rampart, the noise of the little cannon caused his horse to shy out of line. By great good luck [*par un grand hasard*], he did not fall off, and from that moment on he felt himself a hero."[4] "From that moment on": his pride comes from the fact that he remains on the horse. But in fact, the subtle intrusion of *hasard* contradicts Julien's understanding of the moment as his own creation and explicitly dissipates the notion of personal agency. The act cannot be entirely "heroic" when it is as much an enactment, an intrusion from without, as an act; and yet, the incident contributes to Julien's sense of his competence and his place in the world. What is more, it contributes to others' sense of him: at dinner with the Valenod, the guests admire him: "These fine gentry, who knew Julien only by reputation and from seeing him on horseback when the king of _____ came to town, were his most enthusiastic admirers" (112; 141).

Hasard, again and again, intervenes at the precise moments when Julien is most proud of his competence, most sure of himself. In the salon with Madame de Fervaques, for instance, the narrator writes: "He had taken an action, he was less miserable; his eyes fell by accident [*par hasard*] on the Russia-leather briefcase in which Prince Korasoff had placed the fifty-three love letters that were his gift to Julien" (328; 404). And then, on the next page, the narrator reveals that "accident [*le hasard*] had revealed to Julien the path to eloquence" (329; 405). It is true that Julien has acted, that he has done something. But chance has twice intervened to carry Julien through that course of action, handing him both eloquence in the salon and the turn of the head that enables him to remember the letters. Again, though, the eloquence that chance makes accessible inspires Fervaques to admire Julien, and Julien to admire himself. Here, there is a sense that the personal triumph is neither. Indeed, the idea of the personal is complicated, as chance intrudes on the very parameters of Julien.

In his study of chance in nineteenth-century fiction, David Bell underscores the importance of the auspicious (chance) occasion. He writes, "What the strategist forgets or neglects is quite simply the fortuitous nature present at the founding of the law, the unpredictable propensities that gave the law its particular shape and signal its temporary (because nonoriginary) status."[5] Chance produces space, signifies opportunity: Bell describes Stendhal's characters (in *La*

Chartreuse in particular) as strategists or tacticians according to their understanding of this freedom.[6] In *Le rouge*, chance is both the foundation of the plot and the condition of narrative: the sign, as it were, under which the novel is set. Chance places the narrative on a continuous circular pursuit of meaning that becomes, for character and reader, the principal concern of the novel.

THE EPIC FORCE OF CHANCE

To more precisely cast the use of chance in *Le rouge*, I turn to Georg Lukács's account of the transition from the epic to the novel. This transition, as he recounts it in *The Theory of the Novel*, turns on the character's dependence on outside forces:

> Achilles or Odysseus, Dante or Arjuna—precisely because they are guided along their paths by gods—realise that if they lacked this guidance, if they were without divine help, they would be powerless and helpless in the face of mighty enemies. The relationship between the objective and subjective worlds is maintained in adequate balance: the hero is rightly conscious of the superiority of the opposing outside world; yet despite this innermost modesty he can triumph in the end because his lesser strength is guided to victory by the highest power in the world.[7]

In the epic, the "highest power in the world" sustains the hero, who in turn depends upon that power to guide his path. That "highest power" acts both as a spiritual guide for the character and as a cement that unifies the narrative—that connects the episodes to one another and the epic character to the world of action. In the novel, though, this cement comes undone and the nature of the protagonist's path turns suddenly solitary: "The first great novel of world literature stands at the beginning of the time when the Christian God began to forsake the world; when man became lonely and could find meaning and substance only in his own soul, whose home was nowhere; when the world, released from its paradoxical anchorage in a beyond that is truly present, was abandoned to its immanent meaninglessness."[8] The novelistic world is thus one in which the spiritual connection of the hero to the outside world is dissolved, in which the "highest power in the world" (the gods of the epic) gives way to an "immanent meaninglessness." The novelistic character, or a character in a world without God, responds to this meaninglessness by generating a meaning or substance of his or her own: "The inner importance of the individual has reached its historical apogee: the individual is no longer significant as the carrier of transcendent worlds, as he was in abstract idealism, he now carries his value exclusively within himself."[9]

In turning to *The Theory of the Novel*, I mean to discuss the characters' dependence on or independence from outside forces as Lukács does, in spiritual terms. The transferal of "value" from the outside to the inside could be read as a rite of passage or as a gesture of pride, but Lukács narrates it as a response to a world situation. In the preface to *The Theory of the Novel*, he declares the stakes of his discussion by pointing out that for Hegel "Art becomes problematic precisely because reality has become non-problematic. The idea put forth in *The Theory of the Novel*, although formally similar, is in fact the complete opposite of this: the problems of the novel form are here the mirror-image of a world gone out of joint. This is why the 'prose' of life is here only a symptom, among many others, of the fact that reality no longer constitutes a favourable soil for art. . . . And this is not for artistic but for historico-philosophical reasons."[10] Michael Holzman reads the moment in the preface when Lukács writes that "the author was not looking for a new literary form, but, quite explicitly, for a 'new world'" (20), with this statement: "That 'new world' was as little social as literary, and if it was not as specifically sectarian as that of Lukács's friend Buber, it was most certainly religious."[11] Holzman then speaks of reading *The Theory of the Novel* "as a wish, as, in a way, a novel or a fantasy, a search through literary history for exactly those lost Blessed Ages, for immanence, for God."[12]

Based on the schematic criteria that Lukács outlines, Julien Sorel fits the description of a novelistic character, both in his ideological and his historical positions. For one, Julien has an incredulous disposition, a suspicion of institutional religion, a sense that the Church is nothing but a profitable business, and a mistrust of ecclesiastics. What is more, he resists the notions of God and transcendence in a more fundamental sense. He believes that what happens around him—his social circumstances, the conduct of others, the decisions that are made for him—is not the work of God, not an indication of the world as it is meant to be, not about a cosmic master plan, but about social mores and rules, rules whose uniformity is born of artificial manipulation rather than divine ordinance. This belief pushes Julien to position himself as a manipulator and a climber, qualities that he admires in Napoleon. He sees his successes as his own doing ("the credit is all mine") and remains contemptuous of superstition, even his own. He embodies romantic irony as René Bourgeois describes it: "Romantic irony . . . is a philosophical disposition, wherein the world is a theater on which one must play one's role quite deliberately, keeping in mind another universe, one born of the imagination, which stands at once in opposition to and in correspondence with the first."[13] In *Le rouge*, we can understand these opposing worlds as the outside context as Julien understands it and the inner landscape within which he operates. As the narrator writes, "Julien . . . had sworn an oath never to say anything except what seemed false to him" (114; 143); he has promised that the part played on the outside stage will be held at a distance from his inner feelings.

On the one hand, his is the ironic disposition of a cynical mind under Restoration culture, where the entire political structure can be read as a theater with rapidly changing sets and costumes. But more profoundly, Julien's is a secular disposition, a strategic self-sufficiency created for a world without an intrinsic or sacred order, without God. Restoration culture, as critics have observed, resembles an elaborate mise-en-scène, but one without substantial connection to some spiritual force.[14] And when there is no guidance, and thus no substantial source of meaning and direction, the moment comes when the character "carries his value exclusively within himself." Kierkegaard outlines this transposition of meaning from the world into the character in *Either/Or*: "Our age . . . must turn the single individual over to himself completely in such a way that, strictly speaking, he becomes his own creator."[15] Unfortunately, as repeated intrusions of chance demonstrate, the world Julien inhabits is not entirely novelistic, in Lukács's sense of the word, and does not turn Julien completely over to himself, but rather contains a subtle residue of epic structure. Personal freedom and the concept of action must be rethought when chance intrudes (and in this novel chance moments *are* presented as intrusions) on individual agency. When, in the episode where Julien holds Madame de Rênal's hand ("Julien thought it was his *duty* to make sure that the hand was not withdrawn when he touched it" (42; 51, italics in text]), the narrator writes that Julien "had found, almost by accident [*presque par hasard*], enough blind courage to take a single action" (44; 54), *hasard* comes in to contradict the sense of duty. "Almost" shifts the locus of compulsion, of duty, placing Julien somewhere between free choice and unconscious beholdenness to another dimension. Another such intervention, and in some sense the most subversive to Julien's sense of success, appears in the episode that leads him to declare: "My novel is finished, and the credit is all mine. I was able to make myself loved by that monster of pride, he thought, glancing at Mathilde; her father cannot live without her nor she without me" (359; 444, tm).[16] Here again, though, chance has intervened. In that victorious moment in the library, when Julien "makes himself loved by that monster of pride" ("So there she is, that proud beauty, at my feet!" [338; 418]), the narrator writes, "Only accident [*le hasard tout seul*] had brought about this outburst" (339; 419). Again and again, an active and independent *hasard* orchestrates Julien's experiences: "A lucky accident [*Un heureux hasard*] brought Julien into the presence of M. Valenod" (51; 64); "As luck would have it [*Le hasard voulut que*], Abbé de Frilair was on duty that evening" (164; 204); "The singular person whom chance [*le hasard*] had rendered absolute mistress of all his happiness" (296; 365); "The excesses of zeal, of which chance [*le hasard*] had made him the witness" (313; 385, tm).

When chance has a substantial hand in his success, Julien, though he alone is accountable for his actions, cannot claim responsibility, anymore than Achilles or Odysseus can claim sole responsibility for their victories. With the support of chance, as Lukács would put it, Julien "can triumph in the end because his lesser strength is guided to victory by the highest power in the world." But whereas this guidance is fundamental to the epic, it becomes doubly subversive in this chronicle of manipulation and studied orchestration. In Homer, the gods were there to underwrite the virtues of Achilles or Odysseus, not to compromise them. Chance in *Le rouge*, though, functions not to guide Julien but to intrude on and dismantle his fantasies of autonomous manipulation at precisely those moments when the fantasies are at their pinnacle. This inscrutable force prevails at the moments when Julien becomes most enthusiastic about his own value, giving Bourgeois' ironic world another dimension, that of chance, superimposed on and trumping Julien's vision (he carries "exclusively within himself" a value that in fact comes from without). But even more ironic is that this inscrutable force *is* that of chance: the precise antithesis of fate, of epic structure, of everything that made Lukács's epic world a secure and meaningful arena in which to operate.

CHANCE AND THE AUTONOMOUS SUBJECT,
OR THE DOUBLE BIND OF SECULARISM

Sandy Petrey places chance in a political context by finding in it an embodiment of the arbitrary, performative, and content-free nature of Restoration ideology and laws. In a more abstract sense, chance embodies the spiritual situation of a culture from which transcendence has departed but in which secular logic has not taken root. Chance reminds (or threatens) Julien and the reader that an entire alternate world stands outside the realm of human machinations and interpretations. In contrast to the providentialist reading of history that precedes the Restoration, chance dismantles or contradicts the predication of causal chains, of determinism, of all manner of modes of reason, secular and religious, because it renders cause, linear narration, and understanding largely immaterial.[17] The result is a sort of vacuum, a relentless orchestrated failure of modern (and ancient) epistemological strategies that places Julien in a double predicament. On the one hand, the repeated intrusions of chance deprive Julien of the autonomous existential certitude that Lukács finds in the novelistic hero. On the other hand, because the principle of chance is not in fact a principle, not a conferrer of meaning, and furthermore because Julien does not even see chance in operation, the narrative is denied the organic structure and seamless direction that Lukács finds in the epic. When Julien decides to go riding, writes the narrator, "acting only on himself and not at all on Mathilde's mind or heart, he was leaving up to chance [*au hasard*] the disposition of his own destiny" (296; 365). And yet, we know by this time that the disposition of Julien's own destiny is up to chance no matter what he does and no matter how he envisions his actions.

This chronicle of 1830 traces cultural and individual responses to the transition to a nonreligious consciousness. In order to do this, the novel creates that space of transition, creates the particular semiepic and semisecular 1830 that it chronicles. This, again, is the same space of transition to which Hegel responded when he tried to reconcile freedom and the "demands of union with cosmic spirit." Writes Charles Taylor, in a description reminiscent of Lukács and Kierkegaard:

From the standpoint of the autonomous, finite subject, the larger course of events which affects him is distinguished from what he does as what happens to him: his fate. This fate is quite distinct from himself, in the sense that it is not at all an expression of him, something one can only find in what he does. From this point of view, that of separation, the injunction of an earlier time to reconcile oneself to fate, to come to see its necessity and hence make peace with it, can only be understood as a call to surrender, not as an invitation to deeper insight. But the course of things is in some sense an expression of cosmic spirit; and hence to see it as quite other is to define oneself in opposition to cosmic spirit. On the other hand, to be united to infinite spirit, even more to see oneself as its vehicle, would be to recognize in one's fate an expression of a reality from which one could not dissociate oneself.[18]

Le rouge casts chance as a metaphor for this ambivalence about connection to the outside world and, what is more, casts fiction as the arena for its dramatization. Julien follows the directions of chance like the ancient Stoic's dog tied to the wagon; and yet, he has neither the Stoic's attitude of resigned submission nor the Hegelian's deep understanding of the wagon's course and its logic. Implied in the intrusions of chance, which both comprise and undo the "Chronicle of 1830," is an ironic ambivalence about the transition to a secular world. This chronicle expresses on the one hand a desire to be rid of the constraints of the philosophical and ontological structures of the past and, on the other hand, a reluctance to abandon those form-giving structures.

LIVING IN LIMBO: CHANCE AND PROVIDENCE

Chance, as we said, prevents the reader from situating meaning solidly within the world of action or within the world of the mind. The characters, too, seem to sense this problematic function and are much occupied with negotiating the cosmic (or random) spirit of the outside world. Julien regards such spirits with a mistrust that morphs into philosophical detachment: "Hitherto, he had been angry only with his destiny [*le hasard*] and with society" (62; 78); "A poor devil like me, dropped by fate [*par le hasard*] in the lowest rank of society, will never get a chance like this again" (270; 333). And, before he meets his father for the last time: "Chance [*le hasard*] has placed us near one another on the earth" (398; 496). While Julien maintains a sort of brave denial, Mathilde on the other hand sees chance as a fairy godmother: "What could she want? Fortune, noble birth, intelligence, beauty (as everyone kept telling her and as she believed herself) had been piled on her by the hand of fate [*les mains du hasard*]. Such were the thoughts of the most envied heiress of the Faubourg Saint-Germain" (250; 309). And again: "Between Julien and me there is no contract to be signed, no lawyer, everything is heroic, everything is up to the free play of chance [*tout sera fils du hasard*]" (252; 311). And then, bemoaning the modern age: "A man's life was one continual train of dangers [*hasards*]. Nowadays civilization has eliminated danger [*a chassé le hasard*], and the unexpected never happens" (265–66; 327). In the end, there is no great distinction between the respective superstitions of these characters, for the chance that Julien and Mathilde ponder (or welcome or fear) is eclipsed by the narrative chance that actually acts upon them.

While Julien embraces the idea of being his own creator and Mathilde enjoys being the favored daughter of chance, the ecclesiastics, on the other hand, want to weave chance into a sacred narrative of destiny. At the beginning of the second part of the novel, Julien has left the seminary for the Hotel de La Mole. He declares to the abbé Pirard, "My father hated me ever since I was in the cradle; it was one of my greatest griefs; but I shall no longer complain of fortune [*je ne me plaindrai plus du hasard*], I have found another father in you, sir" (191; 236). To this, Pirard responds, " 'Very well, very well,' said the abbé in some embarrassment; then he recalled [*rencontrant fort à propos*] a timely expression from his days as director of the seminary: 'you must never speak of fortune, my child, always say Providence instead [*il ne faut jamais dire le hasard, mon enfant, dites toujours la Providence*]' " (191; 236, tm). Julien has no response to this statement and the narrator no comment.

Pirard's replacement of chance with Providence exemplifies the sort of narrative production, or reduction, that Bell decried in his examination of chance. When Pirard insists on Providence, having "recalled a timely expression of the seminary director," he does not stipulate that his bond with Julien in particular is the work of Providence. He insists instead, in a semantic gesture that seems almost instinctual, that Julien should substitute Providence for chance in every case. Pirard's principled rejection of Julien's way of speaking comes from a long-lived and powerfully developed theoretical point of view, but his manner of articulating it, I would propose, does not so much replace chance with Providence as absorb the one into the other. Pirard, in his capacity as seminary director (and thus as former seminarian who learned from his seminary director, who in turn learned from another, etc.), intends a spiritual paternalism, but in the end, he seems only to fob his student off with a slogan—a slogan that seems surprisingly rote and insubstantial in its application.

Helmut Thielicke writes in *Nihilism*: "Accident is the 'other side' of fate itself," and, "Fate and chance are the same thing, only seen from different sides."[19] Thielicke's book starts, tellingly, with a consideration of "nihil" and "ism," or nothingness (nihil) and absoluteness of position (ism), and the collapse of chance into fate can be read in connection with this reconciliation. When, in the second part of *Le rouge*, Madame de Fervaques makes a cryptic comment about love, Julien thinks: "Either that means nothing or it means everything. These are some of the secrets of language that will be forever hidden from us poor provincials (333; 412)." One of the secrets of language that looms in the *hasard-Providence* episode, in the Fervaques episode, and in the rest of *Le rouge* is the intimate connection—and in a sense the ultimate interchangeability—between meaning everything and meaning nothing. If *a* is *b*, goes the mathematical principle, then *b* is *a*, and while Pirard's substitution intends to minimize chance in favor of Providence, it simultaneously and unintentionally elides the distinction between these propositions. If Providence is a vehicle of meaning and chance a repository of meaninglessness, in other words, then the replacement of chance with Providence brings meaning and meaninglessness into a precariously close proximity. Chance become Providence gains a sudden significance, a sudden substance, but by the same token, that Providence that once was chance retains the sense or shade of meaninglessness—a meaninglessness that, in this novel, continues to surface.

Providence and the Business of Narrative Production

Pirard's substitution of chance for Providence is a testament both to the need for and the futility of narratives: the scramble for the condensation of chance into Providence, of disorder into order, and the continual appearance of more chance, more disorder, to be so condensed. On the one hand, the facile emptiness of the substitution is important for the criticism of Restoration politics that subtends this narration. During the Restoration, as Petrey described: "The characters of *Le Rouge et le Noir* continuously do for themselves exactly what the regime of Louis XVIII and Charles X did for itself,

convert quintessentially performative operations into incontrovert-
ibly referential truths."[20] Among those performative operations was
the insertion of the discourse of sacred order into social and historical narratives.[21] Aside from its political resonance, though, and aside
from its critical implications for the Church and its discourse, Pirard's substitution presents the taming of chance, by whatever means,
as an act of narrative production, and vice versa. At the start of the
chapter entitled: "A Plot [*Un Complot*]," the narrator inserts this epigraph: "Random words, accidental encounters [*des rencontres par effet
du hasard*] turn into conclusive evidence in the mind of an imagina-
tive man, if he has a bit of fire in his heart" (256; 317). *Le rouge et le
noir* both demands and chronicles the production of narrative
strands, the synthesis of "random words" into a chain—for the characters and for the reader. At the same time, it impedes that same
production with a deliberate series of disparate elements that both
demand and resist connection.

The entire plot of *Le rouge*, indeed, constitutes a sort of mosaic
on which any structure remains a false imposition and in which
the search for first causes must remain unsatisfied. Writes Victor
Brombert, "Rapid shifts of point of view, calling for several layers of
simultaneous interpretation, almost totally abolish explicatory transitions."[22] For Shoshana Felman, these "rapid shifts" permeate the
novel's lexicon: "Taking apart (yet with apparent lucidity) rational
clarity and the security of univocal meaning, Stendhalien language
makes reading itself an adventuresome experience, risky and un-
comfortable."[23] And not just paragraphs and words, but the entire
narrative is comprised of various disembodied sections—of bounds
from one episode to another, from one moment to another. In the
episode of the secret note, the narrator compares politics in the
novel to a pistol shot in a concert ("The noise is shattering without
being forceful. It doesn't harmonize with any of the other instruments" [304; 376]). To continue this musical comparison, the world
of *Le rouge* can be read as a discordant orchestra; without what
Brombert called explicatory transitions, the novel resonates not so
much as a symphonic whole as a compendium of various melodies,
one on top of the other. The cacophonous composition of scenes,
for instance, the introduction of Falcoz and Giraud, the episode of
the secret note and Castanède's inexplicable opposition to the
note's delivery, the adjudication scene and the visit of Geronimo,
the encounter with Don Diego Bustos, introduced and then abandoned, the continuous alterations in sentiment, Julien's love for Ma-

dame de Rênal, then for Mathilde, then, suddenly, once more for Madame de Rênal, produce this discordance. So does the continued focus on the present, which Michel Crouzet names the "perpetual discovery which would be the law of the narrative,"[24] and which Brombert described as crucial not just to the narration but to the characters' experience: "Stendhal's heroes discover themselves existentially, through their reactions; and they even discover their reactions as a surprise."[25]

The novel's simultaneous demand for and resistance to consolidation finds further articulation in its continuous erasure of memory. For instance, once at the Rênal house: "[Julien] forgot everything, including his purpose in coming" (22; 25). When M. de Rênal goes away, "[Madame de Rênal] had quite forgotten his existence" (40; 48). Further on, Julien: "If he had stopped seeing M. de Rênal, in a week he would have forgotten him, his house, his dogs, his children, and his whole family" (50; 62). Norbert meets Julien and the next morning "had forgotten his existence" (199; 246, tm). As for his sister, when Julien returns from Strasbourg: "Mathilde had almost forgotten him" (325; 400). On the one hand, these persistent erasures serve to undermine the sentimental bases of romanticism: there can be no permanent adoration when the brain and heart have no retention. But more than this, these erasures undermine the sense of a narration that builds. Crouzet's comparison with the surrealists is perhaps the most apt, for the novel is comprised of these suspensions, bounds from one moment to the other— moments that enter into one another, act on one another, obscure one another, but resist composition and condensation, resist conversion into Providence or even into a reasonable narrative.

The fundamental disembodiment that permeates this novel contradicts the sense that understanding is cumulative, and in so doing undermines the predictive and explicatory function of the past. It also turns the process of reading into an exercise in connecting dots that resist connection. Given these leaps and gaps and interruptions, any synthesis would necessarily be an imposition, and an incomplete one. Readers would necessarily, as Carol Mossman proposes, "extract one series of messages while ignoring the other."[26] At best, the narrator indicates, the mind can generate possible narratives, none of which are complete and none of which come close to encompassing the world in its disconnection and disorder. We can consider for instance the shooting of Madame de Rênal and the punishment that ensues, about which D. A. Miller said: "Each separate motive on its own merits is insufficient, and all the motives taken together do not command a cohesive psychological case."[27] The various plot elements that lead up to the shooting can each be made to make sense, but resist an encompassing narrative. The marquis reacting to Madame de Rênal's letter, for instance, can read as the moral father outraged at Julien's conduct, or, alternatively, as the hypocritical aristocrat pleased at the excuse to banish the peasant. As for Julien, he can represent the jealous lover furious with the Church, the parvenu obsessed with Mathilde, the lover obsessed with Madame de Rênal, the son obsessed with Madame de Rênal, the paranoiac worried about his reputation, the egomaniac who does not want to be misunderstood, or the self-destructive madman. The death sentence, finally, can be read as bourgeois vengeance on the upstart peasant, Valenod's punishment of his rival, the result of Frilair's clumsiness, the simple intrusion of judicial principle, a senseless aberration, and so on. The entire scene, if not the entire novel, reads as a complicated compendium of intersecting and superimposed circles, stories, and readings. Like the sort of children's book that divides into horizontal sections so that the head of a bear can rest on the body of a horse and the legs of a chicken, *Le rouge et le noir* encourages such curious combinations and resists a condensing explanatory narrative.

We know that the transition to secularism poses the problem of where meaning is to be situated, within the character or in the outside world. Chance, both as a dramatic instrument and as a narrative principle, precludes a harmonic vision of the outside world. It turns what Lukács named "the highest power in the world" into a largely amorphous force and so encourages what Taylor described as "disenchantment." And as cited earlier, Lukács wrote that the "individual, no longer significant as the carrier of transcendent worlds . . . now carries his value exclusively within himself." Julien, a novelistic hero ("my novel is finished") certainly seems to want the novel to be about him ("the credit is all mine"), as do readers; *Le rouge* is often called a psychological novel. But it is important to see that the strand of psychological interpretation in this novel, like all its strands of interpretation, is systematically broken or blurred at important points by a disorder that intrudes on the subject from within and without. This blurring undermines the conceptual parameters of character and also impedes the "winning through to self-identity" even in the midst of disenchantment.

CHANCE, THE UNCONSCIOUS, AND THE
DEAD END OF SELF-REVELATION

Some readers propose that chance, in such sentences as "he had had almost by accident [*par hasard*] the blind courage to act" and "accident [*le hasard*] had revealed to Julien the path to eloquence" could be read as indicating the operation of the unconscious rather than the epic intrusion of another dimension.[28] This reading is entirely possible, but not as valuable an instrument of comprehension as it seems. One problem is that aside from moments in which chance could be read as code for the unconscious, it is connected in other instances to a force outside (it would be hard for instance to declare that Julien's unconscious made him remain on the horse); so even the operation of the unconscious would not disable the other sorts of chance that intrude upon him. Another more fundamental problem is that chance, no matter what it is and where it is situated, has already been placed in an ironic contradiction with Julien's understanding, his sense of character, his pride. Therefore, even when we read certain moments of chance to mean that Julien's unconscious is in operation, the fact remains that that unconscious is inaccessible to him, unassimilable, enigmatic. Nineteenth-century psychological discourse, in fact, long describes the unconscious less as an integral part of one's character than as an inscrutable alternate dimension. Henri Ellenberger's *The Discovery of the Unconscious* traces the history of this dimension. Of Schopenhauer, he writes, "man is an irrational being guided by internal forces, which are unknown to him and of which he is scarcely aware."[29] Carus described an unconscious that "is turned toward the future and toward the past but does not know of the present."[30] (This idea could be read as an oracular description of the psyche, an alternative to *Le rouge*'s focus on chance and Providence.) Carus focused, as Jung would, on the unbeholdenness of the unconscious to constraints of time, space, and direct experience. Von Hartmann understood the unconscious in terms of an energy force, as a "highly intelligent though blind dynamism underlying the visible universe"[31] and Nietzsche conceived of psychic energy as being dammed up and discharged in the same way as physical energy.[32] Darwin situates this energy in the nervous system, but echoes the sense that it constitutes an independent mechanism: "Certain actions which we recognize as expressive of certain states of the mind are the direct result of the constitution of the nervous system, and have been from the first independent of the will, and, to a large extent, of habit."[33]

In the course of the century, the unconscious replaced the supernatural as principal character in scenes of drama and madness. Chevreul, in experiments with divining rods and pendulums, attributed to unconscious thoughts and movements phenomena that had been previously attributed to "spirits."[34] Bergson and Janet (both of whom, as Ellenberger writes, "revealed their deep-seated preoccupation with religion late in life"),[35] wrote of the automatic nature of unconscious reasoning. Freud would later describe the instincts as "representatives of all the forces originating in the interior of the body and transmitted to the mental apparatus" and, in a more poetic moment, as "an urge inherent in organic life to restore an earlier state of things;[36] he also introduced the concept of displaceable or sublimated energies.[37] Georg Groddeck, demonstrating that writings on the unconscious used the discourse of the supernatural well into the twentieth century, insisted that "man is animated by the Unknown, that there is within him . . . some wondrous force which directs both what he himself does, and what happens to him. The affirmation 'I live' is only conditionally correct, it expresses only a small and superficial part of the fundamental principle, 'Man is lived by the It.' "[38]

In their readings of *Le rouge*, Shoshana Felman and Michel Crouzet cite the unconscious, much as Bell cites chance, as an obstacle rather than a key to planned understanding. Felman describes Julien's actions in terms of madness, defining madness as a "derangement, a mental sickness,"[39] and as senselessness with respect to an established order: "Madness is relative: it is senseless with respect to sense, which denies it and is then denied by it in turn."[40] Crouzet writes, "This [the sublime] is the dimension from which I want to study Julien Sorel: this character [*personnage*], but is he in fact a character, he whom one cannot grasp without interpreting, without mutilating, this non-character [*non-caractère*] endlessly covered and described in contradictions. His only coherence comes perhaps not from a psychological but from a poetic reading, where he could be understood for his effects. The sublime would be that constant that gives him, in his brilliance and incoherence, a formal definition."[41] And then: "Psychoanalysis, perhaps because it misrepresents or flattens the Sublime, seems deadly for this concept-form so suited to romantic modernity."[42] The unconscious, as fountain of ideas and images, retains the element of the inexplicable or uncontainable. It is not surprising, since psychology is a form of narrative, that the introduction of the science of the mind, as well as of narrative production, accompanies the fading of the sacred master plot. But the unconscious, as we see, like generated narratives, like the replacement of chance with Providence, does not elucidate enigma, but rather transposes it. Psychoanalysis, like psychoanalytic criticism, resonates thus as a Band-Aid over an abyss, for whether Julien throws himself in a fit of madness or is pushed by a cosmic hand, the rise of the unconscious as Stendhal frames it here functions as a Trojan horse returning the vast unreadable to the modern world.

Let us consider the disclosure of Julien's character that operates in the course of the novel. From the start, the narrator predicates a distinction between the character Julien discloses to the outside world and the character that he in fact is (the distinction described in Bourgeois' romantic irony). This distinction, underscored in the numerous references to hypocrisy, to role-playing, to the desire to "rely only on those parts of my character that I've thoroughly tested" (37; 59), to "never to say anything except what seemed false to him," suppose a "him" obscured under the charade—a character conscious of a core concealed within. In the Hôtel de La Mole, Julien is employed as a scribe: he copies the words of the marquis. This occupation, which is also emblematic of his modus operandi (Julien has previously copied Napoleon, Rousseau, Molière, etc.), rests on the distinction between the scripted and unscripted on which the narrator has insisted from the start. In a sense, the entire Hôtel de La Mole is about that distinction and about speculation on what Julien would do in spontaneous moments, in the absence of mimesis, deception, verbatim recitations, and other calculated performances. Critics have commented on the value and substance in this obscured spontaneous Julien. For instance, for D. A. Miller: "The moments when plots falter coincide with moments when Julien seems most closely in touch with himself, at a primary level of being."[43] And for Brombert: "[Julien] is persistently wrong about his feelings and, above all, charmingly unaware of his real qualities."[44] These comments and the narrator's insinuations presume that there is a fundamental Julien, a primary level that can be uncovered. This focus is appropriate to the historical moment; character, as Lukács said, stands as the nucleus of modern fiction, and much of the novel seems to maintain this principle.

For months, Julien is unable to transcend the Hôtel de La Mole, unable to depart. In London, he is praised for his "cool expression, *a thousand miles from the sensation of the moment"* (222; 276, italics in text). And even in Strasbourg he continues to copy, only this time from Korasoff and not the marquis. However, within the frame of his mimetic occupation, there are moments when Julien can escape, when he eludes the bounds of calculation and mimesis. And these moments, curiously, invariably produce senselessness rather than a comprehensible core. The first instance of unplanned originality appears in Julien's first series of copies: "The marquis entered, glanced at the copies, and noted with amazement that Julien wrote *cela* with two l's, *cella*" (195; 241). This spontaneous nonsense word becomes a signature feature of Julien: at dinner, the marquis introduces him as "my secretary, and he writes *cela* with two l's" (196; 243). But this signature feature, this first departure from the script, in this scene, in this house, and in French, has no meaning. As Jared Stark points out, the unscripted Julien (the two l's indicate the presence of Julien Sorel, *sur-l*, Sorel), is the embodiment of senselessness.[45]

Another moment of spontaneous revelation comes when Julien draws a sword on Mathilde—an action that is instantly cut short (the sword, no more than the pen, can function as an instrument of self-expression in the house of La Mole). Another such instance is when Julien discusses Napoleon with Mathilde (abandoning one script to discuss another), and another is when he declares his adoration for her. But the final and most important such moment is his response to Madame de Rênal's letter. When this document arrives, Julien runs from the house, never to return, no longer the scribe. This is his most spontaneous action and it is also, significantly, his most unreadable. From the moment he steps out of the house, his actions are dramatic, erratic, and peculiar. The narrator writes: "On this swift journey he was unable to write to Mathilde, as he had intended to do; his hand formed nothing on the paper but illegible scrawls [*traits illisibles*]" (362; 449). Unable to read or represent himself as other than the manipulated and mediated character that he was in the Paris mansion, Julien cannot make sense. This predicament continues in Verrières at the arms merchant, where Julien "had great difficulty in making him understand he wanted pair of pistols" (362; 449). Not a word is said, from Paris to the church, and the gun transaction seems to be enacted almost without human participation. The inauthentic and mimetic structure of the house of La Mole is broken and the "unscripted" Julien is released. From the Hôtel de La Mole to the shooting in Verrières, Julien is positioned to move from the mimetic to the spontaneous, from the calculated to the natural, from the surface to the nucleus. But when he does move thus, there is nothing to read.

This progression of incidents—the duties as scribe, the restrictions, and then the moment of spontaneous action—prepare the gradual disclosure of what Miller named the "primary level." And yet, the wordless shooting of Madame de Rênal is the most incomprehensible action in the entire novel. What does this action articulate? What is being revealed? For some it is a frustration with God, who had "stolen" Madame de Rênal. For others it is the loss of Mathilde. For some it is the fact that his actual character is exposed, or that his actual character is discounted. Just as during the parade, chance (Providence) intruded at the moment he became a hero, here that outside force (madness, chance, the unconscious, romantic obsession) intrudes at the moment he is to express himself, at the moment the story becomes, in the most fundamental sense, about him. If indeed this is the core of Julien, the essence of his character, a "winning through to a self-defining identity," it is a core or an identity that announces nothing but its unreadable nature. The road from La Mole to Verrières undoes what it pretends to reveal, sending the reader to search elsewhere for an explanatory chain.

Louis Jenrel, or the Oracle

What Lukács named the "highest power in the world" has morphed into chance, and thus loses its form-giving power. Its constant presence, however, precludes "the inner importance of the individual" from "reaching its historical apogee." Though the individual is supremely important to himself and to the reader, intrusions from without continue to undermine his discoveries and determine his movements. Lucidity, once proclaimed, is denied and individual vision remains incomplete. Because this is so, though, because both Julien and the reader are systematically blocked in the pursuit of understanding, we should consider the place of the narrator in this spiritual and epistemological limbo. After all, the intrusion of chance and coincidence, the superimposition of various dimensions of action, the subversion of predictions, and the complication of character readings depend on third-person narration. When the marquis introduces Julien as the secretary "whom I've just added to my staff, and propose to make a man of, if that [*cella*] can be done" (196; 243), his pun, his senselessness, has to be spelled out. In the coach to Verrières, it is the confusion in Julien's writing (*traits illisibles*) that indicates his internal chaos. On the one hand, then, the narrator stands as reporter for a disordered world. On the other hand, the incomplete nature of the individual vision extends to this narrator, making him a participant in rather than a dominator of the culture he documents. The narrator occupies an uncertain space, between mastery and subversion of mastery, between the pronouncement of last words and the retraction or substitution of those last words, postulation of first causes and erasure of those causes.

In order to examine the role of the narrator, and by extension of narrative production, we must turn to the piece of paper that Julien finds in the church on his way to the Rênal house. For though it seems that there exists no absolute word, no superstructure to this world, there is a slender formal element that in some sense decides, or seems to decide, the course of the entire narrative: a subtle Providence, as it were, in the form of the oracle: "He found the church dark and deserted . . . All alone in the church, he took a seat in the finest pew. It bore M. de Rênal's coat of arms. On the lectern, Julien noted a scrap of printed paper, set out there as if for him to read. He glanced at it and saw: *Details of the execution and last moments of Louis Jenrel, executed at Besançon, on the* _____ The paper was torn. On the other side were the first words of a line: *The first step . . .*" (20; 25, italics in text). The oracle, if we can name it that, has most commonly been read as a fanciful detail, rather than as a fundamental force in the plot. Michal Peled Ginsburg writes, "At first sight it seems as if this piece of paper functions as an oracle announcing, at the very beginning, what will inevitably happen at the end . . . At the end of the novel we should be able to recognize how 'the first step' started a chain of events that led with some logic and necessity to the last step—the violent murder attempt and the execution. But this reading is totally unconvincing. Why would the totally formal resemblance between Julien Sorel and Louis Jenrel (their names are the anagrams of each other—a formal resemblance that Julien does not even fully grasp) predict a similarity in their fates? . . . In other words, the oracle-text is presented as almost pure form, as empty of content as possible."[46]

The principal objection here is that there is no reason to read this paper as an oracle, that an anagram in a church with blood-colored curtains does not constitute a prediction, much less point to a causal chain. Ginsburg's objection, entirely valid, brings us back—and it seems that this was the narrator's intention—to the notions of Providence and chance. In some sense, as an explanatory narrative, the oracle embodies the uselessness of explanatory narratives, but this uselessness, this ultimate fusion of chance with Providence, is, I would propose, the point of the novel. The oracle ends—or rather eludes—the search for a line of reasoning through insertion of a causal or at least predictive chain of the sort common in the epic. But even if the paper is not an oracle, even if it is just a coincidence, the fact remains that the shooting and execution would be no more or less assimilable, no more or less explicable as a pure mundane coincidence than as an oracular prediction. In the end, what matters is the fundamentally unassimilable nature of the shooting, the sense that it originates or is readable only in another, ever elusive dimension.

The ultimate fusion of chance and Providence sets in motion an eternal circle of perception similar to that embodied in Julien's prison meditations—a circle of reason and senselessness, first causes and multiple causes, or causes and coincidences. On the one hand, this circle derides the production of master plots, or derides the mind that is prepared to read coincidence as oracle. And this derision in turn undercuts all the master plots that have ever been produced, all the cosmic reasons that have been located and used as explanations from time immemorial, by virtue of its emptiness, its thin presence. On the other hand, because the fact remains that Julien does come to the same end as Louis Jenrel, because the slim formal element that is the oracle-coincidence is the closest we come to a prediction of that "unpredictable" execution, the intrusion of the oracle implies in some sense that a master plot cannot be avoided. This second scenario constitutes a particularly radical act for Restoration culture and a particularly anachronistic epistemological subversion. While readers ponder sources and reasons, while Restoration politicians and ecclesiastics claim an understanding of God's will, while Machiavellian manipulators orchestrate their social ascents ("Nowadays civilization has eliminated danger [le hasard], and the unexpected never happens"), this novel introduces a real Providence, a master cause. The real Providence is the one that no one (character) sees, or that no one (reader) can believe. During the Restoration, as Petrey described, the answer to the question "why" is often absent. But here, that "why" is resuscitated—taken out of the hands of politicians, ecclesiastics, and parvenus, and placed, in some strange sense, in the hands of God. Throughout this novel, the more Restoration politics fabricate a vision of the world, the more the real world recedes. Conversion of chance into Providence seems only to generate more chance, and the more characters (and readers) come to understand the "entire story," the more the "entire story" is displaced. This displacement, I propose, (re)inserts an element of the enigmatic in a culture that depends on and values pure manipulation. If the Restoration means a disingenuous free-for-all, then the oracle represents a fantasy of retribution, of transcendent order, of a means to make truth visible and dominant—a fantasy, ironically, of Providence.

NARRATIVE PRODUCTIONS: MANUFACTURING A VISION OF GOD

The oracle-coincidence serves as an effective instrument of indirect political comment. But as a form-giving instrument, as an actual source of reason, the oracle is rather insubstantial. Emile Talbot writes that the narrator of *Le rouge et le noir* "enjoys highlighting the arbitrariness of his role."[47] But the author of Julien's chronicle is not a Flaubert who guides the hand of God and sends his character to a depressingly unsurprising death. In the end, it is not the arbitrariness of the narrator's role but of narration itself that this narrator underscores again and again. The narrator introduces the oracle and frames it with crimson curtains, but at the same time renders it as slim and coincidental an element as possible. What is more, by the time Julien comes to the same end as Louis Jenrel, the narrator has undermined and all but ridiculed the dramatic and narrative mechanisms that made the oracle possible. We can return, for instance, to the crimson curtains that set the sinister scene for Julien. These curtains, the narrator insists during the course of the novel, are put there by ecclesiastics wanting to produce an impression. The narrator is blatant about this: indeed, the church where the oracle is found functions primarily as an arena where spiritual dramas are mounted. We see the bishop of Agde practice his benedictions before the king's parade. We see in the seminary a sort of actor's workshop where the students practice "significant" acts: "In the seminary there's a way of eating a boiled egg which declares how far one has progressed down the saintly path" (145; 180). The narrator discloses the human hands behind the stage set of the spiritual world and traces the building of that set: the cathedral before it is

decorated, the bishop without his miter and without his benedictions in order, Julien with spurs under his robe, the seminarians in
the process of learning, Julien as a priest-to-be, thus establishing that
human hands manufacture and sustain the spiritual world.

The church produces an entire vision of the universe—a vision of
transcendence and spiritual ambiance. Julien, for instance, understands that the masses depend on his robe to sustain their vision of
heaven: "How will [their seat in heaven] be made visible to them?
By the difference between my exterior and that of a layman" (145;
181). This robe (and the decorated church, the benediction, the discourse of Providence, etc.) is a sort of blue suit for the spiritual
world. When Julien (or someone else, anyone) puts it on, an entire
atmosphere of sacred order and spiritual hierarchy is mounted. This
atmosphere, synthetic as it is, and conscious as Julien is of its synthetic nature, is quite convincing to him. Just as the fiction of the
chevalier de Beauvoisis, the blue suit, and the name of la Vernaye
persuade Julien that he could be the son of some distant nobleman,
so the vacuous emblems of the spiritual world work on him in spite
of their emptiness. For instance, though Julien sees the bishop of
Agde practicing his benedictions and so understands the plastic nature of this action, some months later, this same gesture puts him at
ease: "[Pirard] glanced upward and made a sign of the cross. At the
sight of this holy symbol Julien felt a slight easing of the profound
horror that had frozen him since he entered this house" (137; 171).
Julien is similarly affected by the decoration in the church of Verrières: "Because of a festival, all the windows of the building had been
covered with scarlet cloth. As a result, the sun struck through in
shafts of brilliant light, creating an impressive and religious atmosphere" (20; 24–25). Later, he participates in the decoration of the
Besançon cathedral and so sees the process: "It was necessary, in
one single morning, to cover all the Gothic columns lining the nave
and the two aisles with a sort of red damask that was to be no less
than thirty feet high" (153; 191), but nonetheless remains susceptible to its charms. "Fool that I am! I see a Gothic cathedral, ancient
stained glass; my heart in its weakness forms from those windows a
picture of the priest" (401; 500). The actor or producer in the
drama of the spiritual world can become the audience, a Pavlovian
consumer of his own product. Indeed, in a moment of *mise-en-abîme*,
during the episode of the secret note, the marquis de La Mole
quotes a fable of La Fontaine, *The Sculptor and the Statue of Jupiter* (*Le
statuaire et la statue de Jupiter*): "Shall it be a god, a table, or a pot?"

[*"Sera-t-il dieu, table ou cuvette?"*] (307; 378). This fable describes a sculptor intimidated by the God he himself has made, and is worth quoting in its entirety:

A block of marble was so fair, / A Sculptor purchased it whole. / "What will my chisel prepare?" / He asked, "Deity, table, bowl?"

A god; he'll even have, I say, / A bolt of lightning in his hand. / Tremble, humans; make vows and pray! / Behold the master of the land!

So perfectly the artist did portray / His statue's each and every trait, / That everyone who saw it claimed with no delay: / Jove lacked only power to orate.

Of this artist it was even said: / On finishing his imitation, / He was first to quake in dread / And terror of his own creation.

To match this sculptor's flaw / The poet of antiquity was excellent, / In his great fear, respect, and awe / Of those very gods he did invent.

He was a child in this. / Children always fuss and fret. / Ever take things amiss / Lest their dolls become upset.

The heart is quick to heed the mind / And so it became the fountainhead / Whence pagan error, always blind, / To so many peoples swiftly spread.

Passionate was their embrace / Of their own fantasy's desire: / Pygmalion's love did grace / The Venus he himself did sire.

All try to change to gold, / The dreams that pass before their eyes: / To truths man is always ice cold; / And always eager to swallow lies.[48]

DISTRACTION, OR THE UNBEARABLE ARBITRARINESS OF THE *ARBITRAIRE DU RÉCIT*

Because religion in Restoration France is so inextricably interwoven with economic and political manipulation, the novel's subtle undermining of ecclesiastic dominance and lucidity can be read as pure social criticism. But, I maintain, *Le rouge*'s criticism of this production has to do with atmosphere, with the dismantling not just of power structures but also of instruments of understanding and form-giving. The narrator, significantly, seems as unable to master the narration as do the ecclesiastics, as unable to comprehend the out-side world as Julien. The oracle-coincidence that intrudes on the church, for instance, could easily be read as the instrument of a ma-nipulative, elusive, and secular author. And yet, this narrator prac-tices neither elusion nor manipulation, but rather distractedness and contradiction. When the narrator decorates the church for dra-matic purposes as the ecclesiastics decorate it for political purposes, he shows his own hand. He is also almost parodic in his use of fore-shadowing: when Julien comes to the Rênal house the narrator writes, "He had just ducked his head [*plonger la tête*] in the public fountain. To her great joy, she discovered the timid manner of a young girl in this terrible tutor [*fatal précepteur*]" (22; 27). At the end, of course, the fatal Julien plunges his head, as did Louis Jenrel, into another public aperture.

The fact that the oracle contains as much coincidence as it does sacred direction underscores the emptiness and gratuitousness of these gestures. Furthermore, and here we recall Ginsburg's objec-tion that "while the end meets the beginning, the events that medi-ate fail to constitute a coherent sequence," the oracle is not even the sole reference to an epic or supernatural order that the narrator inserts. Superimposed on the oracle and the falling head is the mo-ment in the opera house, when Mathilde is in her box and Julien, returned from Strasbourg and courting Madame de Fervaques, forces himself not to turn in her direction: "Drunk with love and pleasure, he took an oath not to speak to her. In my opinion, this was one of the finest traits of his character; a man capable of impos-ing such restraint on his own impulses may go far, *si fata sinant*" (342; 425, italics in text). Julien's plans and desires, warns the narra-tor, are useless when the *fata* are in operation. In an epic, these *fata* would mean the gods. Indeed, *si fata sinant*, much more than the oracle, resonates as a subtle reminder of the narrator's dominance. But then again, these dramatic *fata* already have competition: the oracle is already in place. In other words, the narrator introduces this demure prediction (*si fata sinant*) in such a way that the reader marvels not so much at his mastery of the scene, but at the empti-ness, multitude, and contradiction of his gestures. With these ges-tures, the narrator undermines his role and positions himself with the ecclesiastic, the scientist, and Julien, as another generator of fractional narratives.

The insertion of *si fata sinant* in a narrative that already contains a crimson-curtained oracle amounts to a layering of Providence upon Providence, narrative instrument upon narrative instrument. With these instruments, *Le rouge* combines the various sorts of Providence that have driven narratives from time immemorial: dramatic anachronisms epic and tragic that, competing in multitude, underscore the mimetic clumsiness of modern narrative production. As Peter Brooks writes, "The climactic moment of *Le Rouge et le Noir* may be an instance of what is known in classical rhetoric as a 'metalepsis of the author': assigning to the author's agency an action that should normally have been given an agency in the text."[49] And yet: "Constantly referring to the worlds of misunderstanding between his characters, the missed chances and might-have-beens, the narrator repeatedly adumbrates other novels, texts of the might-have-been-written."[50] The "texts of the might-have-been-written" amount to "texts of the might-have-been-explained," which amount in turn to a "could-not-be-explained," impervious to readerly comprehension and authorial mastery.

The process of reading *Le rouge*, again, reproduces the process of living in Stendhal's multidimensional and semisecular universe, but so, it seems, does the process of writing it. All these processes are based on the production of sense-making narratives, the discernment or fabrication of cause and effect. And all those narratives are at the same time bound to be erroneous—bound to discount or misread the actual forces that determine the world of action. The superimposition and intertwining of narrative strands blurs rather than fortifies the narrator's authority. This blurring, this presentation of the narrator as a juggler of narrative strands rather than as some master puppeteer, finds particularly concrete articulation in the descriptions of the Rênal children. When the family is introduced, there are three sons, but when Julien arrives, there seem to be only two. Mossman and Lukacher write that this reduction—the temporary erasure of the middle son—represents the entrance of Julien and the filial nature of his relationship with Madame de Rênal.[51] Indeed, this reading makes sense, as Julien's departure for the seminary restores the original structure.[52] But these mutations also act as a visible representation of the intersection of narrative strands—strands that compromise and undermine one another, that can only be considered one at a time because the mind is bound to a continuous motion from one reason to another, from one narrative to another. There is no master picture, in other words, but only an endless number of stories, a sense of reason that vacillates without resolution from one place to another. One reading eliminates another, which in turn eliminates another. At the end, when Madame de Rênal dies embracing her children, we do not know how many there are. With the variable children, the oracle-coincidence, Providence and chance, and *si fata sinant,* the narrator shows his hand, or hands, subtly but repeatedly. He shows his authorial gestures to be gestures, spectacles, and performances. On the one hand, this narrator is the undisputed master of his chronicle of 1830, but the question remains: what chronicle is that? What has happened? Even the narrator does not seem to have the answer.

I have started this study with *Le rouge et le noir* because the novel articulates subtle and varied responses to participation in a secular culture: subverting readings, welcoming the arbitrary, separating character from social status, recuperating and undermining sacred order. The closest we can come in this novel to an explanatory narrative is something that seems to promise explanation but in fact does not: a disclosure of character that leaves the reader wondering what is so lucid about psychology, or a mise-en-scène of sacred spectacle that makes the sacred ludicrous, an evocation of God that ridicules religion, moments of spiritual contemplation that end up being the result of coincidence, or an oracle that leaves one wondering what was so comforting and harmonic about the epic world. There is a substantial distinction between creating disorder to celebrate authorial manipulation and creating disorder to warn what havoc the human hand can wreak. In the first scenario, the narrator derides the very form and structure of the world he produces. In the second, it is human pretense to authorial status that the narrator mocks. In the first scenario, forces of unsteadiness dismantle the entire frame and leave only the author standing. In the second, the author retains an ambivalence about the implications of that dismantling, about the loneliness that it implies. *Le rouge et le noir* stands in a space between these narrative attitudes, between vaunting and mistrust of narrative production, between celebration and subversion of the individual voice. That space of transition, that inclination to and ambivalence about narrative production, I would propose, accords *Le rouge* a particular sort of emotional and philosophical realism—the realism of gradual transition to a secular consciousness.

2

Flaubert's Superior Joke

In an 1853 letter to Louise Colet, Flaubert writes:

> There is a horde of subjects that exasperate me no matter what end one comes at them from (no doubt, one shouldn't come at an idea from an end, but from the middle). Voltaire, magnetism, Napoleon, revolution, Catholicism, etc, whatever one has to say about them, good or bad, I'm irritated all the same. Conclusion generally seems to me an act of stupidity. Now there's the beauty of the natural sciences: they don't try to prove anything. So what a wealth of facts and what an immense span of thought! We should treat men like mastodons and crocodiles. Do we lose our heads over the horns of the one, the jaws of the other? Display them, stuff them, preserve them, fine, but appreciate them, no. And who are you, then, little toads?[1]

It is around the time that Flaubert writes this letter that European science does in fact begin to treat humans like mastodons or crocodiles. The human organism is studied as the product of the metamorphosis of species, and this metamorphosis as the enactment of natural (rather than supernatural) forces. Scientists describe species without sentimentalities, remaining personally uninvolved with the object of study. For Flaubert, and in particular in *Madame Bovary*, the scientist's detachment becomes the foundation for a narrative mode. Emma is a natural phenomenon to be documented, an organism to be considered. In an earlier letter to Louise Colet, Flaubert described this detachment in other terms: "When will we write the facts from the point of view of a superior joke [*au point de vue d'une blague supérieure*], that is as God sees them from on high?"[2] In this proposition, the dispassionate glance of the scientist becomes the disinterested regard of God.

In this second letter, God's detached vision is presented primarily as a metaphor for narration: the author wants to write as God sees. An ironic and distant God becomes a figure for the obscure, ironic,

49

and contemptuous author: this connection is underscored in Flaubert's famous statement that "the author in his book must be like God in the universe, present everywhere and visible nowhere."[3] Flaubert's obscure and distant God has accordingly been read in criticism as a metaphor for problems of narrative situation, authority, and determinacy. For instance, Pierre Bourdieu writes, "It is here, in this narrative with no beyond, in this narrative that recounts itself, in the irreconcilable diversity of its perspectives, in the universe from which the author has deleted himself but remains, like Spinoza's god, immanent and co-extensive with this creation—it his here that we find Flaubert's point of view."[4] For Jonathan Culler, the metaphoric God is more demonic than Spinozan, but remains the figure of a particular narrative mode: "It is not so much God's objectivity Flaubert desires as his absence: the world will be totalized in a negative fashion, its order shown to be that of an ironic joke, but the author of that joke will be as difficult to pin down as the God who for so many centuries managed to escape, with the aid of his theologians, his obvious responsibility for the world's evil. And just as this evil without an author convinced men that they were themselves guilty of an original sin, Flaubert's *blague supérieure* should have a thoroughly demoralizing effect which men would take as a correlate of their objective condition."[5] In this statement, as in Flaubert's own declaration about God in the universe, the remoteness of God becomes a metaphor for the absence of a dependable narrative source or point of view. The reader is to be demoralized, *as if* confronted with a malicious and vaporous God. But in *Madame Bovary*, God's absence or distance are more than metaphors for a narrative mode. Flaubert says he wants to write as God sees (indeed, also wants others to write as God sees) but, to recast the focus, it seems too that he wants God to see as he writes. Production of a distant and contemptuous God *is* Flaubert's superior joke, a principal concern of *Madame Bovary*.

We know that the nineteenth-century transition to secularism was accomplished not through a direct assault on the idea of transcendent structure, but rather through the gradual conceptual development of a reasonable and harmonic world without that transcendence. In one sense, this replacement is theoretical, an intellectual modification. But it nonetheless produces a considerable mutation in the philosophical and spiritual atmosphere. J. Hillis Miller's comments on a God who has "slipped away from the places where he used to be" belongs to a strain of writing that understands

the disconnection of the world from God as a disorienting philosophical and ontological phenomenon. This disorientation is the
thematic and formal core of *Madame Bovary*. A modern historical
phenomenon, the move to secularism is presented as an occasion
for emptiness and hopelessness and also for narrative manipulation,
as the ironic and secular author eliminates and then comes to substitute for God. Flaubert, with the detachment and entitlement of the
natural scientist, cheerfully seats himself in the place that God has
abandoned, creating a bleak and triumphant portrait of the modern
secular world.

THE SPIRITUAL PURSUIT, OR WILD-GOOSE CHASE

Madame Bovary documents a world run on mundane biological
principles, on natural forces. But one of those principles, one of
those natural forces, is human enthusiasm for the notions of supernatural order and true "meaning," for the residues, however thin,
of God and romanticism. Emma never manages to tire of the spiritual pursuit, and so runs again and again into the idea of God as an
ironic vacuum, an absence that continues to surprise and torment.
Her dedication to a God of absence and hopelessness is crucial to
the superior joke, enables the joke—for in order that God's absence
be ironic, someone has to notice it, to sense it. Ridicule of the spiritual pursuit is one element of this ironic vacuum, one cornerstone
of Flaubertian disillusionment. Some of the novel's most dismal moments are those that mock religious enthusiasm and the desire for
spiritual connection. Emma has three principal episodes of experience with religion: her education at the convent in Rouen, the consultation with Bournisien, and the months of pious ritualism after
Rodolphe's desertion. In Rouen at the age of thirteen, as numerous
critics have commented, Emma finds sensual pleasures, but not
God: "This nature, positive in the midst of its enthusiasms, that had
loved the church for the sake of the flowers, and music for the words
of the songs, and literature for the passions it excites, rebelled
against the mysteries of faith as it had rebelled against discipline, as
something alien to her constitution."[6] Although the "enthusiasms"
are meant to be religious in nature, and although the very word
(God within) implies a religious experience, no such experience is
produced. It is not God who is within, but just Emma. For enthusiasm here remains bound to the natural world, and that world re-

mains antipathetic to God. So it is that Emma "in the midst of her enthusiasms" is closed to religion and faith—a closure that will stand as the foundation for subsequent spiritual failures.

Emma's later spiritual failures are founded on the principle that she cannot reach outside herself. Flaubert's God, it could be said, is amused when Emma attempts this. But this episode's focus on the mind, on its limitation within fantasies, does not at first read as a superior joke, but as a natural modern fact. Writes Georges Poulet, "For the first time in the history of the novel, human consciousness shows itself as it is, as a sort of core, around which sensations, thoughts and memories move in a perceptible space. Thus it becomes possible to discover and express the depth of the human mind; a depth which can be conceived as an expanse through which radiations diverge [la conscience s'épandant dans toutes les directions], or, conversely, as the convergence of all peripheral life upon the sentient being."[7]

In the natural world, Poulet states, the mind "radiates" out to what is around it. "S'épandant dans toutes les directions" implies the mind's vast and perhaps boundless domain, its extension into and onto the world around it. So it is for Emma in Rouen. But it is worth noting that this extension, while celebrating the range and centrality of the mind, stands at the same time to eliminate God and the notion of the outside. In Poulet's reading, dreams and thoughts and fantasies incorporate, or absorb, the dreamed idea into the realm of the mind. But when every circumstance described is described through the radiating mind, then there is no space for an "outside." There is no space for God and transcendence, as the mind incorporates God, as it were, and so eliminates the vast transcendent outsideness of the idea. This is the same absorption that J.-P. Richard discerned in Emma's memories: "Confused reveries allow those 'elsewheres' to become 'heres,' making past and present sensations coincide: but one can hardly give the name of 'memory' to this languid invasion by which the past inundates the present. That past is effaced, not recuperated."[8] This elimination of a transcendent "elsewhere" (and of a past) is explicitly an effect of the secular world: everything is here, must be here, since there is no beyond. Indeed, this concentration on the "here," on the radiating mind, is the defining characteristic of a secular world or at least of a secular fiction. As Georg Lukács puts it, and as cited in chapter 1, "The inner importance of the individual has reached its historical apogee: the individual is no longer significant as the carrier of transcendent worlds, as he was in abstract idealism. He now carries his value exclusively within himself; indeed, the values of being seem to draw the justification of their validity only from the fact of having been subjectively experienced, from their significance to the individual's soul."[9] And then, to explain this phenomenon: "The individual, the vehicle of the utopian challenge to reality, was crushed by the brute force of reality; here, defeat is the precondition of subjectivity."[10] In Lukács's interpretation, consciousness (subjectivity) eclipses the outside world because that world recedes or becomes inaccessible. It is no longer a home; the "brute force of reality" acts on the human soul without comforting it and without strengthening it. The radiating mind, in this interpretation, is reacting to the world's emptiness, building its home—compensating for a transcendence that is no more, or that sustains no more. The problem in *Madame Bovary*, though, is that Emma neither wants nor is able to "carry value exclusively within herself." She is the philosophical and spiritual antithesis to Julien Sorel, for she wants the order around her to *be* an order, to resonate with spiritual meaning and active capacity. The radiation of her consciousness is no triumph, then, but rather a dismal reminder of the departure of transcendence, of the "outside" that the narrator steadily eliminates.[11]

THE DISAPPEARANCE OF GOD, OR FLAUBERT'S PRACTICAL JOKE

When Emma is a young woman in the convent, her resistance to religion can read as adolescent impatience and self-absorption. As a married adult in Tostes and Yonville, though, she is no longer content to remain "in the midst of her enthusiasms." She wants to see spiritual fantasies actuated, to have words (and ideas) "represent an attainable object," as Nathanial Wing puts it.[12] The narrative, though, denies this dream, rendering the outside, and in particular the spiritual outside, more and more inaccessible. Emma's first religious episode in Yonville begins thus:

> One evening when she was sitting by the open window, watching Lestiboudois, the sexton, trim the boxwood, she suddenly heard the Angelus ringing . . . This repeated tinkling stirred in the young woman distant memories of her youth and school-days . . . Then she was moved [*un attendrissement la saisit*]; she felt herself weak and quite abandoned, like the down of a bird whirled by the tempest, and it was unconsciously that

she went towards the church, ready for any kind of devotion, provided that her soul was absorbed and all existence lost in it [*pourvu qu'elle y absorbât son âme et que l'existence entière y disparut*].)" (78–79; 112–13, tm)

Here, Emma desires an absorbing experience of nothingness—of the disappearance of existence. As she leans out the window, into the vast outside, she prepares for this obliteration, this engulfment. But the nothingness that Emma comes to is of another sort. The nothingness, rather than a sublime state of spiritual calm, becomes the simple absence of incident and meaning. She pursues religion in the hope that "all existence be lost in it [*l'existence entière y disparut*]" but finds no "it," no "there" to host or generate this disappearance. Instead of transcendence, Emma comes to the "brute (and secular) force of reality" and of Flaubert's "superior joke."

Much of *Madame Bovary*'s desolate atmosphere comes from the sense that Emma is a moment too late, that she has just missed what she is looking for. At the ball at Vaubyessard, her admiration for the drooling duke is emblematic of this lateness: he is but a shadow of his once (if ever) glamorous persona. The visit to Bournisien stands on the same conceptual foundation, but here it is God that Emma has missed. The episode starts as Emma "suddenly heard the Angelus ringing." But as Emma nears the church and passes Lestiboudois, we read: "Lestiboudois, in order not to lose out on a full day's wages, preferred to interrupt his gardening-work and go ring the Angelus when it suited him best" (79; 113). The ringing bells, then the convent memories, the inspiration to devotion, the trip to the church—these incidents come about because of Lestiboudois' mundane human convenience. Further on, the narrator notes, "Besides, the ringing, over a little earlier, warned the boys that catechism time had come" (79; 113, tm). The Angelus is explicitly not for Emma, but for the children who distract Bournisien from her during the consultation. Indeed, when Emma arrives at the church, it has faded: "The noise subsided with the swinging of the great rope that, hanging from the top of the belfry, dragged its end on the ground" (79; 114).

As the ringing fades, each sound becomes fainter than the one before, until at last no sound can be heard. This diminution is emblematic of the gradual fading of religion from the world of the novel, of Emma's inclination to a God that is no more, that means no more. The studied contamination of Emma's spiritual pursuit continues at the church. As Emma comes to this house of God, she finds only human banalities and cacophonies. Shouting children, rattling marbles, Bournisien's stupid chatter—these are the realities that substitute for God. And these ironically were the same sort of realities that pushed Emma to turn to the church in the first place. Flaubert's "superior joke" insists that Emma's interest in religion brings her to the very terrestrial banalities that she had wanted, through religion, to escape. God has departed: what remains are the emptied ceremonies and discourses of an obsolete cultural delusion.

What Becomes of Repetition in a Secular Culture

The scene of Emma coming to the church as the Angelus fades out is symbolic of the fade of religion in the novel. But this is not the first faded Angelus that we encounter. The first sounds in the description of Charles's lessons: "They were given at spare moments in the sacristy, standing up, hurriedly, between a baptism and a burial; or else the curé, if he had not to go out, sent for his pupil after the *Angelus*" (5; 8). These recitations take place when the Angelus has finished—when the religious moment has symbolically ended. Significantly, neither Charles's education nor Emma's spiritual pursuits, coming in the wake of the faded Angelus, are suited to the modern world. The novel creates in a sense an aftermath of religion, a residue. What becomes of religion and the spiritual pursuit when God has departed? What becomes of meaning? The response to these questions is to be found in the mechanism of repetition that Flaubert uses to disclose and undermine bourgeois cultural and religious discourse and to contaminate the episodes of spiritual enthusiasm.

Ross Chambers, writing of repetition and irony, says of Emma: "She seems not to realize that in trying to escape banality and in searching for something 'new' she is only condemning herself to an existence of repetitions."[13] These repetitions become degradations, and the initial substance is either eliminated or degraded in turn. So it is with the Angelus: the ringing of the bell is a repetition, as are the various instances of ringing, as are religious rituals in general. Charles's education, for instance (which as Chambers observes constitutes the novel's initial and foundational repetitions) is also performed "between a baptism and a burial." This symbolic space of a life becomes, for the priest who performs these ceremonies on a regular basis and for Charles who stands between them, a space between and among repetitions. Existence itself, connected symbolically to these religious ceremonies, is reduced to empty routine, to "spare moments [*moments perdus*]," as is the Angelus for Lestiboudois, as is the fact of spiritual consultation for Bournisien. This repetition continues as the children chant at Emma's departure: "'What is a Christian?' He who, being baptized . . . baptized . . . baptized . . ." (82; 117). This ceremony, and the idea of new life and new naming that it signifies, becomes a repeated word that fades in its turn as Emma returns home. The reiteration of sounds without meaning, of ceremonies without substance, of devotions without object, become in this episode the sole substance of religion.

The "degradation" that Chambers finds in repetition is enacted here as the reduction of religion to a series of emptied discourses that function in turn as emblems of disconnection from God. The author uses his literary arsenal to undermine God and the dream of spiritual solace, as the mechanism of repetition indicates the gradual replacement of spiritual substance with the secular author's deliberate narratological machinations. After the consultation, Emma returns to her house, doomed by the experience to more of the initial frustration of the "inside." The brute force of reality has acted and won. But this brute force is again confronted, and this futile episode repeated, for what Poulet named "human consciousness as it is," despite the sense that God is inaccessible, is nonetheless unable to tolerate God's absence. The "superior joke," the disconnection of God from human experience, also produces Emma's blindness to and incapacity to cope with that disconnection. Lukács's idea of the character that "carries his value exclusively within himself" cannot come to be for Emma, who, in a sort of repetition compulsion avant la lettre, pursues a transcendence that Flaubert steadily erases.

The second time that Emma turns to religion is after Rodolphe has abandoned her; she becomes ill, and believes the end is near:

> Once, at the height of her illness, she had thought she was about to die and asked for communion; and, while they were making the preparations in her room for the sacrament, while they were clearing the night table of its medicine bottles and turning it into an altar, and while Felicité was strewing dahlia flowers on the floor, Emma felt some power passing over her that freed her from her pains, from all perception, from all feeling. Her body, relieved, no longer thought; another life was begin-

ning; it seemed to her that her being, mounting toward God, would be annihilated in that love like a burning incense that melts into vapour. (154; 218)

In this episode, as in the former, the words that describe the spiritual moment are the same words that doom and ridicule it. The moment opens promisingly, with "some power [*quelque chose de fort*]" that seems to come *upon* Emma—to come from outside rather than within her. But this sense of an outside is undone in the next sentence: "it seemed to her that her being, mounting toward God, would be annihilated in that love [*allait s'anéantir dans cet amour*] like a burning incense that melts into vapour." The "it seemed to her" contradicts the "freedom from all perception" and so undermines the eclipsing and engulfing capacity of "some power." Again, the void that Emma dreams of becomes a void of meaninglessness and sameness. So it is with "that love." "That" demands an antecedent, but there is none. What is more, it seems improbable that "her being" would "be annihilated in that love" when "that love" is but an abstract production of said "being." And it seems improbable that that "being" could "be annihilated in" anything at all. "In" implies a receptacle, a space. But here, space means a boundless nothingness, not an enclosure. Like "a burning incense that melts into vapour," Emma's erroneous "it seemed to her" dissipates into thin air, not into the hands of God.

THE DISAPPEARANCE OF GOD, OR PRAYERS UNANSWERED

Here too, the mechanism of repetition functions to evacuate the idea of God. One of the most conspicuous elements in this religious episode, and the most steadily repeated, is the failure of prayer. Emma attempts prayer again and again: "When she knelt on her Gothic prie-Dieu, she addressed to the Lord the same suave words that she had murmured formerly to her lover in the outpourings of adultery. It was to make faith come; but no delights descended from the heavens . . ." (155; 220, tm). In a sense this (repeated) failure can be said to come from Emma's superficiality, from the complete absence of faith, understanding, and patience, and from the use of adulterous discourse in petitions to God. Emma has said the same words to Rodolphe, who has heard them from other women who have read them in other books and possibly said them to other men.

But what is scandalous in this instance is not the fact of repetition, but the transposition from an adulterous to a pious discursive domain. In fact, it is not at all unusual for prayers to be repetitions of words already said, or said by others. In this domain, repetition in word and action is in some sense expected.

Richard Terdiman describes Flaubertian repetition in terms of recitation, a mechanism that discloses the emptiness in ideological discourse: "It appears that the discourse of ideology traverses entire social networks without the slightest alteration. In effect it desubjectifies the subjects who only imagine that they are speaking it."[14] Any articulation, then, risks becoming an unconscious or automatic "performance" of bourgeois discourse, an ironic (re)production of a ubiquitous but nonetheless plastic social order, without subjective force. Prayer, though, it would seem, would be a different sort of articulation. Prayers, as repetitious as any other discourse and in a sense more so, are nonetheless meant to produce a distinct and authentic spiritual connection. They are, paradoxically, repetitions of authenticity, of subjective and objective force. And yet, sacred repetition becomes empty repetition, devoid of revitalizing power, and the objective force of prayer is denied. The dream of a spiritual experience becomes degraded, reduced to meaningless cultural routines, futile mental performances. Rather than participating in an authentic spiritual dialogue, the person who prays in Flaubert's world, desubjectified or not, simply carries out the sort of delusion of connection that plagues Emma both in religion and in her romances. The superior joke becomes palpable here, as Emma, tired of praying to no avail, "arose with aching limbs and with the vague feeling that she was being cheated" (155; 220).

Were God a complete fiction, something fantastic or impossible, then Emma, in her devotion, would have the recompense either of being creative or of being mad, or of living in her own world of subjective accomplishment à la Lukács.[15] Were Emma's impression of being cheated solid rather than "vague," then perhaps she could cope with it. But instead, the absence of God continues both to ambush and to disillusion. That disillusionment constitutes the novel's most vital repetition—in a sense, the novel's only vital repetition—and we sense that it will continue into eternity. Nathaniel Wing comments that "desire, when associated with the nouns which serve as its signifier, can only remain virtual, a possibility forever suspended. When it is articulated as the narrative of fulfilled pleasure, however, desire is linked inevitably with the alienating repetitions of the stereotype."[16] When it comes to God and religion, the desire for spiritual recompense is one that is meant to be suspended. Unlike the desire for love or money, it is not meant to be made substance, not meant to be put to the test in some concrete or immediate sense. Emma's failure to be content with that suspension, the fact that her desire for God is no different than her desire for new clothes, must therefore produce frustration. But the reduction of religion to useless repetitions implies that what is suspended is not completion but more emptiness and disappointment: that there is nothing to hope for, no hereafter to aspire to. This emptiness is demonstrated again and again in Emma's material desires, and it promises to be demonstrated again in the spiritual, as Emma's prayers become "alienating repetitions" of a cultural joke, a vacuous and futile routine.

When Emma's desires for spiritual connection are derailed, when God is denied, what J. Hillis Miller named the "force binding together all men and all things" is eliminated. And that elimination creates, for Emma and the reader, an unpleasant limbo. For although religion has become emptied and meaningless, the secular world in *Madame Bovary* is no more promising. Flaubert's repetition and desubjectification, while undermining religion, also undermine what Lukács described as "subjective experience," or a value carried exclusively within the character herself. Singular experiences and identities, the substance of secular value, are in *Madame Bovary* neither singular nor valuable. Because re-citation desubjectifies not just speech and writing, but thought and experience, the inner life of the individual, which proposes to act as a repository of meaning and value, is unable to do so. The transition from the religious to the secular produces an unpleasant void, a double vacuum comprised of the obsolescence of God and the inertia of the secular world.

What Science Has Done for the Modern World

Important to the "superior joke" is the sense that though religion has become devalued and vacuous, no other source for meaning and substance and promise is possible; that though Emma stands in a wasteland, no return and no progress are possible. What remains in the aftermath of religion in Flaubert's representation is the mundane and invariable fact of the world as it is. One of the reasons that this banality reads as both demoralizing and natural is that the sociological and cultural transition from religion to secularism was in the 1850s a phenomenon in process. Flaubert enacted and thematized this transition by performing and mocking the foundational elements in it—the gradual disconnection from God, the decline of the spiritual pursuit, and the rise of bourgeois materialism—in such a way that the human condition seemed to be set under the sign of decline. Another historical element in this nineteenth-century transition, manipulated and made sinister in the novel, is the rise of the natural sciences.

As demonstrated in his 1853 letter to Louise Colet, Flaubert embraced this rise—not for the understanding it contributed, but for the dreams and grandiosities that it vacated. Science in the 1850s is for the most part detached from religion, concentrating not on the machinations of an ordering God but on the function of natural principles. Biological facts replace the supreme architect. Flaubert uses this replacement, both as a model for his detached narration and as an important ironic component in his "superior joke." For in this novel, the transition from religion to science is more about detriment than about advancement. Instead of bringing an increase in empirical understanding, this transition simply eliminates sentiment and possibilities.

Albert Thibaudet describes Emma's romances: "The two men [Rodolphe and Léon] are nothing more than the male under the entomologist's microscope. The male wants her, pursues her . . . she resists, residues of conscience and modesty linger on the current which attracts her, but something in her and in us knows with perfect certainty [*de science certaine*] that she is headed for a sort of black hole . . ."[17] Thibaudet's comment reads the characters as insects of a sort, bound to natural characteristics. This comment is of particular interest because the detached meticulousness that it discerns in Flaubert's descriptions also characterizes Rodolphe's conversation. Thibaudet notes, for instance, that Rodolphe seems mechanistic and his perceptions of Emma impersonal. Rodolphe's first perception of Emma: "While he is trotting after his patients, she sits there mending socks. And she gets bored! She would like to live in the city and dance the polka every evening. Poor little woman! She is gaping after love [*ça baille après l'amour*] like a carp after water on a kitchentable. Three gallant words and she'd adore me [*cela vous adorerait*], I'm sure of it. She'd be tender, charming. [*Ce serait tendre! Charmant!*]. Yes; but how to get rid of her afterwards?" (93; 134, tm) is indeed impersonal. And Rodolphe's detachment comes, as Flaubert's detachment comes, from a natural scientist's perception.

"Like a carp after water" is a zoological comparison. "Three gallant words" and "She would like to live in the city" are schematic descriptions of nutrition and habitat. There is a rather medical quality to Rodolphe's scrutiny, for as Rodolphe is "under the microscope" of Flaubert, so Emma is "under the microscope" of Rodolphe. And as Flaubert's "microscope" is his means to manipulate and contaminate the hand of God, so Rodolphe's "microscope" is his means to manipulate and contaminate that hand within his conversations with Emma. Rodolphe's seduction of Emma indicates that a scientific detachment and a disinterested manipulation of divine rhetoric are the keys to success. But this detachment, of course, comes at the price of sentiment and substance. Science has come to replace religion, and the microscope, detached and uninterested, to replace the soul.

SCIENCE AND POETIC DISCOURSE

Flaubert admired the natural sciences for their unsentimental regard.[18] One component of the scientist's detachment is the dispassionate use of poetic or sacred discourse. In the episode of the *comices agricoles,* for instance, Rodolphe's declarations to Emma are loaded with the melodious discourse of celestial intervention. For instance: "Two poor souls . . . will come together in love; for fate has decreed it, and they are born for each other" (105; 151), and, "How did we happen to meet? What chance willed it [*quel hasard l'a voulu*]?" (107; 153). And again: "I don't know what force impelled me towards you. For one does not struggle against Heaven" (112; 160, tm). And again, in the letter that ends their romance: "Is it my fault? O my God! No, no! Accuse only fate" (146; 208, tm). These words read as ironic and vacuous, either because these are "serious" words that Rodolphe parodies, or because Flaubert intends them as meaningless sounds. In either case, Rodolphe's "fate" is emptied of meaning, turned into what Terdiman named a re-citation. And once emptied, it remains so. The word is never "restored" to a loftier meaning, nor can it evoke, except negatively or ironically, a nobler world. "Fate" is bound to, and can never be greater than, the discourse that articulates it. God, then, the God of "fate," is imperceptibly but definitively drained from the word—diminished, limited, as it were, to the insincere dimensions of Rodolphe's discourse.

The emptiness in Rodolphe's words is demoralizing not because it obstructs Emma's seduction, but because it does not. Emma does not see the emptiness of the words, does not understand that the transition from a religious to a nonreligious world, from sacred orchestrations to natural realities, has changed the nature of discourse. In a secular world run on natural principles, the word "fate" is not meant to actually indicate the hand of God. Or rather, the concepts of fate and of the hand of God do not, in themselves, explain or lend substance to anything. Fate can be a metaphor for spirit, for force, or for natural principles, but it is a metaphor only, a verbal decoration. Scientists understand this limitation and, in writings on natural selection, separate verbal decoration from concrete substance. When the zoologist Owens lectures in 1858 about natural selection as "the axiom of the continuous operation of creative power, or of the ordained becoming of living things," he adds, "Always, also, it may be well to bear in mind that by the word 'creation' the zoologist means 'a process he knows not what'."[19] Claude Bernard writes, "To act, one must be a materialist, for one can act only on matter. To understand, think, and believe, one must be a spiritualist [*il faut être spiritualiste*], for matter in itself explains nothing. In other words, to act, one must be empirical. To understand, one must be a theoretician."[20] To be a "theoretician" is to discern contexts and patterns. To be a "spiritualist" is to discern in those contexts and patterns a sort of atmosphere. This atmosphere can then be rendered in poetic words and used to adorn the empirical facts. Such decoration is not uncommon in nineteenth-century scientific writing. One instance of it appears in this 1852 treatise on natural selection, published by the botanist Naudin:

> Mysterious, unnamed power, fate for some, while for others, the will of providence [*Puissance mystérieuse, indéterminée, fatalité pour les uns; pour les autres, volonté providentielle*], whose incessant action on living beings has determined, since the beginning of the world, the form, the volume and the longevity of each of them, based on its particular destiny in the order of things. It is this power that brings each member of the ensemble into harmony with the others, adapting it to the function it must fulfill in the general organism of nature, the function which is its reason for being.[21]

Here, the verbal emblems of sacred order (mysterious power, fate, providential will) are used to ornament the phenomenon that is natural selection. That phenomenon, though, would remain intact with or without these words, which do not lend the plants any substance or interest that they do not already have. The scientist's language does not change the nature or origin of the selection process. What is ironic in *Madame Bovary* is that that language does not so much ornament the seduction as enact it. A disingenuous Rodolphe pronounces "fate" and Emma is seduced, animated by Flaubert's ironic hand. As Rodolphe says, "That's a word that always helps" (146; 208). The blatant emptiness in "fate" indicates that ironic replacement, that seduction ex nihilo, that seamless substitution of the hand of the author for the hand of God.

The transition from religion to science is connected with a subtle drain of meaning from the word. And it does not even furnish elucidation as compensation, for science in *Madame Bovary* becomes a repository for practical incompetence and uselessness. This uselessness appears particularly in moments of medical distress—ironically, the arena to which science proposes to bring wisdom and solace. In the episode of Hippolyte's operation, for instance, Homais writes in his article: "that which fanaticism formerly promised to its elect, science now accomplishes for all men" (128; 183, tm). The idea of religious men and women as "fanaticism's elect" deprecates religion and prepares the space for a more modern substitute: Homais proposes science. But because Homais is the author, and Charles the proposed savant, this replacement sounds less than promising. Indeed, the failure of the operation indicates the failure of the substitution: science is to be as absurd and problematic as the religion that it replaces. This sentence and the episode that contains it in effect close both doors. Progression and regression are equally impossible. For this patient, for instance, when science fails, a return to religion ("fanaticism") has already been undermined: "Religion, however, seemed no more able than surgery to bring relief, and the irresistible putrefaction kept spreading from the foot to the groin" (130; 186). As Julien Barnes correctly observes, Flaubert does not believe in progress.[22] Charles, Emma, and the people of Yonville are in a sort of philosophical and spiritual limbo, without the solace of religion and without the foundations and capacities of science. In Flaubert's transition to science, much has been lost, and nothing gained.

The advent of science becomes a gloomy joke once again on Emma's deathbed. When the doctor Larivière arrives at the house, we read: "The apparition of a god would not have caused more commotion" (233; 326): the surgeon has replaced God as the force of salvation. This replacement is underscored with the words: "he would almost have passed for a saint if the keenness of his intellect had not caused him to be feared as a demon" (234, 327). Though there seems to be something otherworldly and powerful about Larivière, saint and demon have become rather dull commodities. Larivière can do nothing for Emma; he turns around and goes to lunch with Homais, and science, in the end, has no effect. Indeed, every declaration about its virtues comes from the bombastic pharmacist or from M. Guillaumin, who comments to Charles that because "a man of science can't be worried with the practical details of life" (200, 281), a power of attorney for Emma is indispensable. Science is brought into *Madame Bovary* not as an admirable explanatory and diagnostic instrument, but as an emblem of modern emptiness and inadequacy. It is represented not for what it contributes, but for what it eliminates—not for what it can do, but for what it cannot.

Overprocessed Discourse, or the
Metaphor of the *Boulanger*

The move to secularism in *Madame Bovary* becomes both emblematic of and responsible for a series of disillusionments. It enacts a series of dismantlings that do not at first seem connected to secularism: the methodological invalidation of meaning, hope, sincerity, and wisdom. These dismantlings are thematic (Emma hopeless, Bournisien imbecilic, prayer useless, science unpromising, the discourse of sacred order insincere, etc.), but also operate within words and sentences. Flaubert recalls Aristotle and medieval theologians and anticipates deconstruction, connecting logocentrism and binarism to the idea of God's infinite understanding. Flaubert uses God as a metaphor for meaning, but at the same time, and more important, explicitly uses meaning as a metaphor for God, making conceptual instabilities and the introduction of uncertainties part and parcel—emblems and consequences—of the move to secularism, and the crumbling of words and meanings correlatives and signals of the departure of God.

Jonathan Culler demonstrated in *The Uses of Uncertainty* how words in Flaubert emphatically do not mean, citing the descriptions of Charles's cap, the houses of Yonville, the wedding cake, the clubfoot apparatus, and so on. I want to point out that the failure to mean is particularly intense in the discourse of sacred order, connected to and evocative of a deliberate separation of word from meaning, of signifier from signified, or of word from syntactical frame. We discussed the separation of words from sentiment, for instance, in Rodolphe's insincere articulations during the *comices agricoles*. But within the articulations themselves, we see sentences come undone and words set adrift, unmoored from meaning. For instance, at Emma's protestation that "one must to some extent bow to the opinion of the world and accept its morality" (104, 148), Rodolphe declares, "Ah! but there are two . . . The small, the conventional, that of men, that which constantly changes, that brays out so loudly, crude and loud like the crowd of imbeciles you see down there. But the other, the eternal, that is about us and above, like the landscape that surrounds us, and the blue heavens that give us light" (104; 148–49, tm). The insincerity in this articulation is obvious but the meaningless in the words is so thorough as to merit further consideration. Rodolphe's second sentence pretends to paint the more important moral order, "the other, the eternal [*l'autre, l'éternelle*]." Detached from the noun it modifies, "the eternal" itself becomes a noun, with the same grammatical and ontological status as the sentence's other nouns: "landscape" and "blue heavens." Furthermore, it becomes reminiscent of its homophone, "l'eternel," the eternal, or eternal one. But "the eternal, that is about us and above" is in fact constructed on the flimsiest of conceptual foundations. A close reading of the sentence discloses a noun that in fact represents nothing, combined with a verb and a modifier that specify nothing. Close reading in this instance *is* deconstruction, disclosing what is not there, rather than what is, revealing to the reader the merest partial semantic residues of God.

The unmooring and evacuation of "the eternal" prepares the ground for twentieth-century theories of deconstruction that connect conceptual and syntactical instabilities to the introduction of spiritual uncertainties. Directly after this moment in the episode, the *conseiller* Lieuvain addresses the audience. His address, a praise of the agriculturist, contains a parabolic chronicle of Rodolphe's poetic manipulations—a metaphoric account of modern meaninglessness. Lieuvain declares, "Who supplies our wants? Who provides our means of subsistence, if not the farmer? It is the farmer, gentlemen, who, sowing with laborious hand the fertile furrows of the country, brings forth the wheat, which, being ground, is made into a powder by means of ingenious machinery, issues from there under the name of flour, and is then transported to our cities, soon delivered to the baker [*chez le boulanger*], who makes it into food for poor and rich alike" (104; 149).

Rodolphe's use of sacred discourse and of "the eternal" mirrors
the bread-making process as Lieuvain describes it. Rodolphe Boulanger is the "boulanger" who turns words into nourishment for
Emma. The words to be prepared are the wheat found in the rich
ground of literature and traditional religious discourse. The difference is that wheat that is "ground and made into a powder" retains
its natural edible substance. Indeed, it must be "made into a powder" and "issue from there under the name of flour" in order to be
edible. But that same sort of mutation processes sonorous words
into vacuous banalities—vacuous reductions (rather than edible ver-
sions) of what the words once were. The "food" that Rodolphe prepares is drained of substance, made barren. At the end of Lieuvain's
sermon, the author, writes, "all the mouths of the multitude were
wide open, as if to drink in his words" (104; 149). This comment
underscores the connection of word to sustenance, but also, invariably, the nonmaterial nature of the word. The audience can no
more "drink in his words" than Emma can access God or sincere
sentiment in Rodolphe's overprocessed discourse.

CHANCE AND THE CON GAME OF LOGOCENTRISM

"Eternal" in *Madame Bovary* is tantamount to a stalk of wheat on
a plate: something to do with food, reminiscent of food, but nonetheless inedible. The discourse of sacred order comes to the same
end as the spiritual rituals and emblems: detachment from its cultural and historical meaning. The formula of one word: one meaning ends up dismantled through the narrator's manipulation of the
word, in particular of words that describe sacred or transcendent
order. Another instance of this dismantling can be found in the use
of the word "chance." Rather than no meaning, this word contains
numerous meanings that compromise and erase one another and
drain the hope from the word.

Early in the novel, "chance" has a rather neutral value. In Tostes,
for instance, Emma had wondered: "She asked herself if by some
other chance combination [*par d'autres combinaisons du hasard*] it
would have not been possible to meet another man; and she tried
to imagine what would have been these unrealised events, this different life, this unknown husband" (31; 46). In this instance, *hasard*
has no particular value, good or bad—it simply refers to the phenomenon of chance. Sometime later, the word has an even more

banal resonance: "All her immediate surroundings, the wearisome country, the petty-bourgeois stupidity, the mediocrity of existence seemed to her the exception, a peculiar chance that had caught hold of her [*un hasard particulier où elle se trouvait prise*], while beyond stretched as far as eye could see an immense land of joys and passions" (42; 60 tm) and then becomes neutral once more: "Like shipwrecked sailors, she turned despairing eyes upon the solitude of her life, seeking afar off some white sail in the mists of the horizon. She did not know what this act of fortune would be [*quel serait ce hasard*], what wind would bring it, towards what shore it would drive her, if it would be a rowboat or an ocean liner with three decks, carrying anguish or laden to the gunwales with bliss" (44–45; 64). In this instance, in this its first appearance, the word mutates and blends into the landscape. In the second half of the novel, though, chance (*hasard*) becomes subtly more promising in Emma's mind, turning into the sort of force that Mathilde de La Mole had in mind when she contemplated with pleasure "everything piled on her by the hands of fate [*par les mains du hasard*]." Rodolphe uses the word in this manner: "'How did we happen to meet? What chance willed it [*quel hasard l'a voulu*]?'" (107; 153). So does Léon: "I sometimes fancied that some chance would bring you [*qu'un hasard vous amènerait*]. I thought I recognised you at street-corners, and I ran after carriages when I saw a shawl or a veil like yours flutter in the window . . ." (168; 239). And "he despaired when he thought of the happiness that would have been theirs, if thanks to fortune [*par une grâce du hasard*], they had met earlier, and been indissolubly bound to one another" (170; 241, tm). Emma too subscribes to this meaning. In Rouen, at the opera, "she tried to imagine his life—resonant, extraordinary, splendid, the life that could have been hers if fate had willed it [*si le hasard l'avait voulu*]" (163; 231). In these latter instances, chance is a source of desire, a granter of grace and miracles in a world emptied of animation. Indeed, it is because of the inanimation in Emma's world that chance does not present a dangerous chaos, but a welcome spirit: the hand of God on an inert landscape. But to continue the comparison with food, Emma, in embracing chance, is in fact devouring a plastic fruit. On the one hand, Emma's fondness for the word "chance" in the second part of the novel resonates as foolish, for it was she who used the word with its neutral meaning at the start. But at the same time, we have the sense that semantic and conceptual foundations are coming undone as the novel proceeds.

The mutating meaning of "chance" presents two problems. For
one, it is emblematic of the evacuation of meaning from a word. Just
as "the eternal" insinuated sacred associations that it did not in fact
possess, "chance" in the novel is contaminated, evacuated in this
first instance. Emptied of its promise and romance, the drained
word represents the barrenness of Emma's hopes, of the idea of
hope, and, in a more general and dire sense, the barrenness of
words. *Madame Bovary* is a narrative recounted in time, but the hopelessness recounted is timeless and spaceless. Culler had stated that
"Flaubert's *blague supérieure* should have a thoroughly demoralizing
effect which men would take as a correlate of their objective condition," but in order that that condition depress, it must be more an
organic phenomenon than a particular historic or economic condition. The references to science and to the end of literary romanticism indicate that the historical transition to secularism is in some
sense to blame, but the dismantling of semantic ground is not limited to a particular moment. The novel rather discloses a simple fact
about words and meanings: an instability that has nothing inher-
ently to do with secularism. Casting chance as the source of Emma's
burden ("a peculiar chance that had caught hold of her") and at
the same time as the force that can ease that burden ("if chance
had willed it") becomes a scandalous ruse in *Madame Bovary*, but this
double meaning also embodies a fundamental (and not at all scandalous) contradiction in Judeo-Christian religious doctrine. On the
one hand, this doctrine is based on acceptance of God's will, on the
sense that the world is just as God wants it and must be embraced as
it is. At the same time, it presents God as the promise or possibility of
a change in circumstances. Whereas reading is based on a consistent
connection of word to meaning, faith depends at times on the
readiness to abandon that connection, to embrace incompatible
meanings or counterintuitive interpretations. The fact that faith embodies numerous contradictions does not mean that disorder is the
norm and must inundate other domains. But when Flaubert transposes epistemological uncertainties into other semantic realms and
demonstrates the problems inherent in them, then the inconsistencies in doctrine become problematic. With this transposition, *Madame Bovary* enacts a crisis of secularism spread into past and future,
a scenario that closes the characters within a prehistoric and presym-
bolic meaninglessness. The suspension of meaning then becomes a
joke not just on Emma, but on any believer who accepts God's will
while waiting for God to provide a way out, or on the reader who

searches for solid meanings while at the same time embracing inconsistencies.

PRIMORDIAL MEANINGLESSNESS, OR THE DISSOLUTION OF BINARISMS

Boredom and its antithesis, burden and escape, past and future, fuse and become one in the word "chance." This fusion acts out the Derridian notion that binarism, the idea of discrete entities and forms, is connected (with logocentrism and with historical time) to the idea of God. Indeed, binarisms of all sorts, including past and present, religious and secular, come undone in *Madame Bovary,* as distinctions philosophical, ontological, temporal, and semantic fade. For instance, as cited earlier, J.-P. Richard described how the future, that time of hope, is compromised before it comes, inundated by the past. The human and the divine also fuse, as the nuns embrace Emma as a future *religieuse,* Léon sees her as an Angel (192), and the Rouen cathedral presents the Virgin Mary as one historical character among many: ("Near him, this kneeling woman who weeps is his spouse, Diane de Poitiers, comtesse de Brézé, duchesse de Valentinois, born in 1499, died in 1566, and to the left, the one with the child is the Holy Virgin. Now if you turn to this side . . . [175; 247]). Mind and body join, as confused representations of Emma's body drift with the confusions of her ruminations, and as Madame Lefrancois describes physical competence as evidence of an admirable priest. Inside and outside fuse, in the representations of Emma's house and garden and in her failures to come to a substantial "elsewhere." Characters, spaces, historical moments, ideas, phenomena, and so on are denied boundaries and distinctions, and emptiness visited on one domain spreads to others. The priest Bournisien, for instance, is tired when Emma comes to see him; in the complete absence of boundaries and distinctions, his weariness spreads to his mind and his spirit, then from there to Emma and her household, from her house into the garden and the streets, from Yonville to Rouen, from one person and one generation to another, from the secular world into the religious world, from present into future and past. No person or place is immune because no person or place *is,* with enough force of being, to resist the atmosphere that reaches across space and time. Good and bad, before and after, here and there, us and them, fuse to turn the entire secular scene of *Madame Bovary* into a sort of indistinct primordial soup.

HOMAIS: THE TRIUMPH OF THE AUTHORIAL VOICE

Of the binarisms and distinctions that *Madame Bovary* undoes, perhaps the most important is that of the individual mind and the outside word, or of the idea as lived by an individual and the idea as abstraction in the public domain. The failure of ideas to become lived ideas, to take vital root in an individual mind, is at the base of the novel's hopelessness. Accordingly, the failure of the characters to constitute themselves through the living of ideas is at the base of those characters' indistinction. Mikhail Bakhtin, writing about Dostoevsky, had declared that "living an idea is somehow synonymous with unselfishness"[23] and had said of *Demons'* Stepan Trofimovich: "He spouts his 'verities' because he lacks a 'dominant idea' which would determine the core of his personality; he possesses separate impersonal verities which because of their impersonality, cease to be completely true, but he lacks a truth of his own."[24] The characters in *Madame Bovary* embrace impersonal verities as dominant ideas without personalizing them in the process, an enterprise that fails for the reasons Bakhtin enumerates. Among these dominant ideas are ideas about the substance of romantic literature, the sentiment of optimism, the idea of progress. Another is the idea of God's presence—an idea embodied and at the same time contaminated in the person of Homais.

Albert Thibaudet writes about Homais' triumph at the end of the novel: "This human adventure [*Madame Bovary*] has as its moral the survival of the fittest."[25] Homais' competence, his "fitness," comes from his versatile nature, his inclination to combine and incarnate without distinction. In his person and in his discourse, mind and world, human and divine, emptiness and substance, wisdom and stupidities, and, not least, God and godlessness, combine into one amorphous mass. And the idea or truth that is most lost in the nonspace between Homais' mind and the outside world (between the domain of the impersonal and the domain of the personal) is the idea of God.

Homais' first dialogue takes place at the Lion d'Or, as he waits with the village residents for the Bovary couple. Mme Lefrançois admonishes him: "Be quiet, Monsieur Homais. You are a godless man;

you have no religion" (54; 79), and Homais protests, "I have a religion, my religion, and I even have more than all these others, with
their mummeries and their juggling. I adore God, on the contrary.
I believe in the Supreme Being, in a Creator, whatever he may be. I
care little who has placed us here below to fulfill our duties as citi-
zens and parents . . ." (55; 79).

In this scene, "You have no religion" means at the same time Catholicism and spiritual feeling. When Madame Bovary the elder proclaims that "someone who has no religion always comes to a bad
end," it is presumed that these meanings go together, that the institutional structure accompanies and houses the personal feeling. Homais separates these out, declaring, "I have a religion, my religion."
This is not a scandalous response, but rather the sort of personal
vision of theism that theologians have called necessary to the main-
tenance of faith in a secular world.[26] And yet, Homais' next sentence, "I even have more than all these others [*J'en ai plus qu'eux
tous*]" undermines this conversion of God into a dominant personal
idea. If the "en" refers to "my religion," it stands to reason that
Homais would have "more" of it than anyone else. With this sentence, God occupies an indistinct place somewhere between the inside and the outside, suspended between the banal landscape of the
outside world and the more banal landscape of Homais' mind, and
rooted in neither.

GOD IN A SECULAR WORLD: HOMAIS' DOCTRINE

Homais continues, "I adore God, on the contrary. I believe in the
Supreme Being, in a Creator, whatever he may be." The denomina-
tion remains unspecified here, but with these words, Homais aligns
himself with those who believe there is a God, who see the world in
a monotheistic manner. He participates in a certain discourse, which
implies (as "I adore God" implies) that Homais' "Supreme Being"
is shared by or at least understood by Mme Lefrançois. "Creator"
(with a capital C) also implies this common understanding. But the
understanding comes apart with "a Creator [*un Createur*]." The abstraction "a" is in a sense crucial if Homais' vision of God is to be
his vision (instead of *the* vision). But the fusion of "a" to "Creator"
does not make sense, for this combination lacks both the pious resonance of "the Creator" and the abstract spiritual significance of "a
creator." "A Creator" is neither a particular religious figure nor an

abstract concept, but a nonidea. Homais' announcement that "I adore God, on the contrary" then reads as vacuous and nonsensical, for "God" is suspended in limbo, denied both the intellectual-empirical worth of the "impersonal verity" and the emotional value of the "dominant idea."

Homais ends this scene with the disclaimer, "whatever he may be [*quel qu'il soit, peu m'importe*]," abandoning his spiritual discourse and dismissing what he has said. But he continues his declamations: "My God [*mon Dieu à moi*] is the God of Socrates, of Franklin, of Voltaire, and of Beranger!" (55; 79). In this lineup, Homais pretends to elucidate his vision of God—to describe "my God" so that Mme Lefrançois (and the reader) can understand it. Socrates, Franklin . . . these men shared an interest in God and personal theism that superceded subscription to institutional religion. Indeed, the evocation of these men is appropriate to the historical moment because, as theologians point out, as the force of the Church declines, personal theism comes to compensate. At the same time, precisely for that reason, Homais' claim to collectivity with these men has no meaning. Had Homais claimed a common philosophy or a common attitude toward theism, then that commonality would make sense: it would indicate common philosophical principles, common spiritualism, common individuality, as it were. But "the God of Socrates" has no universal spiritual significance. As a spiritual force, it means something only to Socrates; as an "impersonal verity," it is a nonverity, a nonentity. The same can be said for "the God of Franklin" or "the God of Voltaire." And yet, because Homais brings out this series of names to support "my God," that "God" does not even have the simple spiritual dignity of being "mine." And in any case, writes Flaubert, Mme Lefrançois has turned away and is no longer listening.

God is one idea, or phenomenon, that is supposed to transcend the boundaries of inside and outside, the boundaries of mind and world, to claim both universal meaning and personal meaning, to subtend and transcend semiotic communities. In Homais' discourse, though, God has neither personal nor universal meaning. That discourse thus introduces an important philosophical and historical problem, the problem of whether God (and language) can survive the end of institutional religion. The transposition of God from the Church into the human mind, in *Madame Bovary*, becomes reminiscent of the transposition of "fate" into the world of Yonville, as Homais' discourse indicates that modern theism might not so much sustain God as deify human stupidities. This possibility is ironic, when we consider theologians' assertions that individual theism is a necessary and natural substitute for fading institutional religions. And it is ironic when we consider that Homais, despite the absence of dominant ideas, is the most clearly delineated and most existentially boisterous individual in *Madame Bovary*. His sentences end with exclamation points, his children are the future of Yonville, and his store is a success. The cross that he receives in the final sentence of the novel is a celebration of individual voice and attainment, in contrast to the collective human "we" ("we were in class") that opened the narrative. What is more, Homais has become a writer, the novel's only producer of literature: "However, he was stifling in the narrow limits of journalism, and soon a book, a major work, became a necessity" (251; 351).

The problem of the survival of God outside the frame of institutional religion can be framed in terms of a contradiction Homais points out in his rant—the ultimate meaninglessness of things in themselves: "And I can't admit of an old boy of a God who takes walks in his garden with a cane in his hand, who lodges his friends in the belly of whales, dies uttering a cry, and rises again at the end of three days; things absurd in themselves, and completely opposed, moreover, to all physical laws" (55; 79–80). The point is of course that these phenomena and characters are not meant to mean "in themselves." Their form and their importance come from the narrative and, what is more, from cultural, social, and personal dedication to this narrative. So it is with Rodolphe's discourse, so it is with any word, emblem, or icon, including the idea of God. Homais' "I adore God!" loses resonance when it is detached from its spiritual foundations and articulated "in itself." At the same time, personal theism demands that meaning stand independent of the institutional frame that once produced it. If the human mind cannot regenerate or sustain meaning and faith, then there is no chance for a continuation of religion. Homais' ridicule of things in themselves thus raises an important problem: we want ideas to stand apart, to transcend, to carry, but once an idea stands out, it becomes unmoored and so (like grain that fails to become flour) loses meaning and substance.

CONTAMINATION OF RELIGIOUS EMBLEMS

Homais' reference to things in themselves, in combination with his role as artiste, brings us back around to the role of the author in the production of this secular atmosphere. When we consider what it is that separates things in themselves from things in their frames, the determinant factor seems to be authorial investment in the form of narrative production: a voice to accord meaning to a word, and a scenario in which that meaning comes to life. The presence of Jonah and the whale in the Bible accords the whale a meaning that, "in itself," it would not have. But as narrative production can accord meaning, it can also take it away. Flaubert's contribution to the process of secularism is a relentless resistance to narratives that make words more than the sum of their letters, or sentences more than the sum of their words, or narratives more than the sum of their sentences, or characters more than the space they take up. Narrative production, as we see from the "things in themselves" that Homais describes, is where God is both made and undone, where contagion is both spread and created. This undoing, in some sense the principal purpose of *Madame Bovary*, connects the elimination of God to the very fact or form of the novel.

A crucial element of Flaubert's superior joke (the element that most devalues the notion of superior and most turns that devaluation into a joke) is the transformation of emblems of sacred order into emblems of narrative manipulation. *Madame Bovary*, that is, narrates an atmosphere of absence and incoherence. But more than this, it uses the instruments of religion to produce and structure that atmosphere, turning spiritual emblems into the narrative building blocks of a glum modern portrait. The sort of appropriation reminds the reader that secularism is a correlative of narrative production, that it both generates and is generated by the action of narration. One element of religion that becomes a narrative mechanism is repetition. We examined the ritualistic repetitions that are denied to Emma: the prayers, the services, the meetings with the ecclesiastics, and so on, that turn into vacuous repetitions for her. But this same force of ritual, denied Emma in love and religion, functions in the narrative to produce disillusionment. The desire for spiritual connection, the effort at prayer, the visit to church, these are repeated. Places of spiritual importance are repeated and revisited, as Emma returns to the Rouen convent and then to the Rouen cathedral. With these visits, the spiritual uselessness of repetition is repeated, and the one ritual that retains some meaning in this narrative is the repeated representation of spiritual places as sources of hopelessness.

The same ironic structuring force found in repetition can be found in Flaubert's manipulation of religious emblems and allegories—a manipulation that not only plots the gradual departure of God, but also discloses the deliberate pleasure and power that the narrator finds in turning that God into a negative. Emma's second religious episode, as we have seen, is initiated with religious emblems (the night table that becomes an altar, dahlia flowers strewn on the floor). The ritualistic preparations for communion are the reasons and inspirations for Emma's spiritual anticipation. As words motivate Emma in Rodolphe's seduction, so emblems motivate her in this sequence. And as the religious episode continues, so does Emma's enthusiasm for religious emblems: "She wanted to become a saint. She bought rosaries and wore holy medals; she wished to have in her room, by the side of her bed, a reliquary set in emeralds that she might kiss it every evening" (154; 219). These emblems, though, of course, do not produce the desired spiritual experience. Instead, the result is an absence of meaning, or a dead space where meaning should be. Each symbol is a negative reminder, vacuous and flat. And each ritual honors the spiritual solace that Emma is denied—celebrates, that is, the denial of meaning.

The pursuit of religion through its emblems and rituals is exaggerated and made ridiculous in this novel, but it is not really so outlandish an endeavor. Religion relies on the meaning of rituals and emblems. When Emma is in the convent, for instance, her fondness for ritual makes the nuns hope that she will become one of them. In a dialogue on religion, Schopenhauer writes about symbols and symbolism, "Religion is truth allegorically and mythically expressed, and so rendered attainable and digestible by mankind in general. Mankind couldn't possibly take it pure and unmixed, just as we can't breathe pure oxygen; we require an addition of four times its bulk in nitrogen. In plain language, the profound meaning, the high aim of life, can only be unfolded and presented to the masses symbolically, because they are incapable of grasping it in its true signification."[27]

The human mind, he proposes, is wired to understand through symbols (the reader of *Madame Bovary*, for instance, has no trouble understanding symbols of disillusionment and emptiness). In this interpretation, the symbolic can and sometimes must be the receptacle for meaning. The symbolic (attendance at church, prayer, the Eucharist, or simply the concept of God) is the door to the "high aim of life," as nitrogen is the sine qua non of breathable air. Flaubert, though, turns this door into a dead end and does not open another. The symbolic does not "mean," or means only negatively. The novel deactivates the symbolic register; this deactivation underscores the ridicule of the spiritual pursuit.[28] But to understand this ridicule as a fundamental aspect of Flaubert's superior joke, of the narrator's contamination of the hand of God, we consider religious emblems as presented in the rest of the novel.

Religious Emblems as Ironic Instruments of Secularism

On her way to the convent, Emma eats from a scratched dish: "The explanatory legends, chipped here and there by the scratching of knives, all glorified religion" (25; 36). On the road to Yonville, the plaster priest statue, already chipped, "thrown out of the carriage by a particularly severe jolt, had broken into a thousand pieces on the pavement of Quincampoix!" (62; 90). The humming of the Angelus "subsided with the swinging of the great rope" as Emma comes to the Yonville church. Religious emblems, in the hands of the narrator, literally come apart, fade out, and are obscured. A similar contamination is visited on religious sacraments: at Emma's tumultuous wedding, "coarse grass and thistles" attach to the dress (20; 29). At Berthe's baptism, Charles's father dumps champagne on the child's head (64; 92). So too with spiritual figures. When Emma visits Bournisien, his cassock has come unraveled and he is weakened from the heat: "Grease and tobacco stains ran along his broad chest, following the line of his buttons, growing sparser in the vicinity of his neckcloth, in which rested the massive folds of his red chin" (80; 114–15).

The disintegration of these emblems and sacraments and figures is concrete and progressive. And these disintegrating emblems, unlike the rosaries and the altar in Emma's room, have a symbolic value—an active and generative value—in the narrative. Victor Brombert reads this value as moral or ethical: "At times, the symbolic detail serves as an ironic punctuation, as it almost graphically plots the stages of a moral evolution. . . . The gradual destruction of the ecclesiastical figure [the priest statue] parallels the gradual disintegration of their marriage."[29] The literal destruction of religious symbols, as Brombert reads it, traces Emma's ethical decline. But it also traces the destruction or dismantling of the symbolic register, reflecting and enacting the continuous unavailability of religious experience and of what Schopenhauer called "the high aim of life." Flaubert's superior joke, here, undoes the religious emblems that Emma embraces and turns them into ironic emblems of narrative authority. Their destruction acts upon and within the story, to "graphically plot" Emma's spiritual failure. God becomes an ironic mechanism in the hands of Flaubert, an automatic narrative instrument of deception and manipulation.

A similar and more obvious use of symbolism is found in the reference to God before each instance of adultery. "God is with us!" announces Rodolphe as he and Emma gallop into the woods for their first amorous experience (114; 163). Léon and Emma visit the cathedral before jumping into the coach for their ride around Rouen. As Bourdieu, for whom symbolic capital equates with power writ large, writes, "Flaubert does not stop at affirming his own potency by objectifying impotence; he also objectifies the principle of this symbolic power of objectification."[30] For if, as Wing finds, Flaubert cannot escape the meaninglessness and delusions of the world he creates, he nonetheless retains the force of representation. With the symbolic he is sustained, maintaining his meaning and structure to the detriment—and with the explicit elimination—of spiritual substance.

J. Hillis Miller found that the disappearance of God brought the eradication of a "force binding together all men and all things." But in *Madame Bovary*, the "binding force" is to be found in the structure of the narrative—an ironic order that binds together all men and all things in an atmosphere of secular homelessness and derision. The elimination of God in *Madame Bovary* is enacted with subtle deliberation. And yet, and most ironically, this elimination reads as natural and realistic. The absence of transcendence and the emptiness of metaphors and emblems manage to read as facts of the modern world, outcomes of the rise of the natural sciences and an interest in natural principles. To return to the fondness for the natural sciences with which this chapter opened, in the voice of the natural scientist, and with ironic delectation, Flaubert represents Emma as a sort of unadapted organism—the unselected. Emma's interest in God and her dreams about transcendence make her unable to flourish in Flaubert's secular world. And this inability reads in its turn as a modern fact, a natural if unfortunate condition that is thematized and made the foundation for the entire narrative. A scientist does not mourn and ruminate on what an unadapted animal could have become in other circumstances, or what could be done to protect it from the world. And Flaubert does not mourn in *Ma-*

dame Bovary. The narration does not resonate with what could have been, had circumstances been different, because, throughout, circumstances are relentlessly and resolutely *not* different. Flaubert stands as scientist and as ordering God, as author and documenter of the "superior joke." This joke celebrates the eradication of God at the hand of narrative authority—the hand that contaminates, parodies, and, in the end, substitutes for the hand of God.

3

Faith in Realism

WE TURN NOW TO *A NEST OF GENTRY*, PUBLISHED IN 1858 BY FLAUBERT'S close friend, Turgenev.[1] In this novel, as in *Madame Bovary*, the narrator comments, in form and content, on his characters' notions of God and sacred order. And in so commenting, he establishes a position with respect to the characters—a distance from them, a sense of admiration or disdain, identification or detachment. And that position, here as in *Madame Bovary*, in turn echoes the narrator's sense of commonality with the characters he represents and, I would propose, with the human community at large. *Madame Bovary* articulated more derision and distance than understanding and closeness, and in so doing implied a sense of authorial entitlement—entitlement to detachment, wisdom, amusement, and manipulation. In *Nest* also, the narrator's position with respect to his characters reveals his feeling about participation in the community he describes. But here, the narration embodies a profound distrust of detachment and superior placement—a reluctance to stand in a place of impact and manipulation. In *Madame Bovary*, the narrator's freewheeling production of an ironic secular atmosphere not only created a dismal world for Emma, but also implied the right of the narrator to such a creation. In *Nest*, on the other hand, the narrator's hesitations, disclaimers, and superstitions articulate a disinclination to orchestrate the lives of others, to orchestrate the outside world, in short, to seat oneself, as Flaubert's narrator had so merrily, in the place of God.

In a garden scene, Liza and Lavretsky declare their sentiments: "'I love you,'—he said again:—'I am ready to give the whole of my life to you.' Again she [Liza] shuddered, as though something had stung her, and raised her gaze heavenward. 'All this is in God's power,'—she said."[2]

Liza is a pious young woman with a spontaneous and ingenuous sense that her world is in the hands of the God she embraces. And

79

yet, *A Nest of Gentry* is not a parable about the victories of the humble. The moment in the garden comes about thus: Feodor Ivanitch Lavretsky has returned to Russia from Paris after discovering his wife's infidelity. He continues to support her, as well as the child that may or may not be his; four years after the separation, he goes to visit his aunt and cousin in the town of O and meets his cousin's nineteen-year-old daughter Liza Kalitin. Liza and Lavretsky come gradually to love one another, but Lavretsky's marriage to Varvara Pavlovna, despite their four-year separation, precludes a declaration. One day, though, Lavretsky discovers an obituary in a French newspaper: his wife has died.

The moving scene in the garden takes place a short time after this discovery. But when Lavretsky returns home that same night, after declaring his love for Liza and having this declaration reciprocated, he finds some unfamiliar traveling cases: his wife has returned. The obituary, she explains, was but a ruse, under whose protection she had planned to return to Russia, to Lavretsky, to legitimacy for her daughter, and to a continuation of her pension. Lavretsky is overcome with despair; Liza, with guilt. She insists that Lavretsky return to and reconcile with his wife. Lavretsky, miserable, pensions Varvara once more and furnishes her with an estate. Liza enters a convent, sure that Varvara's return is a punishment for her "criminal hopes" (242; 270). Before parting, Liza and Lavretsky meet one last time. Lavretsky cries, "Akh, Liza, Liza! . . . how happy we might have been!" (269; 286); to which Liza replies, "Now you see yourself, Feodor Ivanitch, that happiness does not depend upon us, but upon God" (ibid).

As these words are articulated, the reader has witnessed the destruction of Liza's dreams by accidents, calculations, coincidences, misrepresentations, distortions, and some particularly bad timing. These coincidences and calculations do indicate, it is true, that happiness (the Russian word *schastie* also means fortune) does not depend on "us." But the narrative has made clear that "not us" does not necessarily mean "in God's hands"—at least not the sort of God that Liza has in mind.

The idea of divine guidance, and the prospect of a world without it, looms in the form of this narrative and in the minds of its characters as it does in those of the French novels examined earlier. Rather than being a drama about the individual actor though (Julien, Rodolphe, Emma in some respects), this is the story of spectators: the people who want to believe, who want to perceive the attributes of the divine (omnipotence, unity) in the world around them, but who, nonetheless, see those attributes mocked and displaced. And that displacement is relentless, for while the novel disdains those individuals who rush to commandeer the course of the world, the fact remains that their individual power constantly crashes in to fill the void that God's absence produces. Or rather—to fill the void that God's name, and the very idea of divine order, paradoxically keeps open. This is a novel about the divine (or rather, the idea of the divine) as, fundamentally, an instrument of manipulation, an idea that pushes some to slow down and surrender and others to spring into action.

The Case for Submissiveness— The Narrator's Humble Example

In this drama of life, one person is the actor and another the spectator; one the god and another, the mortal. Or, to put it another way, one is the author and another the character, or one the creator and another the reader. *Nest* has been called a mockery of faith as well as a revindication of faith, and various points in between. I would propose that this novel does not so much take a position as articulate a deep ambivalence about the various roles one can play, the power one can exert in one's own life and in the lives of others. This ambivalence is thematized, as we will see, but it is also reproduced in the very form of the narrative.

Stendhal and Flaubert narrated circles—often ironic circles—around their characters. Stendhal's circles were numerous and uncertain, and Flaubert's were progressive and relentless, but in both cases, the narrators generate an order (or an absence of order, or a disorienting multitude of orders) to which the characters have no access. The transition to a secular culture becomes an occasion for narrative manipulation—for the intrusion of chance, simultaneous narrative strands, and ironic use of the discourse of sacred order. Turgenev's narrator, on the other hand, uses hesitation, disclaimers, and inconsistencies to vindicate the characters' subjectivities and to undermine the Western trend toward authorial dominance. Flaubert wrote that "the author in his book must be like God in the universe, present everywhere and visible nowhere."[3] I would propose that this author in his book is by design unlike God anywhere, but rather like a person in the universe, examining questions about the (limited) individual role in political and spiritual communities and in his or her own fate. What this author does with his world, in other words—a world that is for him a theoretically unlimited playing field—is emblematic of ambivalence about the impact that one individual can have on the life of another. On the one hand, this hesitation is of particular historico-political importance because the tension between submissiveness and impatience lay at the root of the political and philosophical debates of the Russian mid-nineteenth century. The political struggles of the 1850s and 1860s, the conflict between Slavophilism and Westernism, were intertwined with and motivated by questions of individual authority that were often religious in nature. But though in this sense historically specific to the nineteenth century, such questions transcend the historical and geographical circumstances and are pertinent to power relations of various sorts. The form of narration we see here is emblematic of a mistrust of individual power: of others,' but much more, and in a sense more importantly, of one's own.

For the narrator of *Nest*, there is something deeply suspect about a person who tries to create, to narrate, or even to speak without going through meticulous processes of observation, contemplation, and, importantly, self-doubt. He demonstrates this suspicion through example: from the start, this is a narration that values gradual approach over rapid mastery. One of the most salient characteristics of his narration is the moment of contemplation that suspends selection of words and reasons—the moment it takes for an image in the mind to become a word on the page. For example, in the description of Lavretsky: "Only in his eyes, which were blue and prominent and fixed, was there to be discerned something which was not revery, nor yet weariness . . ." (41; 161). In the description of Varvara: "From the very sound of her voice, which was low and sweet,—there breathed forth an insinuating charm . . . something which it is difficult to express in words . . . [*shto slovami peredat trudno* . . .]" (84; 184). And again, in an account of Lavretsky's ruminations: "It is difficult to say, whether he was clearly conscious in what that work consisted . . ." (93; 189). About Liza: "No word can express [*slovo ne vyrazit*] that which took place in the young girl's pure soul . . ." (203; 247). Of Varvara: "Precisely what those lovely eyes said, it would be difficult to state . . ." (254; 278). From the start, the narrator inches at the story and at the entire Russian lexicon with trepidation, reaching out a conscientious hand to select words and formulate a *discours*.[4] Sometimes, the narrator does not manage to bridge the distance from word to image, or word to idea. In those cases, the failure is acknowledged rather than concealed, and that humble acknowledgment made evidence of a painstaking narrative methodology.

A word should be said about the words "author" and "narrator" as I am using them here. In this novel, there is a particular narrating voice and persona. That narrating persona is loath to claim the author function; this reluctance, this renouncing of authorial hubris, is one of his most important characteristics and the most germane to the argument at hand. Indeed, this persona is almost as loath even to make the descriptive choices, to claim the authority, the finality, as it were, associated with narration. When the narrator does choose a word, it is with indecision, hesitation—a sense that the Russian lexicon as well as the essence of the world around him stands outside his comprehension. Qualification abounds. For instance: "Through a sort of [*kakoy-to*] dark whirlwind, visions of pale faces flitted before him" (95; 190); "Painful sensations, weighed on his breast with a sort of agreeable oppression" (110, 198); "Her eyes gazed dully, but expressed zeal, and a long-established habit of serving with assiduity, and, at the same time, a kind of respectful commiseration" (115–16; 201); "On his return home, he sank into a sort of peaceful torpor . . ." (120; 203); "He read surprise and a kind of secret reproach in her face" (171; 230); "'Do you know how to play piquet?'—she asked him, with a certain dissembled vexation . . ." (182; 236). "Nastasya Karpovna kept prostrating herself, and rising with a sort of modest, soft rustle" (195; 243); "She did all this without haste, without noise, with a certain touched and tranquil solicitude on her face" (288; 297). When he presents a word without qualification, he does so with careful deliberation, defending his selection: For instance, in the epilogue's portrait of the hold that Varvara has on Panshin: "Varvara Pavlovna had enslaved him, precisely that,—enslaved him; no other word will express [*drugim slovom nelzya vyrazit*] her unlimited, irrevocable, irresponsible power over him" (293–94; 300).

The narrator's lexical scrupulousness implies a conviction that the story (and each element of it) contains a precise and complicated essence that resists facile description—that the *histoire* stands antecedent to the *discours* and must be respected and recounted with care. Hastiness on the part of the narrator would stand to contaminate that *histoire*, not to improve it; the same hesitation and reverence applies to the chronological structure. For instance: "On that same day, at eleven o'clock in the evening, this is what was going on at Mme Kalitin's house" (44; 163). When the narrator "breaks" the narration of present incidents and turns to describe Lavretsky's youth, he says, in parentheses: "(We must ask the reader's permission to break the thread of our narrative [*rasskaza*] for a time)" (46; 164). These words imply that the narrator understands the "natural" order, that he respects and intends to return to that intrinsic temporal structure—indeed, the parentheses mitigate even his small intrusion. The intervening section (Lavretsky's parents, adolescence, and education) reads as research in the service of this "thread": the narrator has momentarily sacrificed chronological order, but only in order to unearth historical circumstances and thus better describe the situations at hand. At the end of the "break," the narrator writes, "We now beg the indulgent reader to return with us" (100; 193).

With respect to the characters of the story, the narrator is careful to intimate that he has not invented anything or anyone: that he is present as chronicler and not as creator, as narrator and not as author. For instance, in the introduction of Panshin: "The young man, with whom we have just made the reader acquainted, was named Vladimir Nikolaitch Panshin" (17; 148). This sentence detaches the act of narration from the character "himself," suggesting that the author did not dream up "Panshin" for the purposes of fiction but instead came upon a man named Panshin and decided to write about him. This same implication subtends the portrait of Varvara Pavlovna's mother: "Concerning his wife, there is hardly anything to say: her name was Kalliope Karlovna; a tear oozed from her left eye . . ." (82–83; 183–84). The declaration that "there is hardly anything to say" implies observation rather than invention. It indicates that the author has come upon Kalliope Karlovna, found her tedious, and determined that spare description is enough. The detail of the little tear, though, intimates that had the narrator wished to dedicate his time to meticulous documentation—had he found that his subject merited that dedication—the descriptions could abound. The phenomenological detachment of the narration from the characters is presented again in the epilogue, as the narrator writes, "But first, let us say a few words about the fate of Mikhalévitch, Panshin, Mme Lavretsky—and take our leave of them [*rasstanomsya s nimi*]" (295; 300). This sentence accentuates the sense that the narration and the story are fundamentally discontinuous—that the characters can continue on as "we" break with them. To further underscore this detachment, the narrator does specify that each of these cited characters survives at the end of the novel (whereas numerous others, Lemm, Marya Dimitrievna, Marfa Timofeevna, etc., do not).

THE VIRTUE OF SILENCE, OR THE
PROHIBITION ON FABRICATION

The narrator sustains his characters' decisions through imitation: through narrative hesitations, qualified pronouncements, reluctance to denounce, or even to declare. There is another component of this imitation (or this modeling) that explicitly connects the narrator's machinations to an endorsement of silent submission, and this is the profound distrust of composition, fabrication, and writing that permeates the novel. From the start, the production of fiction and, more than this, the act of writing, are represented as suspect. This suspicion has to do, I think, with the finality of narration and certainly of authorial creation. Early in the novel, Marfa Timofeevna, Liza's aunt, is sitting in her chair, knitting a woolen scarf. The narrator has introduced her as having "independent character," commenting that she told the "entire truth to everyone, straight in the face" (6; 142). Marfa Timofeevna is working on the scarf when Gedeonovsky, the village gossip, comes to visit. He asks whom the scarf is for, and Marfa Timofeevna replies, "It is destined for the man who never gossips, nor uses craftiness, nor lies, if such a man exists in the world" (11; 145, tm). Gedeonovsky wonders, on hearing this, "But who doesn't use craft nowadays? It's the spirit of the age" (ibid.).

The implicit response to Gedeonovsky's second question is: the person who does not obstruct or distort and does not concoct fictions. This interchange is important because it predicates fabrication-nonfabrication as a measure of character. The scarf is not mentioned again and the narrator does not specify on whom, if anyone, the woman finally bestows it. But he does state that for the childless Marfa Timofeevna, Liza is the "favorite." He also specifies that she had cared for Lavretsky when he was a child, and that he had been "born into [her] arms" (42, 162).

The word meaning "to fabricate stories" (*sochinyat*) also means "to compose" or "to write" (an author's complete works, for instance, are *sochinenniy*). In this novel, substantial distrust is placed on the act of writing and, in some sense, on all artistic production.

When we consider who the artists are in *Nest*, it is not Liza and Lavretsky, but Panshin and, most of all, Varvara. Liza and Lavretsky, the narration specifies, are not writers. When Varvara's obituary comes, Lavretsky simply hands it to Liza with a pencil mark on the death notice. He neither writes an accompanying note, nor even speaks to Liza. Liza, like Lavretsky, is uninterested in the manipulation of words. Her note to him is as short as possible. At the end, we learn that she never even writes letters home from the convent; "news comes through other people" (302; 304). Panshin, on the other hand, composes poems, sings at the piano, and draws in his sketchbook (and in Liza's). Varvara is an even more accomplished *artiste*. When it comes to composition of various sorts, there is nothing these characters cannot do. James Woodward notes that the characters that are the most "fluent musicians" are the novel's predators and that those who are the least talented are the novel's victims.[5] Indeed, Liza and Lavretsky love music but are not talented at its execution, while Varvara is a virtuoso at the piano: she can (and will) play anything that is put in front of her, even when it is unsuitable to the situation at hand (a triumphant aria as she tries to reconcile humbly with her husband, for instance). So too with writing and theatrics: Varvara is a composer of dramatic speeches and posturings (pushing Lavretsky to mutter: "In what melodrama is it that there is precisely such a scene?" [224; 259]). And yet, while she can produce composition, she does not want to be an audience to it: as the narrator says, with a preface phrase that sets him apart from dishonest Varvara, "To tell the truth [*sobstvenno govorya*], literature did not interest her greatly" (254; 277).

Behind Varvara's distrust of literature is the sense, underscored in this narrative, that most instances of writing are either instruments or outcomes of deception and distortion. Indeed, the first instance of writing in the novel comes in the form of the note that Lavretsky finds on Varvara's bedroom floor—the note from Varvara's lover that exposes her adultery. The contents of this frivolous note, written in French, chronicle and at the same time enact a contamination of the narrative of marriage. It indicates a germ of distortion and untruth, entered into a narration that was (or that was thought by Lavretsky to be) sacramental and pure. The second instance of writing consists of the newspaper clipping that announces Varvara Pavlovna's death. This article, like Ernest's note, is a scrap of paper that turns the course of the narrative (its contents, like the contents of Ernest's note, are in French). Unlike the contents of Ernest's note, though, the contents of this note are erroneous, since Varvara is not dead. In fact, she is preparing to return to Russia, and hopes that the rumors of her death will obscure that return. This article, then, is a fabrication, a misrepresentation, the very act of fabrication that Marfa Timofeevna had denounced in the second chapter.

The nefarious and deceptive qualities attributed to these instances of writing extend, subtly, to all composition. All writing, all declaration, even all opinion, stands to be such a fabrication. The works of literature described in the novel are either romantic or surreal. Liza, for instance, reads the novels of Walter Scott: the same works of literature that duped Emma Bovary into waiting for a romantic hero. Lavretsky, as a child, read the book *Symbols and Emblems*:

> This book contained about a thousand in part very puzzling pictures, with equally puzzling explanations in five languages. Cupid, with a plump, naked body, played a great part in these pictures. To one of them, labelled "Saffron and the Rainbow," was appended the explanation: "The action of this is great . . ."; opposite another, which represented "A Heron flying with a violet blossom in his mouth," stood the inscription: "All of them are known unto thee." Cupid and a bear licking its cub was designated as "Little by little." (69; 176)

As a dictionary of symbols, as a reference work, this book is rather unusual. Rather than an elucidation, it provides a sort of lesson in how to embrace counterintuitive descriptions and explanations—a lesson, even, in how to see what is not there, and how not to see what is. Indeed, no literature in the novel, not even the Bible, is accorded authority or truth: Liza, significantly, learns about religion not from the written but from the spoken word. The admirable characters in this novel abstain from writing both because they do not want to mislead others, and because they are loath to assume (even for a moment) authorial dominance. At times, this abstention extends even to verbal production. In the description of Liza's upbringing: "[Liza's nurse] Agafia . . . felt that it was not for her to utter such lofty and sacred words. Liza listened to her—and the image of the Omnipresent, Omniscient God penetrated into her soul with a certain sweet power" (217; 255). Words are imparted hand in hand with a reverence for them (here again, "a certain sweet power"), with a humble sense of proscription. In conversation with Lavretsky, Liza declares: "I have always thought that I . . . had no words of my own," to which Lavretsky murmurs, "And thank God for that!" (159–60; 225). This is the same sort of cult of subtle moderation that pervades the narration, with its hesitations, its qualifications, and its defensiveness.

FRESH AIR THROUGH OPEN WINDOWS

As demonstrated in Liza's moments with Agafia, it is in moments of silence that God is found. Liza's religion is born of listening, and that listening, of her own wordlessness. The narrator's hesitations and disclaimers, his formal and thematic ambivalence about the very act of narration, his apparent concern that to describe is to contaminate and that to opine is to slander, is, I would propose, connected to that same idea of listening, of deference to what is outside. Virginia Woolf, in an article about Turgenev's characters, writes:

> As we notice without seeming to notice life going on, we feel more intensely for the men and women themselves because they are not the whole of life, but only a part of it. Something of this, of course, is due to the fact that Turgenev's people are profoundly conscious of what is outside themselves. "What is my youth for, what am I living for, why have I a soul, what is it all for?" Elena[6] asks in her diary. The question is always on their lips. It lends a profundity to talk that is otherwise light, amusing, full of exact observations.[7]

The privileging of the outside world, shared by Liza, Lavretsky, and the narrator, is fundamentally religious (spiritual) in nature. Whatever or whoever God is, the individual is not God: God is distinct from individual mind and desire. The value accorded to that distinction emerges in the narrative's descriptions of the outside and of nature. The interlude that ends with the declaration in the garden starts thus: "One day, according to his custom, Lavretsky was sitting at the Kalitins'. A fatiguingly-hot day had been followed by so fine an evening, that Marya Dimitrievna, despite her aversion to the fresh air, had ordered all the windows and doors into the garden to be opened, and had announced that she would not play cards, that it was a sin to play cards in such weather, and that one must enjoy nature" (197; 244). At the end of the chapter, writes the narrator, "Everything in the room became still. . . . and the song, mighty, resonant to the verge of daring, of the nightingale, poured in a broad stream through the window, in company with the dewy coolness" (201; 246). The chapter ends, as it started, with the stream of nature into the house. In the next chapter, Lavretsky and Liza declare their sentiments in the garden, accompanied by the nightingale and surrounded by the natural earth.

In this scene, in the narration, and in the minds of Liza and Lavretsky throughout the novel, "what is outside themselves" is of more moment and occupies a more elevated rank than what is within. What is more, to absorb that outside, one must be still; silence is inextricably connected with respect. With this balance in mind, we can turn to the last time that Lavretsky sits on the bench in the Kalitin garden. Eight years after Liza's departure for the distant convent, Lavretsky returns to the house where she had lived. He meets Liza's brother and her sister Lena, who is now herself nineteen and engaged to be married. Marya Dimitrievna is dead, as are Marfa Timofeevna and Lemm. Lavretsky wanders around the house, pausing in the drawing room at the piano, and then goes out into the garden. From inside the house, he hears the sounds of the young Kalitins playing and shouting. "'Play on, make merry, grow on, young forces,'—he thought . . . Lavretsky rose softly, and softly went away; no one noticed him, no one detained him; the merry cries resounded more loudly than ever in the garden behind the green, dense wall of lofty lindens" (305; 306).

In this interlude, the house is seen and heard from the garden. Whereas the air of nature had once streamed into the house, here, instead, human merriment and voices stream out, out of the house, into nature. When he was inside the house, Lavretsky turned his perceptions to the outside. Now that he is outside, he is silent and calm. He has no more words about the nature of the earth; he subsides into the landscape. In the next sentence, the narration refers to Lavretsky and Liza as "people who are still alive, but who have already departed from the earthly arena" (ibid.). To be in the "earthly arena" is to discourse about and interact with nature, and to do so from a distance. Once that distance is eliminated, there are no more dreams to be sustained, no more faith to be articulated. *A Nest of Gentry* comes to an end on this same page.

At the same time, the "outside" is not just the home of nature, the antithesis of what is literally "indoors" and "man-made," but, rather, a place or a time or a perceptual plane where one is not. The outside is what is beyond one's control, on scales both large (historical and social realities) and small (the decisions of others, the voices of others). The crucial element remains that distance, that separation between the individual and the sphere of action, the individual and God.

In one sense, these insertions of distance, these subtle insistences on the characters' independent existence, and the devotion to the outside, produce a realistic effect, in the mode of Stendhal's "the novel is a mirror." More than this, though, they reproduce and thus serve to endorse the perceptual mechanisms of the characters. Richard Freeborn writes, "The relationship of Lavretsky to Liza is approximately the same as the reader's relationship: she is an unknown quantity for both parties."[8] The sort of moderation that infuses the narration also infuses Liza and Lavretsky's ruminations: a reluctance to misrepresent, to wield and misuse a narrator's prerogative, even to evaluate another person or declare what a person or thing *is*. For instance, when Lavretsky discovers Ernest's note, "Lavretsky did not, on the instant, understand what sort of thing it was he had read . . . He lost his senses . . ." (94; 190). And when Lavretsky asks Liza what she is thinking: "Ask me no questions about anything . . . I know nothing, I do not even know myself . . ." (193; 242).

One of the more striking characteristics of this narrative, one similar in form to Liza's preternatural acceptance of her unfair and unfortunate circumstances, are the times when the narrator demonstrates reluctance to pass judgment on his characters. In a description of Liza's suitor Panshin, the narrator writes, "In soul he was cold and cunning, and in the midst of the wildest carouse his clever little brown eye was always on guard, and watching; this bold, this free young man could never forget himself and get completely carried away. To his honour [*k chesti ego*] it must be said, that he never bragged of his conquests" (19; 149–50). These sentences open with an account of Panshin's character—an account without mediation or distance. "In soul he was cold and cunning" is pronounced with entire authorial certitude. And the reference to the "little brown eye" in Panshin's wild moments further underscores the narrator's attentive vision; at this point, the narration reads as a detached and meticulous documentation of character. But the words "to his honour it must be said" indicate another stratum of authorial prerogative, or rather, more precisely, of a narrator's obligation or principle. "Honor" resides not with Panshin (the narrator writes that Panshin's soul is cold), but with the narrator and his code of action.

The characters share the narrator's unwillingness to denounce.

When Lavretsky and Liza contemplate Panshin: "Really, it strikes me that Panshin is not worthy of her," meditates Lavretsky. "But what is there wrong about him?" (111; 198). And Liza, asked whether she loves Panshin, replies, "No. But is that necessary? Mamma likes him; he is amiable; I have nothing against him" (177; 234). The narrator comes at the narrative as Liza and Lavretsky come at their world: not with the enthusiastic mastery of the manipulator or the author-manufacturer ex nihilo, but with the hesitation and distance of one imbued with profound reverence, deserved or not, for the unfolding story, the unfolding world.

THE VIRTUE OF SELFLESSNESS

The value accorded to the outside, combined with an insistence on distance, represents a code of submissiveness that permeates the characters through and through. On the one hand, this code has a political relevance, forming an organic part of the Slavophile position as articulated in Lavretsky's political discourse.

In the debate between Panshin and Lavretsky, Panshin proposes: "'Russia has lagged behind Europe; she must catch up with it. People assert, that we are young—that is nonsense . . . The best heads among us,'—he went on,—'les meilleurs têtes —have long since become convinced of this; all nations are, essentially, alike; only introduce good institutions, and there's an end of the matter. One may even conform to the existing national life [narodnomu bytu] . . . but . . . the institutions will transform that same existence'" (198; 244–45). And then: "Clever men must reform [peredelat] everything" (199; 245). To this "Lavretsky did not get angry, did not raise his voice . . . and calmly vanquished Panshin on every point. He demonstrated to him the impossibility of leaps and supercilious reforms, unjustified either by a knowledge of the native land or actual faith in an ideal, even a negative ideal; he cited, as an example, his own education, and demanded, first of all, a recognition of national truth [narodnaya pravda] and submission [smireniya] to it—that submission without which even boldness against falsehood is impossible" (199; 245–46).

In contrast to Panshin, who wishes to "reform" the country in the most absolute sense, from its foundation to its details (or rather, from its details down to its foundation), Lavretsky presumes the immovable nature of that foundation. To the Westernist's desire for reform, Lavretsky counters with preservation. To the Westernist's desire to orchestrate, he responds with acceptance. When the contemptuous Panshin then demands what Lavretsky intends to do in Russia, he replies: "Till the soil, and try to till it as well as possible" (200; 246). This plan embodies Lavretsky's sense of honor: the earth is for him the origin and embodiment of truth, and better to farm it than to raze it in the name of reformation. Richard Gregg calls Lavretsky the "mensch" who emerges victorious from this debate, pointing to the moment when Lavretsky "crushes" his opponent. But he triumphs, paradoxically, through passivity; for in this system, the one who evinces the most preternatural acceptance emerges victorious.

The narrator's scrupulous hesitations are embedded in an entire philosophical, political, and cultural code of submissiveness and acceptance. Turgenev has been called "an outspoken Westernizer and an agnostic,"[9] and some Russians consider him to be more a French than a Russian writer. And yet, the entire narrative is geared to the sort of hesitation that characterizes the Slavophile position. Indeed, in his contrasting of Lavretsky and Panshin, in his espousal of the Slavophile political and cultural position and his unwillingness to undermine or contradict the characters associated with that position, he is explicit about what side he is on. And, more fundamentally, he is explicit about the fact that his narrative mode has a "side"—that submissiveness and hesitations are not just stylistic preferences, but crucial emblems of a national and, I would venture, spiritual code.

"FRENCH DRESSES, FRENCH IDEAS, FRENCH FEELINGS!"

The characters in *Nest,* while all Russian (except for Lemm), are divided by national language and *philia.* Varvara Pavlovna and Panshin are the novel's Francophiles and French speakers. Varvara is described in the French newspaper as "*Une vraie française par l'esprit*—there is no higher encomium for the French" (92; 188–89). It is in French that Varvara coldly mocks her hostess ("Elle n'a pas inventé la poudre, la bonne dame"). French becomes the code for emotional detachment: connection with France means aloofness in a character, and use of French to describe means aloofness from that aloofness. About Panshin, the narrator writes, "Where it was requisite, he was respectful; where it was possible, he was insolent, a capital companion, *un charmant garçon*" (18; 149). About Varvara, we are told, "All her thoughts, all her feelings, circled about Paris" (253; 277). We know that Varvara's "feelings" are rather limited, and so Paris becomes a locus of emptiness, a whirlpool of vacuousness, as well as of a rather tautological conceit. Interestingly, the narrator's description of Varvara anticipates Count Rostopchin's diatribe in *War and Peace.* "'How can we fight the French, Prince?' said Count Rostopchin. 'Can we arm ourselves against our teachers and divinities? Look at our youths, look at our ladies! The French are our Gods: Paris is our Kingdom of Heaven.' He began speaking louder, evidently to be heard by everyone. 'French dresses, French ideas, French feelings!'"[10]

I point out the connection of Varvara Pavlovna's Francophilia to Count Rostopchin's tirade in *War and Peace* because it demonstrates an instinctual connection between a bold reformist Westernist ethos and an intrusive, invasive nature. When Count Rostopchin gives his speech, the French are in the process of invading Russia. That moving, that sense of expansion and incursion, is emblematic of Frenchness as seen through some Russian eyes. The French fabricate, compose, produce, reform, invade, while the Russians contemplate, observe, consume, protect. The French move outward, the Russians turn inward. But more than this, the French move outward onto the Russians, and the French mode of being becomes thus unseemly and violent in its antagonism. There is no war on in *Nest*, but Varvara nonetheless occupies the role of predator from beginning to end: on meeting Liza, "*Mais elle est délicieuse!*" (243; 271); and on leaving the Kalitin house, "On arriving at home, Varvara Pavlovna sprang lightly from the carriage,—only fashionable lionesses know how to spring out in that way—" (258; 280). Varvara is prepared to devour Liza, as Napoleon was prepared to devour the Russian army, as Panshin is prepared to devour Russian institutions, to scatter Westernist political methods over Russian soil.

In presenting France as the spiritual antithesis of Russia, I am interested not so much in the political histories or ethe of these particular countries as in their respective roles in the drama of secular culture (which, as we see, is much the same as the drama of a culture that has maintained the legitimacy of divine authority). These roles, while schematically coded here along national lines, are easily transposed through place and time and culture. In this particular drama, France, broadly stated, is identified with the author function, and Russia, with the book; France, with a turning outward, and Russia, with a folding in. So it is that Panshin sees Russia from the outside, while Lavretsky tries to sense it from within, to be its autobiographer and defender. At issue in these roles, again, in the portrait of Francophile Varvara, the political discussion between Panshin and Lavretsky, the representation of the fresh outside air, and the unwillingness to pronounce or even describe, is of course not just political, but also and more fundamentally, spiritual identity. To "till the soil as well as possible" is to act in balance with the outside world, to not rock the boat or reinvent the wheel (even if the wheel could arguably use reinventing), but to accept the "natural" boundaries of human power.

The idea of a reverence for the soil comes up again in the episode in which Lavretsky goes to church with Liza. In this episode, Liza bends her head and prays to God, while Lavretsky, unaccustomed to the church, "had not appealed to God for a long time: and even now, he did not utter any words of prayer,—he did not even pray without words, but for a moment, if not in body, certainly with all his mind, he prostrated himself and bowed humbly to the very earth" (189; 240). Lavretsky's desire to turn to the earth, to till it, to draw from it, matches Liza's desire to do God's will. Indeed, an admirable spiritual inclination as represented in this novel is based neither on institutional religious association nor even on devotion to God per se (even the extremely devout Liza is not particularly bothered by Lavretsky's lack of religion as such), but on humility, on a reluctance to dominate, manipulate, or orchestrate. To grab the reins, or to seize the pen, puts one on the wrong side of this nearly Manichean conflict between action and submission.

SUBVERTING WESTERN REALISMS

Le rouge et le noir and *Madame Bovary* showed the use of the discourse of fate to manipulate others. *Nest* shows those who use that discourse to understand and tolerate another's manipulation. It is a different paradigm, based on the human being not as writer but as reader and character. As we have seen, the narrator demonstrates in both theme and form the suspect nature of authorship. And in so doing, he adds a different cast to discussions about realism. One principle that this novel contradicts is that of realism as connected to secularism. Another is the principle of realism as connected to (the idea of) empiricism.

The representations of Panshin and Varvara, the mocking of reformists, and the ridicule of Francophilia articulate political and cultural criticisms of Westernism. But the entire mode of narration also embodies an aesthetic or literary critique of the West: of the Western version of realism, or of the Western association of realism with secularism and "objectivity." Elizabeth Allen's *Beyond Realism* defines Turgenev's realism thus: "A definition of Realism becomes possible as soon as it is sought not in an idea of the real but in an image of the ideal. In fact, it is an image of the ideal, specifically a normative or prescriptive ideal of human life—that is, what human life *should* be like—that truly distinguishes works of realism."[11] In her estimation, Turgenev's "realism" is in fact idealism—a reaction to a world in need of some ornamentation that she explains in terms of Nietzsche's concepts of Apollonian art:

> Apollonian art does not assert that the harmony, tranquility, and order it presents are objectively true to life. It embodies an original conception of life, a subjective conception envisioned by the artist irrespective of whatever reality (whether hidden or overt) may inhere in the world beyond art, for this harmonious, tranquil conception of reality is generated by the artist's imagination and hence is admittedly a fabrication, even a deliberate untruth. Nonetheless, by virtue of its ordered coherence and comprehensibility, this conception can provide meaning to life, whereas disordered, incoherent, incomprehensible reality cannot.[12]

According to this formulation, Liza's insistence on the presence of God ("Now you see yourself, Feodor Ivanitch, that happiness does not depend on us, but upon God") would be an Apollonian fabrication, similar in nature (if not in mood) to the explanatory narratives readers construct around the shooting of Madame de Rênal and the execution of Julien Sorel. The real would be the machinations of Varvara Pavlovna and the arbitrariness of the characters' unhappiness: the ideal the introduction of the idea of God as salve to render that arbitrariness more tolerable. But the realism in *Nest*, I would propose, is not about resistance to the real, but rather about a meticulous dedication to locating the real. The narrator's numerous qualifications, his careful defense of his word selections, and his code of hesitation serve to uphold the sanctity and even inaccessibility of the real. The criterion of the ideal in *Nest*, in other words, resides not in notions of good and bad, or pretty and not pretty, but in notions of true and false. What reads as masochistic denial could in fact (who is to say?) be a dedication to truth *as* the highest ideal.

Allen's comments on Apollonian reconstruction are reminiscent of the Western aesthetic (and entirely aesthetic) criticisms of realism published during the nineteenth century. *Le roman russe*, the work in which E. M. de Vogüé introduced Russian literature to the French intellectual public, advertises Russian literature precisely as a more "charitable" alternative to French realism:

> Realism responds to one of our demands when it studies life with rigorous precision, when it disentangles the most minute roots of our actions; but it deceives our surest instinct when it voluntarily ignores the mystery beneath rational explanations, the possible element of the divine. I would not have realism affirm truths about the unknown world. But at least it must pause and tremble at the door of this world. Religious sentiment is more indispensable to realism than to any other art form: it lends it the charity it needs. And realism becomes odious when it ceases to be charitable.[13]

As Vogüé sees it, secular realism is an artistic and spiritual fiasco: odious, in a word. But the "odiousness" is based not on its falseness but on its poetic emptiness. The word "charity" implies that "religious sentiment" is a donation—an indispensable donation, perhaps, but nonetheless an element introduced from without, and not an intrinsic part of realism. I would propose, though, that to the narrative standards established in *Nest*, a realism that obscured the element of the divine and divine will would not be so much uncharitable, as simply unrealistic. The idea of secular realism is rooted in a particular cultural and intellectual tradition, and Vogüé has French literature (and French romanticism and French aesthetic standards and French intellectual dominance and French fantasies of religious grandeur) in mind when he speaks of charity. The ultimate equation of realism with godlessness has little application, indeed little realism, for a culture that God has never abandoned—for a culture that does not connect understanding with secularism, or humility with humiliation.

THE MYTH OF OBJECTIVITY, OR RESISTANCE TO NARRATIVE AUTHORITY

The critique of Western realism articulated in this novel goes beyond the argument of the world as it is versus the world as it is not, realism versus unrealism. For once the secular standard of realism is

put in doubt, then human reason has declined in value or importance, and when this happens, in turn, the binarism of "is" and
"should be" or "is" and "is not" starts to evaporate. As modern literary criticism has demonstrated, the entire paradigm of a calcula-
ble realism breaks down when "is" becomes a matter of consensus.
Furthermore, the idea of declaring what the real is or is not smacks
more of hubris than of realism in a culture that sees hesitation and
uncertainty as crucial elements of realistic narration.

In many ways, the narrative construction of *Nest* can be read as
a subtle defense of subjectivity—a defense that in turn undermines
objective definitions of realism and the real and flies in the face of
French fondness for authorial dominance. For this narrator, for one,
there is little realism and documentation that operates without the
mechanism of perception, of witnessing, direct or indirect. Moreover, there is no mechanism of perception and witnessing that is in-
herently or absolutely immune to contradiction. In this description
of the Kalitin prayer service: "Nastasya Karpovna kept prostrating
herself, and rising with a sort of modest, soft rustle; Liza took up
her stand, and never stirred from her place, never moved; from the
concentrated expression of her countenance, it was possible to divine [*mozhno bylo dogadatsya*] that she was praying assiduously and
fervently" (195; 243). "It was possible to divine" predicates subjective interpretation as the sine qua non of narration, and indeed, of
vision. In this novel, narrative descriptions are often preceded by an
implied "it was possible to divine"—imbued with the sense that all
narration, all declaration, comes from a combination of intuition
and sensorial clues. Again during the Kalitin prayer service: "Marya
Dimitrievna stood in front of them all . . . she crossed herself with
enervated carelessness, in regular lordly fashion,—now glancing
around her, again suddenly casting her eyes upward: she was bored"
(194; 243). Because the declaration of fact ("she was bored") is preceded by a description of visual clues, it reads as a conclusion at
which the narrator, having watched Marya Dimitrievna, has arrived.
This construction presents perception and deduction as crucial
steps on the road to realism and, in so doing, substitutes the world
as it is read for the (increasingly contingent) "world as it is."

The narrator's reliance on visual clues and the characters' hesitation in the face of the clues that confront them embody two fundamental obstacles to a solid definition of realism. On the one hand,
empiricism and deduction are all we have: only that which is seen
can be known. And yet, as the characters insist, and as the narrator

lets them insist, even empiricism does not tell the entire story. Put in other words, *even* that which is seen cannot be known. Faith leaves a space in this narrative—a space for alternative interpretation or, more often, for a deferral of interpretation. This space, which comes out in the narrator's moderate descriptions ("to his honour, it must be said . . .") and the characters' modesties ("But what is there wrong about him?" "I have nothing against him.") also creates the distance between the narrator and "what happened"—or between the narrator and the real.

"WHO KNOWS? WHO SHALL SAY?"

One element of the narrator's cautious treatment of the real is his reference to moments of direct witnessing or visual interpretations, as in the aforementioned instances. Another and in some sense more striking such element is his refusal to contradict the perceptions and interpretations of his principal characters. This resistance is most present in the narrator's treatment of Lavretsky. For one, the narrator echoes Lavretsky's submissive tone, his hesitations, his reluctance to evaluate, his sense of honor, and his insistence on respecting the truth of things. But he also at times echoes the content of Lavretsky's perception—at moments, interestingly enough, when those perceptions are most at odds with Western standards of realism. In the episode when Lavretsky encounters Liza in the Kalitin garden, it is night; Lavretsky wanders for some time with no particular direction on the village paths, and soon finds that he is standing at a garden gate. He pushes the door, enters the garden, and is astonished to find that it is the garden to Liza's house. She comes to the door at the sound of his step, and the scene of declaration ensues.

As Lavretsky wanders, the narrator writes, "a narrow path fell before him [*popalas emu*]" (204; 248, tm). The construction of this sentence has the path as animated subject and Lavretsky as destination. He walks on this path, and comes upon a gate. "He tried, without himself knowing why [*sam ne znaya zachem*], to push it open: it creaked softly and opened, just as though it had been awaiting [*slovno zhdala*] the pressure of his hand" (ibid.). When the narrator does turn to describe Lavretsky's sentiments, it is as though he and that character were of one mind: "This has not happened for nothing [*eto nedarom*]," (ibid.), thinks Lavretsky as he stands at Liza's house. When Liza comes into the garden, he declares, "I did not think to come here. I was brought [*menya privelo*]" (207; 249, tm).

The narration of Lavretsky's wanderings approaches the fantastic (the fact that the gate opened "as though it had been waiting" becomes especially curious when we learn that as Lavretsky tried to leave the garden, the gate was locked and he had to climb over it). Semifantastic sentences such as "a narrow path fell before him" and "it creaked and opened, just as though it had been waiting . . ." can be read as decorations on a prosaic world, but this entire garden interlude demonstrates that the parameters of realism are not to be measured to the standards of an objective secular reality, but to the standards of the narrator. In other words, this interlude uses the French convention of narrator privilege to undermine narrator privilege—and, in the end, to argue the possibility of a mystical realism. Woodward writes, "Nature, the greatest character in all Turgenev's works, is the 'force' that leads him irresistibly to the gate."[14] And, "To the 'forces' which dictate their attitudes and actions corresponds the 'force' represented by their predictive portraits. Their freedom is as limited in the fiction as in life, and in this sense the form is a mirror of the content."[15] But what emerges most in this episode is not the narrator's omniscient statement of any particular worldview, but his echo of the characters. The narrator maintains a cautious distance from the omniscient position, and resists imposing limitations.

There is another moment when the narrator hitches himself to Lavretsky and moves with him through the story. In the epilogue, when Lavretsky returns to the Kalitin house, the narrator sets the scene by announcing which characters have died in the past eight years: Marya Dimitrievna, Marfa Timofeevna. Then, when the conversation starts, Lena announces these same characters, and puts in another name that the narrator had not included in his exposition: "And M'sieu Lemm." To which Lavretsky exclaims, "What? And is Lemm dead also?" (301; 303). Lavretsky shows surprise only about Lemm, though in fact it would be much more reasonable that the elderly Lemm had died than, say, Marya Dimitrievna, who was younger and more vigorous than he. With this response, it is as though Lavretsky already knew about the deaths of the others: as though he were with the narrator, reading him or hearing him and understanding what he understands. This doubling means that Lavretsky cannot be surprised or trumped or duped by the narrator in the way that some of the characters in French novels are duped by their narrators. The narrator's reluctance to take the upper hand, to know more than someone else, to claim some sort of authority, is part and parcel of his insinuation that nothing and no one is wrong: that all is but a matter of perception—that, in a sense, there is no objectivity, or if objectivity there is, it is not for him to claim it. With this insinuation in mind, we can return to the concepts of Apollonian and Dionysian art that Allen cites in her definition of realism, concepts about which Nietzsche wrote:

> Metaphysics, morality, religion, science—in this book these things merit consideration only as various forms of lies: with their help one can have *faith* in life. 'Life *ought* to inspire confidence': the task thus imposed is tremendous. To solve it, man must be a liar by nature, he must be above all an *artist.* And he *is* one: metaphysics, religion, morality, science—all of them only products of his will to art, to lie, to flight from "truth," to *negation* of "truth." This ability itself, thanks to which he violates reality by means of lies, this artistic ability of man *par excellence*—he has it in common with everything that is. He himself is after all a piece of reality, truth, nature: how should he not also be a piece of *genius in lying!* Love, enthusiasm, "God"—so many subtleties of ultimate self-deception, so many seductions to life, so much faith in life! He enjoys the lie as his form of power.[16]

God in this formulation is an idea generated in response to the experience of life—a fiction created for a sense of mastery. Most Western writers second this idea of contrast, this sense that the religious ideal is but a fictitious response to the secular real. Charles Bovary and his "It's the fault of fate," to which the narrator instantly adds, "Rodolphe, who had conducted that fate . . ." as well as Emma's episode of fanaticism that functions as a satire of itself, are emblematic of this realism. Examples of such ironic repudiations abound, instances when the narrator represents the voice of secular realism, trumping and ridiculing his characters in moments of religious enthusiasm. In *Nest,* though, the voice of the narrator operates in the service of another vision of realism. And indeed, if, as Nietzsche has it, "God" stands with love and enthusiasm as an organic component of the human thought mechanism, then the extraction of the real from the morass of misperceptions becomes rather complicated. God, and this is certainly the case in *A Nest of Gentry,* is not an emblem of conscious Apollonian artistic revision, but, instead, an instrument of vision in the first place.

"THE MEEK MAY INHERIT THE EARTH, BUT THEY WON'T KEEP IT LONG": THE DOWNSIDE OF SUBMISSIVENESS[17]

The narrator's sympathies and his formal example of modest restraint validate a suspicion about pronouncements, about the pretense to objective evaluation, about the Western binarisms of true and false, real and ideal, subjective and objective, natural and fantastic, mythical and authentic, and, importantly, winner and loser. The characters' most poetic moments are those in which they come to terms with their misfortune, the cards life has dealt them. "I have almost held in my hand, the possibility of happiness for my whole life— it has suddenly vanished; and in a lottery, if you turn the wheel just a little further, a poor man might become a rich one. If it was not to be, it was not to be [*ne byvat, tak ne byvat*],—and that's the end of the matter" (262; 282), murmurs Lavretsky. And Liza declares, "Now you see yourself, Feodor Ivanitch, that happiness does not depend on us, but upon God" (269; 286). Liza's final declaration that happiness depends upon God has a poetic resonance precisely because it marks a surprising detachment from the path of frustration and resentment, an embracing of compliance at the moment when instinct (self-preservation) would seem to reject it. Liza's gentle acceptance, articulated in the narrator's delicate outlines, is what makes Ford Madox Ford (who watched his mother cry as she read *Nest* over and over) call this novel the "most beautiful book ever written." And yet, for all this beauty, for all the sublime calm of Liza's resignation, the narrator nonetheless subtly mediates his celebration of passive acceptance and articulates a profound ambivalence about submissiveness. While unwilling to ironize Liza and Lavretsky, while unwilling to gallop over their world, he does nonetheless question what becomes a gradual slide into immobility, an excess of submissiveness that dooms them and represents the treacherous underside of compliance.

The narrator never does give us a wholesale contamination of the idea of God. To do so, whether in theme or form, would amount to the sort of direction—orchestration—that he has denounced by example. The message is not "there is a God" versus "there is not a God," but rather an examination of what uses and misuses the idea of God can be put to—an assessment of the price of belief.

The Narrator's Cult of Reticence

As cited earlier, the narrator often hesitates before the act of description, vacillating at the selection of a word or at the prospect of (negative) evaluation. There are even times when this narrative mode becomes exaggerated, leaving conspicuous vacuums where description and evaluation could stand. For instance, about Lavretsky: "He himself was not able clearly to make out what he felt" (194; 243). "For some reason or other, Lavretsky felt inclined to smile uninterruptedly, and say something amusing . . ." (195; 243), "Without himself knowing why he did so . . ." (196; 244). And then: "It was a secret to herself; so let it remain for all others. No one knows, no one has ever seen, and no one ever will see, how that which is called into life and blossom pours forth and ripens in the bosom of the earth" (203; 247, tm). One envisions this narrator, like his characters, moving with care to examine that venerable phenomenon that is the real, and trembling to disturb it.

There is a moment in Dostoevsky's *Demons* (to be examined in chapter 5) when the narrator ridicules the Turgenevesque character of Karmazinov for this precise narrative approach. When Karmazinov takes the stage at Yulia Mikhailovna's evening, the narrator writes, "Mr. Karmazinov, mincing and preening, announced 'he had flatly refused to read at first' (much he needed to announce that!). 'There are lines,' he said, 'which so sing themselves from a man's heart as cannot be told, and such a sacred thing cannot simply be laid before the public' (why was he laying it, then?)."[18] The *Demons* narrator notices the moments at which delicate prudence becomes gratuitous, at which a diplomatic touch becomes a spectacle of silence. At some point, Karmazinov's scrupulous qualifications, testaments to narrative precision, slide into a cautiousness that impedes perception—into a sensitive reluctance that goes too far and functions as an obstacle to understanding, or at least to expression. The same impediment operates in *Nest*. The narrator of this novel does wield a sort of mastery: but it is the mastery of the gatekeeper, of the obstacle to understanding. It seems that he is narrating in a small corner, or narrating himself into a small corner, wary of the very act of pronouncement.

The narrator's slide into silence and inaction, the construction of the small corner, the modest abstentions that Dostoevsky would ridicule, reproduce the subtle slide that operates in Liza and Lavretsky.

Hesitation, for these characters as for the narrator, is not just careful-ness and precision. It becomes an entire mode of life, expanding to include a prohibition not just on injudicious action, but on all ac-tion, on all words, opinions, ideas, and even thoughts. It is guarded-ness with respect to the very idea of comprehension, the very idea of opinion. Just as the narrator comes to a point when reluctance to fabricate becomes reluctance to declare an opinion or formulate im-pressions of any kind, the characters come to a point when reluc-tance to impose becomes reluctance to act.

The narrator writes of Lavretsky in the closing chapters: "In the course of those eight years the crisis had, at last, been effected in his life; that crisis which many do not experience, but without which it is not possible to remain an honourable man to the end: he had really ceased to think of his own happiness, of selfish aims. He had calmed down [on utikh], and—why should the truth be concealed?—he had aged, not alone in face and body, he had aged in soul" (304; 305). This becoming tranquil, indispensable as it is to "remaining an hon-ourable man to the end," is also the sort of slowing down that be-comes antithetical to action. In many ways, in their resistance to precipitous action, Liza and Lavretsky are dedicated to silence and immobility. Declares Lavretsky to Panshin, "We must submit to truth"; to Varvara: "But I perceive that I must submit. You will not understand that word; . . . it matters not" (279; 292). And in his ruminations alone at home: "May the irksomeness here sober me, may it soothe me, prepare me so that I may understand how to do my work without haste" (122; 204). In addition to this validation of submission, the characters also abdicate voice and opinion, articu-lating a complacence that seems to be bred in the bone. Liza, for instance, when Lavretsky asks her about her intentions to marry Pan-shin: "I am listening—I am taking nothing upon myself" (178; 234); "Ask me no questions about anything. . . . I know nothing. I do not even know myself." (193; 242).

Liza and Lavretsky's reluctance to pass judgment on Panshin, cited earlier, extends onto other objects of contemplation. During his boring months with Varvara in Paris, for instance, Lavretsky in-sists, "I am not wasting time . . . all this is useful" (93; 189). And when Varvara returns and comes to visit the Kalitin house, "Insult was audible to [Liza] in this [Varvara's] exclamation; but she made up her mind not to trust her impressions" (243; 271). That hesita-tion soon turns into a leaden force: "A strange insensibility, the in-sensibility of the man condemned to death, had come upon her"

(247; 273). When Liza admits that she "[had] always thought that [she] . . . had no words of [her] own," Lavretsky responds with pleasure ("And thank God for that!"). But the absence of words, for her as for him, morphs into a lamentable and even irresponsible abdication of desire. Henry James wrote, "One by one, for thirty years, with a firm, deliberate hand, with intervals and patiences and waits, Turgenev pricked in his sharp outlines."[19] So too with the characters. And at some point, these characters come to a point at which hesitation becomes inertia, and the pricking in of outlines, a complete silence.

THE SLAVIC CULT OF IMMOBILITY

Some of the narrator's most poetic moments are those in which he "pricks in his outlines" instead of rushing at the page with an enormous brush. But there are also the moments, as we see, when trepidation comes with diminishing returns. And these moments do have a political and cultural polemic resonance. Neither a fervent Westernizer nor an unambivalent Slavophile, Turgenev walks a line between Slavophile respect for tradition and Westernist fondness for reform. We have seen how this narrator seconds and sustains his characters' apprehensions—how he seemed loath to undermine (and entirely unwilling to ironize) Liza and Lavretsky. But he also points out that their world vision, their inclination to acceptance, is not the most propitious to happiness—not the most propitious to a full flowering of human potential. This becomes the criterion on which visions of the world are evaluated: not on the bases of true and false, or real and unreal, but on the bases of whether or not the visions are livable. And indeed, for all the portraits of fresh air and warm summer winds that permeate this narrative, there are also numerous images of immobility and sadness, images that connect the characters' faith in the outside to a fundamental and fatal aversion to action.

A narrator who evinces such trepidation at description, character evaluation, and narrative construction is unlikely to introduce a piece of paper in the church, as Stendhal did, or a "Varvara, who had conducted that fatality," à la Flaubert. Instead, he gestures at the futility of a passive nature. When Lavretsky returns to his house in Russia, he tours the premises and there finds the yard dog: "[the dog] had already been fastened up for ten years with a heavy chain, bought by order of Glafira Petrovna, and was barely in a condition to move and drag its burden" (116; 201). Lavretsky "ordered the chain to be removed from the watch-dog, who only barked a little, but did not even move away from his kennel;—and on his return home, sank into a sort of peaceful torpor" (120; 203). As we see from his "torpor," Lavretsky and the other characters have absorbed their yokes as thoroughly as the dog has absorbed his chain. And we can compare the chained dog (and chained Lavretsky) at Lavriki to Varvara, the "leaping lioness" who zips from house to house in her carriage.

So it is for the peasants: "'And now,' wailed the old man, who was already over eighty years of age, 'there's been so much ground cleared, so much plowing everywhere, that there's nowhere you can go'" (124; 205, tm). The clearing of ground, the opening of the roads, paradoxically produces a sense of constraint. Indeed, at various points in this narrative, we get the impression that the prospect of vast possibilities is more unpleasant than promising. For instance, in this statement by Lemm: "Everything is possible in this world. Especially here, with you, in Russia" (183; 210). "Everything is possible" is a menace rather than a promise, having to do not with a broad range of possibilities, but rather a broad range of perils. "You Russians" in this formulation do not so much take things to extremes, but instead, let things go to extremes by not mounting resistance when resistance is called for. In fact, this is the same sentiment that is articulated in *Demons* by Karmazinov, the Europeanized Russian writer whose artistic contemplation translates into a precipitous dismissal of the entire nation and an embracing of the German ideology: "Russia is preeminently the place in the whole world where anything you like can happen without the least resistance . . . Russia as she is has no future. I've become a German and count it as an honor."[20]

Motionlessness, here, has political and cultural as well as personal consequences. The same inclination that keeps the unchained dog in its kennel keeps the characters from action and volition. After Varvara returns, for instance, Lavretsky berates himself for having wanted to come out of his proverbial kennel: "The news of your freedom came, and you discarded everything, forgot everything, you ran like a little boy after a butterfly . . ." (261; 281, tm). Lavretsky, like the other characters, is accustomed to immobility, whether from nature or from nurture. As a child, we learn, "He was waked at four o'clock in the morning, was immediately drenched with cold water, and made to run around a tall pillar, at the end of a rope" (71; 177). As an adult, he is mentally tethered to that childhood, announcing to Mikhalévitch, "It proves, that they dislocated me in my child-hood" (144; 216), as well as to the idea of a circumscribed existence. Liza is also tethered to her childhood—and to the idea of childhood as tether—having absorbed the patience and silence of her nurse-maid and taken on the guilty conscience she associates with her father: "I know everything, my own sins and the sins of others, and how papa acquired his wealth; I know everything. All that must be atoned for by prayer—atoned for by prayer" (291; 298–99). For both of them, contemplation and consciousness are enemies of ac-tion—not the silence of the humble who stands to inherit the earth, nor even of the dramatic penitent who luxuriates in the wearing of a hair shirt, but rather of the one who, for reasons she herself does not understand, is slowing herself into an early grave.

The Role of the Individual and the Role of the Narrator: Form and Content

In *Nest* as in *Madame Bovary*, the complicated interaction of indi-vidual and world is defined and evaluated through narrative form, and in particular, through the narrator's placement with respect to the characters. There is one moment in *Nest* that does more than any other to present the narrator as a Westernist, to undermine Liza and Lavretsky, and at the same time to demonstrate the signifying power of narrative form.

The narrator's one direct contradiction of the characters' desires and perceptions is also his one rousing endorsement of a secular vision of realism. And not surprisingly, it comes in a moment of ironic authorial detachment from the principal character. Varvara has returned, and Lavretsky's dreams for happiness with Liza are ru-ined: "'Can it be,'—he thought,—'that I shall not be able to con-quer myself,—that I shall give in to this—nonsense?'" (261; 282). The narrator then writes, in parentheses: "(The severely-wounded in war always call their wounds 'nonsense.' If a man could not de-ceive himself,—he could not live on the earth)" (ibid.).

This parenthetical aside is the closest the narrator comes to a sur-reptitious undermining—the closest he comes to Flaubert's "Ro-dolphe, who had conducted that fate . . ." The message articulated validates the contrast between realism and idealism, between the

characters' visions and the facts of the world, and anticipates Nietzsche's notion of the human as a "genius in lying" ("so much faith
in life!"). To name the characters "self-deceivers" is in a sense to
describe them as dupes. Being wrong in a French novel is generally
a more humiliating proposition than being wrong in a Russian
novel: this criticism, then, based as it is on the shame of error, embodies a Western rather than a Russian mode of censure. And yet,
the narrator never does completely cross the line from Slavophile
submissiveness to Western pride. Even as he moves out for a moment to call Lavretsky a self-deceiver, a "genius in lying," as it were,
he retains the sense that there is something greater than Lavretsky
that makes him a genius in lying, or that makes lying a crucial element of terrestrial survival. The narrator's intrusion translates most
precisely as "If it is not for a person to delude himself, it is not for
him to live on earth [*ne obmanyvat sebya cheloveku—ne zhit emu na
zemle*]." The content is one of secular pessimism, an equation of
faith with delusion; and yet, the sentence's dative construction gives
it a homiletic tone and implies some structuring principle, some
force of action and decision.

Parentheses give this aside a similar ambiguity. On the one hand,
they distance the narrator from his characters, thus preparing the
conditions for manipulation and ironic sabotage. And yet, on the
other hand, these same parentheses insert mediation, suggesting a
reluctance to compromise this gentle story with an ironic moment
of outright pronouncement. When the author intervenes, he does
so not "like God in the universe" but like a hesitant narrator, who
both indicates and effaces his authorial intervention with parentheses—rather disinclined, it seems, to directly contaminate the morbid
optimism of Russia with the West's hard repudiations.

This one parenthetical intrusion (or parenthetical excursion, as
the case may be) embodies the narrator's treading of the line between identification with the author and identification with the
character. Indeed, the narrator's proximity to or distance from the
human community he describes is the most reliable measure of his
philosophico-political stance. The further he (or any narrator)
stands from his characters, the freer a hand he has in evaluating
them. When that distance diminishes, so too does the breadth of
the narrator's mastery. And when that mastery decreases, when the
opposition of the narrator to the characters weakens, so too do
other oppositions fundamental to secular realism: that of the real to

the ideal, of the objective to the subjective, of secularism to foolishness, of the one who knows to the one who knows not.

The narrator's soft-pedaling, particularly in the instance discussed above, indicates, I have argued, a reluctance to wield narrative dominance. "Pricking in his outlines," as James put it, represents as much a spiritual as a stylistic decision; it has to do with a cultural or individual bent that condemns or at least profoundly mistrusts the desire for individual agency. It is perhaps because of this mistrust that the narration sometimes takes the form of a series of vignettes, and that the narrator refrains from wholesale, form-giving assertions. Even those moments that point out the downside of humility are "pricked in," even when the stakes of this downside are high (Varvara's domination is a microcosm of the ironic fact that tsarism flourishes in a humble populace, for instance). The description of the chained-up dog at Lavriki and the comparison of Varvara Pavlovna to a lioness have something of the fable to them—fables, however, without a clearly articulated moral, without closure, without an authorial evaluation or interpretation, without form. Rather, these are scenes, moments, that arouse emotion rather than inciting to thought. At the end of the novel, the narrator writes, "Who knows? Who shall say? There are moments in life, there are feelings. . . . We can only indicate [*ukazat*] them,—and pass by" (307; 307). This is narrative authority on a subtle leash, echoing the silence and restraint, advisable or not, reasonable or not, of those who wish to sense the good, and the true, in the world around them.

4

The Joy of Mystification

Wʜɪʟᴇ *ɴᴇsᴛ* ᴜsᴇs ᴜɴᴅᴇʀsᴛᴀᴛᴇᴅ ɢᴇsᴛᴜʀᴇs ᴛᴏ ᴇɴᴅᴏʀsᴇ ᴛʜᴇ ᴄʜᴀʀᴀᴄ-
ters' faith and humility, *Bewitched* (*L'Ensorcelée*) comes out with what
seems to be a resounding indictment of secularism. The idea of
"secularism" has numerous meanings in this story and on the surface, none of them seem particularly desirable. One is the idea of
"without God" as a philosophical bent, an intellectual decision (an
erroneous one) to abandon God as an explanatory principle and
search elsewhere for causes. Another related meaning is "without
God" as a spiritual desolation or disorder caused at least in part by
that intellectual decision—a disorder apparent both on the individual and on the social level. (The dismantling of the monarchic regime and the Church as dominant sociopolitical institution, the rise
of democratic ideologies, and the dissolution of social hierarchies
would be emblematic of this disorder on a social scale; confusion
and disillusion would arise for the individual.) Another meaning or
function of secularism in this narrative, however, is "without God"
as an aesthetic tone or mood—a sense of crisis, boundlessness, incer-
itude, or morbid pessimism. Related to this function is "without
God" as a thematic or structural void, an absence of direction that
enables dramatic Manichaean struggles (at the level of theme) or
narrative interventions (at the level of form). Throughout this narrative, I argue, the narrator deploys secularism even as he deplores
it, using the arsenal of narrative mechanisms to both produce and
promise protection from a sense of imminent and disastrous god-
essness.

In the opening chapter of *L'Ensorcelée*, the narrator writes:

Enslaved by second-hand ideas, Society, the old housewife, has nothing
new but her current needs; she dodders about her enlightenment; she
has no understanding of the divine ignorance of the mind, that poetry of
the soul which she would exchange for sorry and incomplete knowledge,

admitting only the poetry of the eyes, hidden yet visible beneath the apparent futility of things. Should this frightful movement of modern thought continue, we shall hardly have, in a few years, a scrap of land [*un pauvre bout de lande*] where imagination can set its foot to rest and dream, as the heron does on one leg.[1]

The end result is a decline in "imagination" but the initial cause is the desire to trade "divine ignorance" for understanding. The substitution of science and rationalist principles for the idea of a transcendent order is for this narrator an intellectual wrong turn that then becomes the source of spiritual disaster. This chain of events connects social, spiritual, and ontological crises to the decision to abandon God as conceptual mediator between mind and world. The first element of the narrator's criticism of secular culture is therefore his criticism of this decision, which comes in the form of a sort of parody. To demonstrate that to exchange "divine ignorance" for "incomplete knowledge" is in fact a poor exchange, the narrator addresses that exchange on its own terms, that is, the terms of intellectual progress. Throughout, the narrator both imitates and undermines the core of "modern thought"—science—through a series of (deliberately) derailed clarifications and epistemological obscurities. Not only is this exchange spiritually unadvisable, he reveals; it does not even provide an intellectual reward. When Barbey introduces his story with the ironic condition "if the sophistication of our day [*la sagesse de notre temps*] permits us to tell it" (2; 556), the point is that secular "sophistication," the proposed recompense for the abandonment of religion and faith, is in fact not wisdom, but a pale substitute for it.[2]

The Uselessness of Science

As Barbey writes in the *Revue du Monde Catholique*, the publication he edited, "The Revue has been battling since its first day the many headed dragon of modern rationalism."[3] Without God, then, for the author as for the narrator, science becomes a flimsy and arbitrary discourse. It does not replace the *divines ignorances* that were so valued, but rather, unwittingly, perpetuates an ignorance that is far from divine. Throughout the story, the narrator demonstrates or rather produces this ignorance, proposing scientific explanations only to undermine them. "There was no reason to look about for a malefactor [*de creuser jusqu'à l'idée d'un maléfice*]" (30; 577), he writes of Tainnebouy's wounded horse; he then speculates that Jeanne's problem comes from within her. "Can I make you understand this character? If it is not understood the story will be unbelievable. We should be obliged to return to the conceptions of Maître Tainnebouy, and these conceptions no longer belong to our times" (135; 647). He does then "make you understand this character," but the natural explanations that he provides are in each case so far from explaining that they read as mockeries of the science of the mind. His meticulous insistence on the discourse of natural principles thus becomes incomprehensible, for it elucidates nothing and produces no real sense of the person described. This discourse, in fact, becomes more and more the discourse of disorder, an obstacle to and a subversion of understanding.

LIVES WITHIN LIVES, OR THE DRAGON WITH MANY HEADS

The narrator's insistence on natural principles (and his subsequent critique and near-mockery of those same principles) is most prevalent in his descriptions of unconscious forces. These descriptions become more and more obscure, more enigmatic, as the story continues. The first character that the narrator probes is the farmer Louis Tainnebouy, an uncomplicated man. The narrator writes, "He emerged from inside the tavern, showing himself, to my agreeable surprise, one of those fellows of fine appearance who need no certificate of good life and morals from mayor or priest, for God had written a magnificent and readable one in every line of his face and figure . . . I saw at once what sort of man I had to do with" (10; 561). And then, "What became him most was that he had always kept his place, that he was one with his life [*faisait corps avec sa vie*]; he adjusted himself to his fate like a glove to the hand" (23; 571–72). The person in these sentences conceals no inconsistencies or deficiencies or secrets; his experience balances with his character, which in turn balances with his countenance. God, we read, has made him so. And yet, even within this harmonic representation, there is a germ, a discursive hint, of the disorder to come. In the phrase, "showing himself, to my agreeable surprise, one of those fellows of fine appearance [*montrant à ma vue agréablement surprise un de ces gaillards de riche mine*]" the "fellow of fine appearance" is conceptually separated from the man who incarnates and "shows" him. Because Tainnebouy "was one with his life," the phenomenological separation of "fellow of fine appearance" from "Louis" is at this moment neither conspicuous nor problematic, but it does become so further on.

This same sense of compartmentalization imbues the description of Mère Giguet, proprietor of the Taureau Rouge: "She . . . gave one of those complicated explanations, utterly unintelligible, in which the sly malice of the peasant, foreseeing the embarrassment of others and enjoying it beforehand, is mixed with [se mêle à] the vagueness of the dull and naturally cloudy minds of the people of the lower classes" (9; 560–61). Giguet in this formulation is a sort of unconscious custodian of "the sly malice of the peasant" and "the vagueness of dull and naturally cloudy minds"—forces that produce her actions, and on which her discourse and her character depend. So it is too with Marie Hecquet: "She had kept a woodcutter's faith [cette foi du charbonnier] which makes virtue efficacious, urges good works and sends the heart's charity into the muscles of the hands" (51; 591). Whether the action of "kept" be conscious or unconscious, it is the "woodcutter's faith," a seemingly independent neurological force, that pushes and determines her choices and shapes the nature of virtue.

In a sense, these passages are but lyrical descriptions of a dynamic psyche. And yet, the depiction of characters as compendiums of autonomous forces prepares for the supernatural (or super-natural) disorder that ensues. As it turns out, the fact that Tainnebouy "was one with his life, adjusted himself to his fate like a glove to the hand" is not based just on his modest nature but on a narrative moment that, for this man at this time, happens to place experience, circumstance, character, and internal forces in a harmonic relation. It is the last time that the narrator gives us such a coincidence. When the narrator introduces Jeanne Le Hardouey, the phenomenological separation of the forces of character from their bodily envelopes becomes a dangerous fragmentation, a germ of disorder. The transition from poetry to possession is subtle, but through it, the narrative comes to undermine modern conceptions of the natural and, in so doing, to dispute the competence of science to name and master human phenomena.

When Jeanne Le Hardouey first notices La Croix-Jugan in church, the narrator writes, "For the rest, she felt more than anyone in the church of Blanchelande, her soul being different from other souls [parce que son âme n'était pas une âme comme les autres], what all the congregation felt in different degrees" (70; 603, italics in text). The priest's monstrous aspect is not the principal cause of the obsession, nor is demonic intrusion—the cause is in Jeanne's soul. The biological nature of this soul is underscored in the description of Jeanne's genealogical history, when we read that it comes from her mother: "Louisine had transmitted her strength of soul, like a divine breath [*qui respirait en elle comme un souffle de divinité*], to her daughter" (88; 615). This force of the soul, in one sense an element of Jeanne's natural composition, becomes at the same time an autonomous and enigmatic machine that enters Jeanne and breathes within her. Further on, in the portrait of Jeanne's friendship with la Clotte: "Jeanne, who kept in her soul an immortal wound to her pride, found a certain joy, an avenging of all that her marriage had made her suffer, in her relations with Clotte . . . Her repressed patrician soul rose [*se dilatait*] when she was with this old woman . . ." (115–16; 633). Here, the internal receptacle of a wounded pride responds and acts on its own terms, and the patrician soul beats within the character: a life within a life. When Jeanne is found dead, the narrator mourns "this noble girl who had long hidden under coarse clothing a patrician soul, long restrained, long overwhelmed, but suddenly breaking free [*éclatant*] at the approach of a soul of her own race, thus killing her happiness and ruining her life" (212; 699). From breathing to rising up to breaking free, the soul has become an entity to be contained—the internal mechanisms as sovereign and unpredictable as a visitation from beyond.

Numerous critics discern in *L'Ensorcelée*'s character descriptions an intersection of the natural and the fantastic. Some read this intersection as a strategic problem of codes or as a deliberate source of epistemological uncertainties.[4] Others propose that for Barbey, the natural is tinged with the supernatural and cannot be separated from it.[5] I would contend that the indeterminacies caused by the fusion of the natural and the supernatural (is it possession or is it not?) are in fact quite ideologically determinate: they are part of the narrative's program of dismantling the claims of science and disclosing the deleterious impacts of science on our understanding of the world. Pierre Leburruyer writes of the story: "Magic or power of suggestion? It hardly matters,"[6] and Evelyn Bloch-Dano and Jacqueline Zorla second: "Was there a bewitching? Or did Jeanne imagine it once she already loved the abbé? Doesn't it amount to the same thing?"[7] These comments, made about the narrative's resistance to interpretation, also indicate how little the narrator's language of psychology differs from the language of superstition. But what makes the comments of Leburruyer and Bloch-Dano and Zorla of particular interest is that as the nineteenth century progresses, the discourse of modern psychology does in fact come to resemble the discourse of the supernatural in just this way. The dramatic and rather demonic partitioning of Jeanne into separate compartments would be replicated in real-world scientific writings.

The narrator, ever mistrustful of "explanations," proclaims, "It is always what one understands least that one explains best" (143; 652). And in the nineteenth century, as we saw in the first chapter, "explanations" of the human mind abound.[8] When the narrator of L'Ensorcelée states in a poetic turn, "This blood [of the Feuardents] produced in her an inextinguishable flame the moment it was fanned by that old witch Destiny [cette vieille sorcière de Destinée], who so often rouses the passions in our drowsy veins with a lighted brand" (88; 615), his dramatic neurological discourse is notable not for its extravagance but for its resemblance to that which would be published as science in the decades to come.

In his replications of the discourse of science, the narrator seems to intend not so much to return to the fantastic notions of Louis Tainnebouy as to disclose that science had never really left those notions behind. His phrase, "Modern science, which takes note of such facts and explains or thinks it explains them, will never fathom the secret of the influence in such colossal proportions of one human creature upon another" (142; 651), denigrates not the ability of science to name a natural rather than a supernatural cause (soul, character, inspiration, instinct, the unconscious, rather than enchantment, possession, fate, magic), but the notion that that naming amounts to some actual mastery. The inclination to ascertain reasons and principles, which the narrator imitates in his character descriptions, can for him but perpetuate the same arbitrariness that characterizes superstition. Lévi-Strauss noted that "the ultimate goal of the human sciences is not to constitute man, but to dismantle him,"[9] but in L'Ensorcelée, this dissolution is less a discursive mechanism, less a stop on the road to understanding, than the product and embodiment of an incurable modern bewilderment.

Soundness of Mind, or the Intrusiveness of Ideas

Barbey's characters, again, are constructed to disintegrate under the microscope of psychological investigation. Causes are named but nothing is elucidated; explanations are given but no meaning is produced. The representation of internal forces as unpredictable and dangerous phenomena implies that science (the naming of these phenomena) is in some sense a futile enterprise. But more than this, it raises doubts about the competence of the human mind to even conduct this enterprise. None of the characters is particularly sound of mind (in any sense), not Jeanne and Thomas Le Hardouey, susceptible to visitations from within and without, not la Clotte, absorbed in the "religion of her memories" and seduced since adolescence by the "supernatural ascendance" of the priest, not the obscure and inscrutable (and in some sense remarkably self-absorbed) La Croix-Jugan. When the human mind is separated into autonomous factions, as it is in *L'Ensorcelée*, when it becomes as a dragon with many heads, the status of consciousness and subjectivity becomes problematic.

Another force that intrudes on Barbey's characters is that of ideas. For instance, in the church, the narrator describes "this new preoccupation, so sudden and so demonic, of which she afterward became [*dont elle devait plus tard être*] the victim" (78; 608). And again: "Now, it was decreed that this evening Jeanne could not separate herself from the thought [*ne pourrait se séparer de la pensée*] of this sinister being . . ." (99; 622). At supper with the curé, "a reverie . . . had seized her [*une rêverie l'a saisie*]" (108; 628). The problem then becomes, what or who is the *res cogitans* in a being so affected? Can there be thought in such a mind? As Jonathan Culler writes, following Lévi-Strauss, "What the human sciences have done is to chip away at what supposedly belongs to the thinking subject until any notion of the self that is grounded thereon becomes problematic."[10] In *L'Ensorcelée*, that chipping away becomes literal, as "thought" sets up shop and starts operating on its own. Ironically, the only character that is not so chipped away and driven is Tainnebouy, who, the narrator has declared from the start, is resistant to and uninterested in "modern thought." In the end, Barbey represents a modern world dissected into nothingness, to the detriment of thought and of thinkers.[11]

The chaos that this story associates with modern thought is at its most vigorous in the human mind, in the form of madness and confusion. When La Croix-Jugan shoots himself at the start of the narrative, the bullets radiate through his head like roads through the *lande*. "The face of the suicide was crossed and lined with inextricable furrows of wounds. The rifle had had five or six balls in it and

coming from the barrel they had radiated in diverse directions . . ."
(51; 590). The traces of this violence permeate to the bone. "I saw
that his face was more horrible than it had been in life, for it was
like those which roll out in cemeteries when they dig up old graves
and uncover old bones. Only the wounds which had marked the
abbé's face were more deeply marked on the bones" (273, 739).
And this permeation, in turn, this absorption of aimlessness and disorder into the core of the principal character, establishes the disorientation—the deep unfathomability—of the human organism in
the secular world. Or rather, of the human organism as seen
through a secular lens. For in this narrative, the decision to see the
world as devoid of transcendent order and celestial mechanisms is a
deliberate and, for the narrator, a disastrous one.

The decision to replace divine ignorance with terrestrial principles is for this narrator an intellectual and aesthetic blunder; but
more than this, it is the source of a large-scale contamination of the
world's spiritual ambiance. L'Ensorcelée is set under the sign not just
of epistemological confusion, but also of a spectacular spiritual dis-
turbance. Readers have long discerned in L'Ensorcelée (as well as in
Barbey's other writings, fiction and correspondence) a nostalgic
mood and a desire to recuperate a departed sensation or order.
Emanuel Mickel writes of a "poetic, spiritual death" that the author
mourns.[12] Amélie Djourachkovitch comments that "the text insists
on the freshness and purity of a time before the disaster, Revolution
or guilty passion"[13] and Andrée Hirschi finds "not only recreation
of the past, but a resistance to rupture, to separation."[14] Such a poetic and spiritual death is a crucial result of the epistemological mutation that replaces transcendent order with scientific principles.
But that "spiritual death" is not limited to the agnostic. Secularism
in this story, that is, is bad for everyone, not just the devout who had
faith and then lost it, or the atheist who never had it, or the scientist
who has it but nonetheless looks to scientific principles for "real"
understanding. Still another definition of "world without God"
here is secularism as an atmospheric and historical disaster, a cata-
strophic punishment, a plague of sorts, that corrodes order and understanding across the board.

THE RUINS OF THE CHURCH

From the start, this entire narrative is placed under the sign of
the waning influence of the Church. And from the start, that sign is

relentlessly bleak: the drama of La Croix-Jugan opens on an uniden-
tified Chouan, wandering desolate after the battle of la Fosse. The
narrator links this battle, and the entire Revolution, to the deterioration of religion as an institution:

> It was whispered about that frightful scenes took place [in the Monastery
> of Blanchelande] just before the revolution burst forth. What credence
> must we lend such whispers? . . . Or why, indeed, in those days when
> faith faltered in the worn hearts of the people, should incredulity not
> already have germinated corruption in the consecrated shelter of the
> most saintly virtues? Who knows? No one. The fact remains that, true or
> false, these alleged scandals at the very foot of the altar, this gossip hid-
> den by convents, this sacrilege which God finally punished by a social
> cataclysm [*un foudroiement social*] more terrible than any thunder from
> the clouds, left, right or wrong, a trail of stories in the memory of the
> people . . ." (5–6; 558)

One might wonder what sort of God would punish misdeeds without
regard for whether they are "true or false." One might also wonder
what sort of God would punish (rather than shore up) a "faltering
faith," much less with a broad-reaching *foudroiement* that assumes
universal guilt and smites both believers and nonbelievers, but first
let us look at the atmosphere that the *foudroiement* produces. When
the abbé attempts suicide at the close of the final Chouan battle and
the Revolution, the deterioration of religion is connected to the end
of life. It is as though the decline of religion as an institution obliter-
ated what Alain Toumayan named the "principle of cosmic, social,
political, and moral order,"[15] and produced what Djourachkovitch
named "the empty sky";[16] under such a sky, it would seem, existence
must end. But it does not end, for among these numerous finishes,
it is life that goes on, as if by accident, disfigured and distorted.
From this moment on, the obscure and ominous nature of the narrative is connected to the dismantling of religious (and political and
philosophical) order. Secularism, that is, which started as a "faltering faith" or a "movement of modern thought," has paradoxically
become, or provoked, a torrent of divine punishment.

This aforementioned chapter, which had started with a near
death, ends with a renaissance: the reopening of the church. This
reopening is intended to restore the social, philosophical, and religious order that the Revolution had disturbed. But the atmosphere
in the church is somber and obsolete, more demonic than angelic;
its spirit has in some sense departed. When the narrator comes at

last to name the enigmatic Chouan, he writes, "It was the former monk of the devastated abbey, the famous Abbé de La Croix-Jugan" (62; 598, tm). Before he is the "Abbé de La Croix-Jugan," he is "the former monk," his religion already inscribed as absent, former, abandoned. Pierre Tranouez commented on La Croix-Jugan: "He enters the narrative in the manner of heroes departing, dying, and having scarcely appeared,"[17] and the same can be said of his spiritual vocation. A similar obsolescence permeates the description of the church: "Because of the season and the late hour, the church of Blanchelande had begun to veil itself in grey tints, the darker for the mysterious and somber reflections of the stained-glass window when the sun no longer enlivens them with its rays. These windows, mingled with common windowpanes blackened by time, remained from the destroyed abbey" (63; 598–99, tm). The sinister aspect of the church is blamed on the absence of the sun, which is in turn blamed on the season and the hour. But this "late hour" is further emblematic of the end of an era; at the moment of the Chouan's suicide, "the sun had just disappeared" (50; 590, tm). The church, though technically open, is in some sense extinct. Its fundamental spiritual aspect, the sun of God and of intelligibility and vitality, is absent. And that absence, in the course of the narrative, becomes the occasion for both its sinister aspect and its resistance to interpretation. On the foundation of a dismantled church structure, the narrator enacts a crisis in meaning. One indication of this crisis is the emptiness of religious emblems and ceremonies, which in turn represents a destruction of the symbolic order. For instance, when Marie Hecquet recites the Angelus and makes the sign of the cross, this movement attracts the attention of the *Bleus*: "But what ought to save us sometimes brings ruin. This sign of the cross was her misfortune" (54; 592). The gesture that is intended to summon celestial protection in fact summons violent antireligious enemies who torment La Croix-Jugan. Later, the ringing of the Angelus marks the last time that Jeanne is seen alive. When the Bleus come into Marie's house, the most repugnant among them is bearing "a change of shirt stolen the day before from a priest" (59; 595). Church properties are bought and sold by the secular bourgeoisie.[18] The properties and emblems of religion, displaced, come to indicate the sometimes furious and always sinister denial of religion. This displacement is particularly conspicuous when Jeanne encounters the shepherd at the Vieux Presbytère, "the ruin, abandoned long ago, of the former rectory" (75; 607, tm). The vagabond sorcerer, who threatens Jeanne and may be responsible for her murder, replaces the priest as occupant of the house, as mediator of the supernatural, and, in the end, as consultant to Jeanne and her husband.

Another word can be said about the ringing Angelus. Emma Bovary had run out of the house to an Angelus that, in the end, had been sounded at random by a beadle who did so at his convenience. The ringing in this episode is also somewhat of an ersatz Angelus, and must be, since the churches are not open: "It was not the feeble bell of one of the mossy hermit chapels built formerly in the depths of the woods, for the churches were not yet reopened. It was a little bell in some sabot-maker's hut which marked the hours and the end of labor and the day" (53; 592). The imitation Angelus, an ironic source of disillusion for Emma, becomes a source of disaster for Marie Hecquet. The decline of religion forces imitations, which, denaturalized, are necessarily pernicious phenomena.

The absence of religious order finds further expression in the departure of religious figures, embodied in the shepherds' displacement of the priests at the Vieux Presbytère. Another element of this departure is the conspicuous absence of priests in moments of crisis. For instance, when the sixth commandment is being broken during Jeanne's funeral, "The priests were no longer there; they had gone back into the church" (222; 706). And when they do emerge, "The curé and the priests, who heard the cries of the excited mob, came out from the church and tried to penetrate to the grave, the theater of a drama becoming bloody. But they could not" (224; 707). At the end, when La Croix-Jugan is murdered in the middle of the Easter Mass, "There were two distinct scenes in the chaos: the crowd pushing to the portal and, at the grille of the sanctuary in the choir, the priests out of their stalls [*les prêtres jetés hors de leurs stalles*] . . ." (258; 730). In these moments, as in the shooting in *Le rouge* ("the priest had left the altar"), the priests are unable to intervene.

Julien Sorel was a former seminarian shooting at his former married lover for having compromised his future (some would say shotgun) marriage, and this is a husband shooting at the priest who has perhaps put a curse of sexual obsession on his wife. In both cases, the church is of more value to the story as a scene of drama ("theater of a drama becoming bloody") than it is to the characters as a locus of spiritual experience. But where for Stendhal that unbalanced value was ironic, for Barbey, it becomes tragic. And where Stendhal had Julien's shooting of Madame de Rênal chase the priest from the altar, Barbey has the priests' departure from the cemetery precede, and in some sense become the condition for, the murder of la Clotte. Disorder begets disorder, and the ascendance of the priests diminishes as the narrative continues.

SUPERNATURALISM

When the narrator laments the substitution of scientific investigation for the *divines ignorances de l'esprit,* when he writes of the Revolution as the source of *foudroiement social,* or divine punishment for a decline in faith, he seems on the one hand to wish for a return to a more humble or pious social consciousness. On the other hand, though, the very dire nature of that lamentation, combined with various discursive elements in this chronicle, indicates that his principle concern is neither with a return to religion nor with the spiritual desolation or even the intellectual poverty occasioned by a secular consciousness, but with the drama of the *foudroiement social.*[19]

Ancien régime religious practice may have made for a more ordered society and *divines ignorances* for a more humble populace, but secular consciousness opens the door to more gripping and dire scenarios. Secularism, here, is at once a plot device and an atmosphere: an occasion for an ominous mood, and a chance—here as in *Le rouge et le noir*—for dramatic narrative interventions. The narrator, in other words, uses the idea of secularism as code and as occasion for demonic surprises, for sensational demonstrations of narrative power *ex machina.* One such demonstration comes in the symbolic convolutions that permeate the story. Another comes in the connection between the madness of the characters and the decline of the ancien régime: Jeanne's soul flares up ("killing her happiness and ruining her life") when reminded of the abandoned social or religious order—in the reconstructed church at its first reopening, in the presence of la Clotte, and in encounters with La Croix-Jugan. Another such demonstration of the dramatic uses of secularism is to be found in the turns of phrase that endow the poetic discourse of the supernatural with actual narrative force. A manner of speaking (which, in a secular world, is a category unto itself) thus becomes a concrete force to be reckoned with, as conventional conceptual divides between the rhetorical and the real come undone. For instance, "In her own eyes Jeanne-Madelaine must for a long time have been bewitched—as other people thought, and as they still thought in the time of Maître Tainnebouy. The menacing prediction of the shepherd had sunk little by little [*s'était peu à peu enfoncée*] into her soul. First she had laughed at and insulted its influence, but the strength of this thing that she felt [*la force de ce qu'elle éprouvait*] made her believe in it. Otherwise she never could have understood what happened to her" (153–54; 659–60). In the phrase, "In her own eyes Jeanne-Madelaine must for a long time have been be-witched," Jeanne considers her emotion (the *histoire*, as it were) and then creates for it a *discours*: the shepherd's prediction. In one sense, then, the shepherds are a mere spectating chorus to explicate the drama enacted. But "menacing" raises the stakes of "prediction" because to predict and to threaten imply disparate intensities of im-plication and action, disparate authorial distances and capacities. What is it that "had sunk little by little into her soul": the force of the curse itself, or the subsequent idea of the curse as force? The words, "First she had laughed at and insulted [*bravé*] its influence" with their intimations of combat, contribute to the sense of action. But the last sentence, "Otherwise she never could have understood what happened to her" reintroduces a chronological displacement and so once more turns the "prediction" into a mere idea, a remem-bered moment.

This interlude, in which *discours* becomes *histoire*, and *histoire dis-cours*, contains an important lesson for those who turn to the idea of the supernatural to elucidate or come to terms with the incompre-hensible. It implies that the terms to which one turns are not just terms, or not just disembodied, gratuitous, or ornamental terms, but inspired ideas, visions of true causes. This coincidence of prediction as cause and prediction as idea presumes a particular connection to the supernatural, a connection maintained via words and ideas. To understand that connection, we can consider a rather unsubtle ex-ample from the late twentieth century. A radio evangelist argued for the existence of God by noting that in moments of crisis, when a car is crashing or a painful scene unfolding, people tend to exclaim, "Oh, God" rather than, for instance, "Oh, nothingness." The fact of that articulation, the instinctual or automatic nature of it, proved to this preacher the disingenuousness of any pretense to atheism. For him, that there are no atheists in foxholes makes a point not just about cultural conventions nor even about human nature, but about the organic, theologically realistic connection of human to word, and word to substance. This narrator's braiding of explanatory strands implies this same organic connection.

Another instance when word becomes cause, or secondary narrative strand becomes cause, arises when Jeanne's husband is riding across the *lande* during the night. He hears voices, but sees no one: "Strong-minded as was Thomas Le Hardouey, these human sounds without bodies, in this country filled with the chimeras and monsters of the popular imagination, produced a singular and new effect upon him and doubtless prepared him [*le disposèrent sans nul doute*] for the unheard-of scene which was to follow" (174; 673). This sentence contains the same combination of the concrete and the metaphoric, of discourse and substance. Up until the words "to the scene," this interlude seems to focus on the evocative power of atmosphere. Thomas listens to the sounds and is unnerved, susceptible to insinuation, "strong-minded as he was." The scene that ensues, however, has Le Hardouey encounter the wandering shepherds (theirs were the voices he had heard; the shepherds were crouched in a trench, intoning). Among them is the shepherd who had cursed Jeanne, whose "menacing prediction" we considered earlier. This shepherd shows Thomas Le Hardouey a small mirror. Le Hardouey peers into it and sees Jeanne and the abbé de La Croix-Jugan seated before a fireplace, cooking a human heart on a spit. "'Yes, it's a heart they are cooking,' said the shepherd, 'and it's yours, maître Thomas Le Hardouey!'" (183; 679).

This scene is narrated neither as a dream nor as a delusion, but rather as an actual incident. But because it is no dream sequence, the narrator's statement that "these human sounds . . . prepared him" becomes problematic. For though it could be said that Le Hardouey was inclined to speak with the shepherds (rather than to ride in the other direction or to ridicule them, for instance), it could hardly be said that he was "disposed" to the scene as it is narrated. In the first part of the interlude, the sounds create the sort of ominous sound track that warns horror movie audiences that the murderer is in the room. But no one would claim that the ominous sound track of a horror movie "disposes" the poor victim to be murdered. The sound track is atmospheric accompaniment and the murder is an event, and never the twain shall stand on the same narrative line. The use of *disposer*, like the reference to prediction, is a polemical instrument that argues for the force of words (or, here, sounds). Michel-Eugène Chevreul, in an 1854 experiment with divining rods and pendulums, attributed to unconscious thoughts and movements phenomena that had been previously attributed to "spirits."[20] Here, the narrator reverses (or rather collapses) Chevreul before the fact, demonstrating that ideas that the secular world has demoted to the domain of ghost stories (superstitions, fantasies of resolution and outside intervention) are in fact genuine elements of the natural world. The narrator tries here to erase the schism between words and substance, between the "Oh, God" of the crashing car and the God of theological realism, and in so doing to reintroduce the supernatural not just as metaphor but also as principal actor in real-world theaters.

In these two episodes, the force accorded to prediction, sounds, and insinuations indicates that words are more than secondary sound tracks or instruments of understanding; they are agents of action. And yet, when spoken in the service of understanding, these same words become unwitting magnifiers of incomprehensibility. For each explanatory action, there comes an equal and opposite reaction, a bubbling up of the inscrutable, an expansion of the supernatural that bursts its verbal envelope.

LAST WORDS OR THE CURSE OF NARRATION

The secular world in *L'Ensorcelée* is contaminated with a cataclysmic disorder that the mind is unable to correct. Indeed, a cataclysm that the human mind or desire could remedy would not be much of a cataclysm; the point is that in this chronicle, a "world without God" functions as an occasion for narrative intervention as well as a felt spiritual condition. This distinction, this supremacy of function, comes out in the narrator's attitude toward narration. At first glance, this attitude seems imbued with a restraint and hesitation of the sort that was present in *Nest*. The narrator writes, "And if in place of being a story [*une histoire*], this book had the misfortune to be a novel, I should be forced to sacrifice truth to probability a little and to show that this love might not seem impossible, how and by what attractions a normal woman, of sane mind, a pure and strong soul, could fall in love with this monstrously disfigured man of the Fosse. Thank God all this psychology is useless. I am only a simple story-teller [*simple conteur*]" (153; 659).

With this disclaimer, the narrator of the chronicle of La Croix-Jugan evinces relief at not having to fabricate explanations. (God, though perhaps absent from the churches of Blanchelande, has nevertheless had the goodness to accord the narrator this freedom.) A *simple conteur* can embrace the *divines ignorances de l'esprit* instead of scrambling to meet modern standards of elucidation. Such scrambling, it seems, is always a fool's errand; indeed, this entire story the-matizes the limitations of narrative. Just before his attempted suicide, for instance, La Croix-Jugan's final act is to tear up and eat the "hidden parchment which doubtless held important instruc-tions" (48; 588). This parchment is the last instance of writing to precede the close of battle, the last instance of writing to represent the former religious order—and the chronicle of La Croix-Jugan, the first to represent that order's deterioration. Dodille has com-mented that narratives abound in this story, and that nearly every character is a narrator or a *narrataire,* but it is important to note that most of these narratives are erroneous or incomplete, vain attempts to dispel a sense of impotence.[21] When la Clotte wonders what is wrong with Jeanne: "'I am going to tell you,' replied Jeanne, with an air of mystery" (165; 667), becoming a narrator at the moment that she loses control and rushes out to her death. Tainnebouy nar-rates in contemplation of the death of his son, which he is unable to understand or undo. Instead of producing resolution, narrative in each case underscores complication and desolation. The chronicle of Dlaide does not deter Jeanne but worsens her obsession. At Jeanne's funeral, the spectators come to trade stories about her death, and then turn from narration to an act of destruction. Pierre Cloud (was it a drunken hallucination or an authentic witnessing?) generates more problems than resolutions with his account. Narra-tives, intended to elucidate, either generate or perpetuate the disor-der in this story.

On the one hand, this story contains a subtle prohibition against narration—a hesitation that it would seem to share with *Nest.* At the end, when the narrator admits that he has not gone to the church and thus has not verified whether the Croix-Jugan story is true or false, that admission indicates an incompetence to narrate, the ab-sence of a tale to tell. This silence at the end constitutes the denial of a last word in this narrative that so distrusts last words; the wisest narrator is thus the one who abstains from narration, in the mode of the *Nest* narrator who mused, "Who knows? Who can say?" On the other hand, though, this restraint has less to do with a humble silence than with a warning insinuation that narrative sense-making is useless in the face of modern disorder. For one, the *foudroiemen social* is so broad in its reach that individual silence has no particular virtue—no one is spared the ominous atmosphere that penetrates this chronicle. For another, where the narrator of *Nest* promoted hesitation by example, thus showing it to be in some sense its own reward, this narrator does not: the manipulation of religious emblems and the subtle evolution of the narrator's criticism of modern science constitute a deliberate calculation (Susanne Rossbach, in an article on the author's dandyism, writes that narration "represented for the author an ideologically charged and aggressive act").[22] The idea that speech can do nothing but drown out the voice of God, already subdued and distorted by the machinations of the *pensée moderne*, is subsumed in this case to the pleasure of mood setting and scene-creation. The distinction between novelist and storyteller is more rhetorical than substantive; this storyteller does not renounce fabrication, but rather simply claims association with a storytelling tradition. And yet, what is traditional—or even moralistic—about this chronicle? The entire story is more a modern horror story than a fairy tale, sinister even by Barbey's standards, with a menacing, monstrously disfigured priest, murderous mobs, attempted suicide, torture, various deaths by drowning, stoning, and shooting; even the minor characters at the Taureau Rouge ("the sly malice of the peasant, foreseeing the embarrassment of others and enjoying it beforehand, is mixed with the vagueness of the dull and naturally cloudy minds of the people of the lower classes") suggest nothing so much as a nineteenth-century French precursor to *Deliverance*.

A Crisis of Spiritual Proportions

I have proposed that the idea of secularism is for this narrator primarily a dramatic instrument—a means to create a sense of menace and unease, a fear of God's retribution (or God's abandonment, which in this scenario amounts to a similar thing). Thus, while on the one hand the narrator of *L'Ensorcelée* recalls the narrator of *Nest* with his vaunting of a supreme force and his announced deference to the power of words and ideas, he also demonstrates a fondness for sinister atmosphere and Manichaean conflict. With this fondness in mind, we can look within the drama of secularism to discern what in fact *religion* means to this narrator. What is the real nature of this narrator's anachronisms, the nostalgia that he shares with the principal characters? What does God mean to him? We saw that the narrator deplores the move to secularism and the rise of human pretense to understanding ("modern thought"). We saw that he values contemplation and silence and accentuates the perils of narration, that he is full of warnings about human bravado and the force of the supernatural, full of demonstrations of the power of intonation and insinuation, full of fondness for the poetic discourse of the supernatural. He is pleased to see Tainnebouy remove his hat when he speaks the name of God; is moved by the visions of Marie Hecquet's response to the Angelus and of the sun shining during the Easter season. He is saddened at the melancholic unresponsiveness of La Croix-Jugan on the point of suicide and bemoans the closing of the churches. His insistence that he is but a *simple conteur* connect him with what Walter Benjamin would mourn in "The Storyteller" ("The art of storytelling is reaching its end because the epic side of truth, wisdom, is dying out. This . . . is only a concomitant symptom of the secular productive forces of history, a concomitant that has quite gradually removed narrative from the realm of living speech and at the same time is making it possible to see a new beauty in what is vanishing").[23] We saw, as one could not help but see, that a sense of anachronism pervades this narrative; that the narrators and the principal characters (Jeanne, la Clotte, La Croix-Jugan, Tainnebouy) miss the ancien régime. We see that the end of the Chouannerie marks the start of the chronicle and that La Croix-Jugan and the other characters wrestle from start to finish with this unwelcome historical closure. But the true nature of the narrative's anachronism resides not in the desire for spiritual solace, but in the desire for glory. If the idea of secularism creates a mood of fear and obscurity, the idea of religion produces for this narrator another sort of drama: the drama of human grandiosity and domination.

Broadly stated, Turgenev's narrator demonstrates trust in God by placing himself and his characters in relation to and at a humble distance from that God. Barbey's narrator, in contrast, shows his fondness for God by placing himself and his characters in league with that God—by using, in his narration and in his vision of others, the ominous tone, the haughtiness, the mystification, and the poetic discourse that he associates with the grandeur of religion. In the end, for this narrator, the desire for spiritual presence gets subsumed to or absorbed into a desire for adventure, drama, and hyperbole—the sort of drama that religion confers. The grandeur of religion is thus founded and centered in, even as it makes possible, the grandeur of human characters.

One indication of what the narrator and the characters miss in their nostalgia can be found in their reminiscences. It is not the Church that is pined for, nor social hierarchies, nor the presence of the monarchs, nor the simple solace of a religious culture, but adventure, the war, and social hierarchies. Without the thrill of war, La Croix-Jugan and Montsurvent do not even bother speaking to each other: "For since the Chouan war was over and he had no hope of reviving it in this miserable country where the peasants will fight for nothing but their own dunghills, he had nothing more to tell me and we had no further need of speech" (265; 734). This, I would propose, is not the silence of spiritual desolation, but the silence of letdown when the party is over. Again and again, the desire for God is subsumed to the desire for commotion.

TANTRIC CATHOLICISM

The narrator's nostalgia anticipates the description of convent tedium in *Madame Bovary*: ("Accustomed to calm aspects of life, she turned, on the contrary, to those of excitement [*elle se tournait, au contraire, vers les accidentés*]. She loved the sea only for the sake of its storms, and the green fields only when broken up by ruins")[24]—a turning that has pernicious implications for her religious vocation: "This nature, positive in the midst of its enthusiasms, that had loved the church for the sake of the flowers, and music for the words of the songs, and literature for its passional stimulus, rebelled against the mysteries of faith as it grew irritated by discipline, a thing antipathetic to her constitution."[25] Like Emma, the characters in *L'Ensorcelée* are interested in God for the adventure God represents. And like Emma, they are more interested in sensual experience than in spiritual vocations. Indeed, even when the characters do reminisce about the ancien régime rather than about the Chouannerie per se, their concentration is not on the nobles' pious decorousness but on their orgies. To read this narrative, it would seem that those decadent evenings were the principal attraction of the ancien régime, the sine qua non of the aristocratic position. Jeanne's noble ancestors are straight out of *Bluebeard*: "Her father, the lord of Feuardent, had crowned a life of excesses and of vice by a marriage which had cut him off, so they said, from all the nobility of the country round" (81; 610). And: "Sang d'Aiglon de Haut-Mesnil was a man much more vicious and discredited even than Feuardent was. . . . The last of a race made for great things which, decrepit though still physiologically potent, ended in him in an immense perversity; he was impious, debauched, a duelist, a contemner of all divine and human laws" (ibid.).

The culmination of the excesses of the ancien régime in the Revolution is couched throughout the narrative in erotic terms, as the frenetic culmination of a century of passion. And once culminated, it seems, this passion cannot be reanimated: such is secularism's dismal contribution to the world. Secularism is connected with the end of the war, which is in turn connected with the end of pleasure and romance. In *L'Ensorcelée,* Jeanne dies when she has no more contact with La Croix-Jugan, and that contact ends when the opportunity to return to war is eliminated. "As to the Abbé de La Croix-Jugan, when the project he had so boldly prepared had once more been betrayed by the ill fortune of his cause, he had become rougher and blacker than ever and ceased to come to Clotte's. He had nothing more to do there" (162; 665). The end of the war means the end of romance—the end, indeed, of the very possibility of romance. Or, in other words, the end of the ancien régime is the end of the orgy, as la Clotte notices: "Perhaps if he could crush all the Blues at once under your mattress he might sleep with you" (170; 670). Without the Chouannerie, there is to be no action, no drama, no romance, and, what is more, no sex.

The ultimate sublimation of the spiritual to the sensual (for this is explicitly about sublimation rather than connection) is underscored through the narrative's focus on the body. The body, and in particular the aristocratic body, becomes the principal locus of disorder, chaos, and fear—the arena, both metaphoric and concrete, where the entire drama is enacted. It is the wound, the corporeal drama, one of the most gruesome in nineteenth-century literature, that cements La Croix-Jugan as the nucleus of the drama: "[The Bleu] walked up to the Chouan's bed and, seizing the bandages of his face with his nails, he tore them off with such force that they cracked, broke, carrying away lumps and pieces of living flesh from the wounds which had just begun to close. It could be heard rather than seen, for night had fallen entirely, and it was so frightful to hear that Marie Hecquet fainted away" (61; 597). This description forces a concentration on this tortured body, its senses, its experience. For contrast, we can consider the description of Tainnebouy: "one of those fellows of fine appearance who need no certificate of good life and morals from mayor or priest, for God had written a magnificent and readable one in every line of his face and figure . . ." (10; 561). Tainnebouy seems untroubled, his body unharmed. But precisely for this reason, because he is humble, pious, decent, simple (and not an aristocrat), he has no place at the grisly core of this narrative.

Tainnebouy is the closest this story comes to a Turgenev "mensch," but his numerous spiritual qualities pale in comparison to the ecstatic devotion accorded to La Croix-Jugan: "The face of the unknown [*le visage de l'inconnu*], beautiful, though marked by a fatal scar [*un sceau fatal*], seemed to be carved out of green marble, it was so pale!" (46; 587). Just as the paths in the *lande* spread out from the Taureau Rouge ("several parallel paths streaked across the moor and, as they went on, spread farther and farther apart, ending all of them at points far distant from one another" [15; 565]), so the paths of this narrative spread out from La Croix-Jugan. He is the corporeal and spiritual nucleus of the narrative: both in terms of plot and because he wears on his face ("The face of the suicide was crossed and lined with inextricable furrows of wounds. The . . . five or six balls . . . had radiated in diverse directions") a microcosmic version of the story's dissipation, disorder, and intersecting geological and narrative paths.

The establishment of the body as source and repository of modern drama is accentuated in the scene of torture, where La Croix-Jugan consumes rather than being consumed in the fire: "'And now,' said the execrable sergeant of Hell's Brigade, 'salute the Chouan with fire!' And all five took red coals from the fireplace and strewed them on that face which was no longer a face. The fire was extinguished in blood and the red coals disappeared into the wounds as if they had thrown it into a sieve [*comme si on l'eût jetée dans un crible*]" (61; 597). The blood from La Croix-Jugan's body puts out the fire and thus makes him more elemental than the elements, more demonic than the "sergeant of Hell's Brigade." When he appears in church, all of Blanchelande stands in horror and wonderment: not at the gods of the ancien régime, vanished into thin air, but for this grotesquely disfigured nobleman who has survived them and, in surviving, replaced them.

"WOUND CULTURE"

The transition from the ancien régime to the nineteenth century, from a religious to a secular culture, is couched in terms of transition from pleasure to pain. This mode of representation underscores the anguish of secularism, but it nonetheless does so in such a way as to accord a particular privilege, a particular centrality, to the body. In contrast with the pleasures of the ancien régime, the

secular world of *L'Ensorcelée* becomes the arena for torture, the
scene, more precisely, of numerous gruesome head wounds. The
foundational wound is Croix-Jugan's gunshot wound, of which he is
both perpetrator and victim. And this wound, like the wound of the
Revolution, leads in turn to others—radiates out, as it were. For instance, the narrator recounts how Jeanne's mother earned the name
of Louisine-of-the-Hatchet (*Louisine-à-la-hache*): "Then seizing the
hatchet from under her arm she struck [the intruder] on his forehead, as skillfully as a butcher strikes cattle between the horns and
kills them, the head broken with a single blow. She left the hatchet
in the wound and jumped over the bandit's body . . ." (84; 612).
(This success charmed Loup de Feuardent, thus leading to the
union that would produce Jeanne.) When Jeanne comes to visit la
Clotte: "So bent now was the coif with the fixed thought which she
bore on her brow as a bull bears the axe which has struck it [*emporte
la hache qui l'a frappé*]!" (160; 664, tm). When her husband sees the
vision of Jeanne and La Croix-Jugan cooking his heart on an open
fire, "The vision was so horrible that Le Hardouey felt as though he
were struck on the head by a club and he fell to the earth like a
stunned ox [*comme un bœuf assommée*] (183; 679). La Clotte's murder
starts out thus: "A stone thrown from the midst of the crowd, outraged by Clotte's inflexible disdain, struck her forehead, whence the
blood spurted, and flung her backward" (223; 706). And when
Pierre Cloud witnesses the Midnight Mass of the phantom La Croix-
Jugan through the bullet holes in the church: "I have heard him say
himself that the nine strokes brought out the sweat on his back and
that he dropped to the earth—excuse me, sir—as if the strokes of
the bell had fallen upon his head, thick as the hammer on the anvil"
(270–71; 737).

These visceral scenes, centered on and in the human head, endow
the body with a particular gravity—not the gravity of spiritual pro-
fundity, but the gravity of grimness. This grimness is underscored
in the numerous comparisons of the characters—in particular the
wounded characters—to beef and bulls and cows. These comparisons and the numerous descriptions of blood (in Jeanne's face, on
la Clotte's forehead, on La Croix-Jugan, etc.) separate the concentration on the body from the spiritual dimension. For these characters are not sublime sacrificial emblems, but rather brute victims of
brute violence. In these concentrations on the body we see life at its
most primitive, animals at their most rudimentary: not in some sub-

tle connection to a supreme force, but in their most primal and terrestrial biology.

Mark Seltzer, writing on trauma in the late twentieth century, says,
"The convening of the public around scenes of violence—the rushing to the scene of the accident, the milling around the point of
impact—has come to make up a *wound culture*: the public fascination
with torn and opened bodies and torn and opened persons; a collective gathering around shock, trauma, and the wound."[26] He then
goes on to suggest that "the very notion of sociality is bound to the
excitations of the torn and opened body, the torn and exposed individual, as public spectacle."[27] Seltzer's twentieth-century "fascination with opened bodies" is germane, curiously enough, to Barbey,
whose opened bodies are glorious spectacles unto themselves. The
bodies in *L'Ensorcelée* generate a cult of corporeal fascination: it is as
bodies, and not as emblems or sites or spiritual entities, that they
stand at the grand center of the narrative.[28]

With its concentration on sensual pleasure and pain, this narrative slides away from spiritual connection and into the realm of secular materialism. Fascination with God becomes fascination with
religious feeling, which in turn becomes simply fascination with
feeling, which in turn becomes fascination with the body. This entire movement, this reduction or shift in the arena of action, finds
particular expression in the almost ritual repetition of human
names. When La Croix-Jugan comes to see la Clotte, she cries: "You
are the same Jéhoël who overawed us all in our mad youth. Ah, you
great lords, what can efface in you the mark of your race? And who
would not recognize what you are by the mere bones in your body
asleep in the tomb?" (133; 645). When la Clotte then introduces
Jeanne Le Hardouey as the daughter of Loup de Feuardent, La
Croix-Jugan exclaims, "Loup de Feuardent! The husband of the
beautiful Louisine-of-the-Hatchet, dead before the civil wars!"
(134; 646). When Jeanne announces to la Clotte that she is in love
with the priest: "'Listen,' she said with a wild look, 'I love a priest;
I love the Abbé Jéhoël de La Croix-Jugan!'" (166; 668). When no
interlocutor is present or willing to pronounce the ancien régime
names with reverence, the characters do it for themselves. Warns la
Clotte to Auge: "'Silence, son of an executioner!' she said. 'It
brought no good luck to your father to touch the head of Clotilde
Mauduit!'" (222; 706). La Croix-Jugan, presenting himself to la
Clotte: "Do you recognize, Clotilde Mauduit, in this remnant of torture, Ranulphe de Blanchelande and Jéhoël de La Croix-Jugan!"

(133; 645). And alone in the *lande*. " 'Ah,' he said pushing back the pistol in the holster of the saddle, 'you will always be the same sinner, insensate Jéhoël! Thirst for the enemy's blood will always dry up your impious mouth'" (230; 711). On the one hand, these moments are reminiscent of the pronouncements of a Greek chorus, watching with admiration a drama in process, vocalizing reverence for history. But at the same time, these pronouncements constitute moments of quasi-idolatrous veneration. The ritual repetition of names, which purports to represent respect for tradition, in fact ends up as a worship of human identities. And that worship, that articulation of adoration, becomes in turn a spectacle. These characters are absorbed in a passion of adulation that becomes the focus of the narrative.[29] From start to end, the narrative's most dramatic moments are those that describe the characters' obsessions (sexual obsessions, usually) with one another. We see the rending of clothing, for instance, as Jeanne tears out to find La Croix-Jugan and leaves a piece of her apron in la Clotte's hand. These instances of torment and obsession might seem strange manifestations of wistfulness for a more pious historical period, but they become less strange when we understand that in this narrative, that historical period was more about state-sponsored grandiosities than about God. The dramatic instruments with which the narrator traces the dangerous decline of religious order are rooted in human emotion, desire, and sensation.

As we examine this story's focus on human grandeur, a word should be said about ancien régime conceptions of the noble constitution and about the gothic and romantic foundations of Barbey's writing. First, the sort of fascination with the "race" described in Barbey is common to French literature and thought in the ancien régime and is thus not surprising in this chronicle of anachronisms. And in some sense, commenting on Barbey's grandiose discourse, pathologies, and perversions is like shooting fish in a barrel, for the themes of violence, sex, religion, and aristocracy permeate his fiction across the board (see *Les diaboliques*, for instance). What I want to emphasize in this chapter is that Barbey, editor of the *Revue du Monde Catholique* and one of the most Catholic writers of the French nineteenth century, the most devout, the most explicitly resistant to the idea of a world without God, nonetheless presents a narrative more dedicated, in terms of proportion, to adoration of the human than to adoration of God. Read in comparison with the sort of distance from God created in the Russian narrators, the devout narrator in Barbey comes out in near idolatrous veneration of the human body, name, and mind. His studied repudiation of secularism returns like a moth to a flame to the pleasures of creation—creation of human-centered narratives.

THE JOY OF MANIPULATION

The narrator's veneration for the human characters, their bodies, their aristocratic ancestries, their bellicose adventures, and their melodious names broadens to include veneration for the force of the human voice and mind. From the start, the human mind is vaunted as a locus of action and inspiration. The focus on the turbulent unconscious and on the force of the soul is emblematic of this concentration. So too is the narrator's earlier cited wistful: "Should this frightful movement of modern thought continue, we shall hardly have, in a few years, a scrap of land where imagination can set its foot to rest and dream, as the heron does on one leg" (2). And then: "Imagination will continue to be, for a long time hence, the most powerful reality in the lives of men" (4; 557).

In one sense, these sentences articulate a mere fondness for rumination—a respect for the inner landscape. But because this is a narrative of possession, the stakes of "imagination as most powerful reality" are raised considerably. "Imagination," during this entire narrative, tends not to be content to remain within the inner worlds of the characters; instead, it wants a concrete outcome. The episodes of the "menacing prediction" and the acts of "disposition," for instance, testify to the constitutive force (or at least to the fantasy of constitutive force) of utterances and ideas. In the first instance, it is the shepherd's words ("menacing predictions"), and in the second, sounds ("these human sounds"). In one sense, the value of these words and sounds can be said to indicate a human connection to something greater than human, but I would propose that it comes from a vision of the human *as* that greater something. When the characters become frustrated, it is because their imaginations, their adventures in the realm of ideas, fail to act on the outside world. The silence maintained by Croix-Jugan and the countess of Montsurvent implies that unless words are to have a constitutive effect, then there is no use in speaking.

In one sense, the dream of a return to the word-made-flesh enactment of aristocratic desire, nurtured by La Croix-Jugan and Montsurvent, is primarily political in nature. At the same time, I would propose, aristocratic frustration at losing grasp on France becomes emblematic of a particular vision of spiritual connection. The narrator's initial rumination on secularism: ". . . we shall hardly have, in a few years, a scrap of land where imagination can set its foot to rest and dream," is crucial because it connects—even subsumes— spiritual and aesthetic decline to the decline in the scope of the imagination. In the end, I would contend, restrictions on the competence of human words and ideas to act on the outside world loom for this narrator as the principal disaster of secularism. In his rather petulant phrases, we are in some sense reminded of the La Fontaine fable mentioned in *Le rouge et le noir*, in which the sculptor turns his dream into reality through force of desire ("The heart is quick to heed the mind / And so it became the fountainhead / Whence pagan error, always blind, / To so many peoples swiftly spread. . . . All try to change to gold, / the dreams that pass before their eyes"). For these anachronistic characters, to "change to gold" the "dreams that pass before their eyes" seems a right rather than a privilege, and the failure of that alchemy an unacceptable deviation from the divine right of influence.

The creator of this narrative is no possessor, but he nonetheless demonstrates a particular fondness for the intricacies of his own creative processes. From the start, he articulates a scrupulous consciousness of his own consciousness, of his narration, of his contemplations.[30] When Tainnebouy starts to talk about the Chouannerie, he comments: "The word Chouans . . . evoked at once in my mind's eye [*aux yeux de mon esprit*] those phantoms of a former day before which the present reality paled and was effaced" (31–32; 577). Much of his introduction concentrates on the importance of the mind—his mind—as the crucial arena for the action. For instance, when he prepares to launch into the embedded story: "I spent the time thinking it over, and that is the best I can say for myself [*je passai mon temps à y songer, et c'est ce que j'en puis dire de mieux*]" (41; 584).

When we think of *Nest*, we can envision Lavretsky articulating this last sentence. And we can imagine that articulation being a moving admission of ultimate powerlessness. On a number of levels, though, Barbey's narrative assumes a continuous connection from the inside to the outside, from the world of the mind to the world of action. And whereas in *Nest* that connection is one of adaptation ("till the soil, and till it as well as possible," responds Lavretsky when asked his plans), the inclination of these narrators and characters is to impose inner desires on the outside landscape—to produce new soil, as it were. When the narrator praises the imagination as the most powerful *reality* in the life of man, and when he does so in the introduction to a carefully constructed narrative, a narrative of possession set in an atmosphere of waning religious influence, he intimates a desire for—and, what is more, a subtle sense of entitlement to—real-world impact. When he declares that he has spent time "thinking it over," he endows that act with considerable value: a value that combines the power of transfiguration with the delicacy of artistic meditation. With these praises and preparations, creation in *L'Ensorcelée* crosses a line that it does not in *Nest*, insisting on a broader arena, a greater impact.

That *L'Ensorcelée* is at the same time a repudiation of secularism *and* a celebration of the force of the word *and* an exaltation of human grandiosities *and* a quite self-consciously manufactured narrative underscores the disparities in focus and proportion between various visions of spiritual and secular existence. Those disparities inform and are revealed in others: dissimilar visions of the meaning of writing, of narrative, and even of contemplation. While the *Nest* model uses language carefully, poking at reality, peering in at it, mindful not to disturb or disrespect it, this narrative tends to believe, at some level, in the productive function of words. The notion that narrative voice should operate in a vacuum, be restricted to the inner landscape, be a means of mere escape rather than action, seems for this model in some way unacceptable.

While in the present discussion, these models or modes are divided along cultural lines (the Russian reverence for the "outside" in *Nest* versus the French grandiosities of *L'Ensorcelée*), they transcend these national envelopes to represent various uses of (and responses to) the idea of secularism. On both the social and individual levels, there are numerous such responses, and much room for variation within them. For instance, a considerable gray area (as well as considerable overlap) lies between the grandiose orchestrator and the passive surrenderer—between God as a discursive instrument of manipulation and God as a source of spiritual solace. *L'Ensorcelée* is emblematic of such an ambivalent position both as it is produced in narrative and as it is lived in a historical moment. The desire to claim some spiritual connection combines with the simultaneous desire to master the terms and harvest the fruits of that connection.

For this narrative, as it undermines secularism and deplores the de
parture of the sacred and supernatural, at the same time disclose
the simultaneously reverential and narcissistic nature of human in
vestment in that supernatural—and of modern visions of what it can
mean to stand and write on the side of God.

5

The Narrator Who Knew Too Much

CRITICS OFTEN COMMENT ON THE INCONSISTENCIES IN *DEMONS'* NARRATIVE voice—on the numerous moments when the narrator, at times meticulous and conscious of his limitations, blithely describes something (a person, event, dialogue, feeling, etc.) that he could not possibly have witnessed. These leaps have been variously read in criticism as unimportant (D. S. Likhachev sees a narrator "about whom one must forget to a certain degree")[1] or as careless (J. Zundelovich comments, "We will linger over the narrative changes of face and show that they are a stylistic indicator of the novel's flawed quality and its ideological and artistic defectiveness").[2] In this chapter, I concentrate on two modern interpretations of these inconsistencies. Both interpretations treat the human narrator, the gossiping Anton Lavrentevich G, as a reporting character who both lives in and documents his world. The distinction between the readings arises in those moments where the viable limits of human perception are surpassed. In these moments, one critical vision, the more common, sees the narrator recede, while the other sees him launch into creative action.

Ralph Matlaw describes Dostoevsky "dropping the narrator to act as an omniscient author when reporting private conversations."[3] In this reading, the author, or authorial figure, assumes and discards the persona of a human narrator. In situations that preclude human witnessing, Anton Lavrentevich is pushed aside and the author replaces him as narrator; the situation passed, Anton Lavrentevich recommences his chronicle. Another reading, introduced by Vladimir Tunimanov and elaborated by Gene Fitzgerald, sees Dostoevsky "present a plausible witness-narrator [Anton Lavrentevich] who is also an authorial figure in his own right . . . In such a case, an author not only surrenders his omniscient point of view by imbuing his narrator with certain authorial skills, he also surrenders some aspects of his 'authorship' as the narrator is given the responsibility to choose the novel's structure, the material to be included in the novel, and the manner of presentation of that material."[4] In this reading, Dostoevsky does not "drop the narrator to act as an omniscient author," but rather turns the narrator himself into an author and creator.

These two visions of the narrator, both viable, and which combine and intersect throughout the novel, represent two different narrative ethe. Let us consider these readings side by side. One describes an omniscient author who at times takes on the attributes of a human narrator. The other proposes a human narrator who at times takes on the attributes of an omniscient author. These visions, I propose, represent crises of embodiment—crises of the intersection between finite and infinite that are fundamental to the political and philosophical substance of the novel. To cast these critical interpretations in the philosophical terms of the novel, one chronicler, the one proposed by Tunimanov and Fitzgerald, reads as a human-God, a person who sometimes transcends or disregards his limitations and launches into creative action. We can then understand the other narrator as a God-human, an omniscient creator who alternately assumes and discards the cloak of human limitations. These two narrators cross the barrier between observation and creation, hesitation and fabrication, deference to truth and invention of "truth," though in different ways and to different effects. These narrative visions are crucial because crossings of that barrier, the barrier that separates finite and infinite, subtend the philosophical and political crises narrated in the novel. *Demons'* narrative construction articulates a rich and nuanced criticism of those crossings; an elucidation of the variegated crises produced not simply in nineteenth-century Russia, but in numerous instances when human pretends to fuse with God.

NARRATIVE INCONSISTENCIES

From the start, the narrator is an ostentatiously humble and meticulous presence. Matlaw describes him as "a malicious gossip and busybody," "a spokesman for attitudes and reactions of his society, incapable or unwilling to consider the real issues involved or to have a view of his own," "entranced with himself."[5] He is indeed entranced with the act of narration, absorbed in his turns of phrase, his selection of words, his manner of presenting the world, his formation of the narrative's order. The foundation of this entrancement, though, he declares, is an acute consciousness of his shortcomings and perceptual limitations: he articulates these again and again. In the first sentence of the book, the narrator points to a lamentable want both of talent and of powers of decision: "In setting out to describe the recent and very strange events that took place in our town, hitherto not remarkable for anything, I am forced, for want of skill, to begin somewhat far back."[6] Implied in this phrase is a meticulous dedication to the task of narration and a simultaneous consciousness of his limitations. In the second paragraph, he seems concerned about the precision of his words. Stepan Trofimovich is, "so to speak, an 'exile'" (8; 7), "If one may put it so" (8, 204; 8). (Though, as Matlaw comments, "numerous other words, used incorrectly or idiosyncratically, are not qualified at all.")[7] Aside from these hesitations, the narrator also has a deliberate and tentative manner of using adjectives. For instance: "'Nothing,' Dasha repeated softly, but with a sort of [kakoy-to]sullen firmness" (67; 56), and "Varvara Petrovna shrieked with some peculiar irritation" (68; 57). When Sofya Matveevna speaks with Stepan Trofimovich, "His lips quivered as if [kak by] convulsively" (653; 498). Apparent here is a hesitation to use words, an uncertain vision of language. Also present is the sense that the world that surrounds the narrator is alien to him: "Strange talk, the existence of which I mention just to warn the reader" (211; 168). And, "It was a peculiar time: the facts were generally more or less known . . . besides the facts, certain accompanying ideas appeared . . . there was no way to adapt and find out just exactly what these ideas meant" (21; 20). "What our troubled time consisted of, and from what to what our transition was—I do not know" (462; 354). In these instances, he seems to experience his historical moment and social milieu—as well as the lexicon available to him—as beyond his comprehension.

In addition to these concerns about interpretation and expression, the narrator articulates uncertainties with respect to facts. For instance: "Generally, as far as I can recall" (302; 237). And: "I know almost positively" (438; 377). At times, the narrator seems unable to evaluate what is worth recording: "It also turned out that [Stavrogin] was quite well educated, and even rather knowledgeable. Of course, it did not take much knowledge to surprise us. . . ." (43; 37). At other times, he is uncertain about his choices: "Somehow almost without intending to (what on earth possessed me?) [dernulo zhe menya i tut] I went up to him as well" (483; 370). "To this day I do not understand and marvel myself at how I could have shouted that to him then. But I had guessed perfectly: it had all happened almost exactly the way I said, as turned out afterwards" (500; 384) or even about what he has done or seen. For instance, when Karmazinov drops his satchel, the narrator reports: "I am perfectly convinced [*ubezhden*] that I did not pick it up" (87; 71). Again, in a description of Stavrogin's conduct in the salon: "Ten seconds later his look was cold and—I'm convinced I'm not lying—calm" (205; 166).

Because the narrator admits numerous shortcomings, he tends to compensate with substantial justification. One of the first times he presents a fact, he claims the certitude of a human eyewitness, predicting a doubtful response: "Perhaps I shall be asked how I could have learned of such a fine detail. And what if I myself witnessed it?" (14; 12–13). This argument is repeated further on: "Thus their real relations were disclosed to me, for this time I listened to the whole conversation" (303; 238). And later, "He told it to me himself the next day" (502; 385). He also claims a serious dedication to fact finding. In the "Filibusters" chapter, there has been a riot and the narrator wants to ascertain the minutest facts:

> Many people here were talking about a woman from the cemetery alms house, a certain Avdotya Petrovna Tarapygin, who, as she was crossing the square on the way back to the almshouse, supposedly pushed her way through the spectators, out of natural curiosity, and on seeing what was happening, exclaimed: "Shame on 'em!"—and spat . . . And what then? It turns out that there never was any such almshouse Tarapygin woman in our town at all! I went myself to inquire at the almshouse by the cemetery: they had never even heard of any Tarapygin woman." (445; 343)

With this research, the narrator separates himself from others, less rigorous, who accept rumor as fact. Vision and hearing, human senses, are presented from the start as the bases of narrative authority. Indeed, the narrator has presented himself as incapable of narrating or even of seeing the world without the strictest of methodologies. What is striking, however, and important for the present discussion, is that the narrator's ostentatious disclaimers come to nothing. The scrupulousness and humility that he claims one moment are abandoned the next, not with subtle indiscretion but with blatant disregard for former prudence. For instance, early in the text: "Virginsky spent the whole night on his knees begging his wife's forgiveness . . . Though he never spoke of his domestic affairs with us. Only one time, as we were returning together from Stepan Trofimovich's did he begin speaking remotely about his situation" (33; 29–30). In another instance: "One must do Stepan Trofimovich justice: he knew how to win his pupil over. The whole secret lay in his being a child himself. I was not around then [menya togda eshe ne bylo], and he was constantly in need of a true friend. The boy knew that his mother loved him very much, but he hardly had much love for her. She spoke little to him, rarely hindered him in anything, but he always somehow morbidly felt her eyes fixed upon him, watching him" (40; 35). "I was not around then" is meant to demonstrate Stepan Trofimovich's loneliness, but it also serves to underscore the absence of a direct testimonial authority. And yet, the moments when the narrator is "not around" are invariably described with as much precision as the moments when he was around—when he was on hand to "witness it himself." Furthermore, those moments when the narrator was not around, when indeed human witnessing is a practical impossibility, are the most important in the novel: the conversation between Peter and Kirillov, between Stavrogin and Marya, Stavrogin and Tikhon, must occur in closed spaces outside the earshot of the narrator.

This narrator who proclaims his dedication to meticulous documentation repeatedly and blatantly abandons his narrative delicacy. From the humble servant of the narration, he becomes its master. This morphing of scrupulous hesitation into its opposite (and back again, and again) is underscored in the narrator's comments about time constraints. In one moment, the narrator writes, "I had no time to go to Liputin" (83; 68). Here, the speed and content of the narration is determined by the packed schedule of Anton Lavrentevich: the pen cannot describe what the eye had no time to witness. And then: "I cannot avoid a detailed account of this extremely brief meeting" (380; 295). Here, the narrator is scrupulous in not leaving anything out, seemingly repeating the mechanism of his first demural: "I am forced to begin somewhat far back . . ." But in still another scene, he comments, "It is a pity the story [rasskaz] must move on more quickly and there is no time for descriptions" (284; 223). Here, there is no apparent reason for the rush: why must the story move on more quickly? Every narrator (and every reporter) can determine what is to be said. But with this statement, with this abrupt transition from modest disclaimers to demonstrations of random dominance, the narrator shows the arbitrariness of his power. The leisure to dispose of time indicates authority: for instance, when the narrator describes the "Olympian" ruling circle, he writes, "These were very serious and very polite people; they bore themselves well; the others were evidently afraid of them; but it was obvious that they had no time [*im nekogda*]" (22; 21).

These inconsistencies, these oscillations between hesitation and boldness, scrupulousness and grandiosity, limited and unlimited perceptual and creative capacities, are of more than technical narratological interest. These oscillations can suggest a fusion or confusion of the human and the superhuman, a fusion with considerable political, social, and spiritual resonance.

THE IDEOLOGICAL FUNCTION OF THE NARRATOR'S DISCREPANCIES

The competing visions of the narrator represent the two principal spiritual and philosophical scandals treated in *Demons*—the subtle moves in position that troubled Dostoevsky on both the moral and the political planes. In the one scenario, in which a human narrator (Anton Lavrentevich) assumes and discards the omniscience of an author, those moments of creation constitute a disingenuous abandonment of the narrator's humble disclaimers, a precipitous seizing of power. In the other scenario, in which the author assumes and discards the voice of a human narrator, the constant articulation of disclaimers represents another sort of disingenuousness: a false and gratuitous humility. The first is the scandal of arbitrary manipulation and power: the intrusion of authorial machinations where humble hesitations had pretended to stand. In the second scenario, the scandal is not one of manipulation but rather of a pretended modesty—a gratuitous and insincere concentration on discretion, humility, and hesitation. The first scandal reproduces the Westernist political discursive and strategic machinations as embodied in Peter Verkhovensky, the megalomaniac who practices manipulation and a sort of ventriloquism to political ends. The second represents Westernist narrative manipulations as embodied by Karmazinov, the writer who, in the very creation of fiction, in fact retains as his principal focus his own unassuming discretion. These schemas both represent, though in differing incarnations, the scandalous crossing of the line between finite and infinite, hesitation and boldness, witnessing and creation, or human and God.

THE NARRATOR AS GOD

The first scenario represents a human who assumes and discards the voice of a God and the second, a God who assumes and discards the voice of a human. Throughout *Demons,* philosophical and political questioning is framed in terms of the human connection to God. The characters are forever examining that relationship. Shatov "will believe in God." Stepan Trofimovich believes in God "as in a being who is conscious of himself in me" (37; 33). Kirillov declares that "he who dares to kill himself, is God." But before he proceeds to act out that dare, he claims that "Man has done nothing but invent God" (617; 471). Matryosha commits suicide from a fear that she has "killed God." The question of the intersection of the human and the divine is articulated by nearly every character and is also made crucial on a cultural and national scale. Shatov claims that "the aim of all movements of nations, of every nation and in every period of its existence, is solely the seeking for God, its own God" (249; 198), and goes so far as to declare that an "atheist cannot be Russian . . . he who is not Orthodox cannot be Russian" (250; 197). The narrator, however, describes that same nation's elite as comprised of "Olympians." The distinction between respecting God and posing as God is fundamental to the political and philosophical content of the novel. So it is in the novel's form, where the narrator's moves in position represent a problematic crossing of the human-God line.

That the narrator enacts an ethical and spiritual problematic rather than simply raising theoretical questions of narratological prudence is made more clear when we consider the narrator's role within, as well as his power over, the narrative. Omniscience and omnipotence are in a sense capacities that the act of narration automatically confers, or can confer, though usually not in the deliberately uneven formations featured here. But this narrator, as a human character, as the young man Anton Lavrentevich G–v, has a particular place within the world and culture that he chronicles. He is an interlocutor, a listener—a confidante for Kirillov, Shatov, and, importantly, Stepan Trofimovich. He creates for himself the role of a vital and respondent presence. Of Stepan Trofimovich, for example, the narrator writes, "He was unable to be without me even for two hours, needing me like air and water" (81; 66). The narrator listens to Stepan and the former's presence, more than any other's presence, other than Varvara Petrovna's, enables Stepan to articulate his experience and to continue his existence. When Liza wants to send for Shatov and be introduced to Marya Timofeevna, she turns to the narrator: "I'm counting only on you, I have no one else" (135; 108). Insofar as he combines the capacities of narrator, creator, facilitator of action, calm witness, consoling interlocutor, and ubiquitous presence, the narrator explicitly embodies, though in a disordered and continuously shifting manner, the attributes of God. In other words, he reads as a God figure, not merely as a metaphoric vehicle for demonstrating a narratological God problematic.

Moments of narrative manipulation can signify, with varying degrees of explicitness, human assumption of divine force. At times that signification is metaphorical only, but in *Demons*, it takes the form of a more literal and more scandalous embodiment. At the end of the novel, for instance, when the narrator describes the conversation between Stepan Trofimovich and Sofya Matveevna: "'You must read it to me: I'll tell you why afterwards. I want to recall it literally. I need it literally.' Sofya Matveevna knew the Gospel well and immediately found in Luke the same passage I have placed as an epigraph to my chronicle. I quote it here again [*privedu ego zdes opyat*]: 'Now a large herd of swine was feeding there on the hillside . . .'" (654; 498). The quoted passage recounts Jesus' miraculous relocation of the demons, from the man into the swine, thus reminding us of God's power and the force of the superhuman. What is more, the entire episode stands as part of Stepan Trofimovich's spiritual experience, his return to Russia, as it were. And yet, the narrator's words remind us first and foremost that there was an epigraph—that this is a constructed chronicle, one that the narrator took some trouble and time to put together. Introduced with the words, "I quote it here again," the passage has two simultaneous functions. On the one hand, it is an important moment in the story, a turning point for Stepan Trofimovich: "'My friend,' Stepan Trofimovich said in great excitement, '*savez-vous*, this wonderful and . . . extraordinary passage has been a stumbling block for me all my life . . .'" (655; 499). On the other hand, the words "I quote it here again" (rather than "Sofya Matveevna read," or some such) reminds the reader of the passage's effect—not its spiritual effect, but its dramatic effect. The "I" in "I quote it here again" accentuates the fact that this moment is not so much serendipitous as smartly orchestrated, and that the narrator's particular superior talent is not for witnessing moments of spiritual connection, but for authoring them.

THE NARRATOR AS PETER VERKHOVENSKY

In his study of *Demons*, Vaclav Cerny writes that Stavrogin, Kirillov, and Peter Verkhovensky represent the three "major theological predicates of God": absolute pride (Stavrogin), absolute existence (Kirillov), and absolute power (Peter Verkhovensky).[8] These predicates also describe the narrator, who stands as detached witness, creator, and empathic interlocutor. And yet, this composite position has different sorts of resonance depending on how we read the narrator. I said that the two scandals or inconsistencies enacted in the narration represent the two principal spiritual and philosophical scandals that are treated in *Demons*—that of political manipulation and power, and that of pretended humility. Let us consider the first scenario, the "narrator who is an author figure in his own right." In this scenario, as Fitzgerald described, the narrator chronicles what he sees, hears, or experiences. When these means of access are unavailable, he becomes a creator. In those moments, then, the story splits into two strands—the strand of the real (which the reader does not see, because the narrator cannot see it) and the strand of the fabricated, which the narrator presents to the reader in lieu of the (inaccessible) real. Dostoevsky is particularly adept at making palpable the fact we never can know the *fabula* directly, that all we ever know of a narrative is the *sjuzet*.[9] This consciousness may come from his interest in crime/police fiction, where the inquest, like the *sjuzet*, sets out to uncover the story of the crime, the true *fabula* (the point that Todorov of course makes). *Demons* plays with these superimpositions and limited perceptions. During the narrator's moments of viable witnessing, one plot (*sjuzet*) narrates one story (*fabula*). In moments when witnessing is impossible, the *sjuzet* abandons the inaccessible *fabula* and composes a second *fabula*, to substitute for and conceal the absence of the first.

Important to this particular narrative dynamic are the smooth transitions from moments of chronicling to moments of composing. As we see, the narrator does not announce when he is abandoning the role of witness for the role of composer. And though one can discern the transitions on the basis of whether or not witnessing is possible, even when a distinction is made between what is real and what is not real, that distinction becomes immediately untenable. As Fitzgerald writes, "In all works in which witness-narrators emphasize that they have composed their worlds after the novel's conclusion,

only the 'narrating' perspective realistically exists . . . Whenever the
'experiencing' perspective is used, it is at the choice of the narrator's 'narrating self,' and is an indication of his ability to control and
manipulate the narrative point of view."[10] The fabricated element
intrudes on and weaves into the narrative and so determines the substance of the real. Once the narrator fabricates, though, both the
caution and the realism articulated in his disclaimers are compromised. This reading of the narrator is of particular pertinence to the
novel's political actors and their discursive strategies. Let us turn to
the political "salon" discussion in the episode "With our People"
and to the words and actions of Peter Verkhovensky.

During his address to the group at Virginsky's, Peter uses much of
the same subtle deceptions, the same inconsistencies of position, as
the human-God narrator. The second section of the chapter opens
with Peter coming in and "greeting almost no one" (394; 305).
When asked, "Verkhovensky, do you have anything to state?" he replies, "Precisely nothing" (401; 310), and then declares that he is
not even listening. He is poised for indifference and, what is more,
since he is not even paying attention, for ignorance. From his introduction, Peter seems a recessive presence, nothing more than an an-
nouncer of Stavrogin: "And imagine, Varvara Petrovna, I came in
thinking to find he'd already been here for a quarter of an hour"
(180; 144) and a humble narrator: "I'm a poor describer of feelings" (187; 149).

When Peter does listen at Virginsky's, he does so with contempt
and unconcern: " 'That's a lot of nonsense, however!' escaped, as it
were, from Verkhovensky. Nonetheless he went on cutting his nails
with complete indifference and without raising his eyes" (404; 313).
"Well, I just knew I was letting myself in for it," he mutters as the
lame man orates. Indeed, he seems to distrust not just these interlocutors, but all political theorists, all those who articulate an opinion:
"I think all these books, these Fouriers, Cabets, all these 'rights to
work,' Shigalyovism—it's all like novels, of which a hundred thousand can be written. An aesthetic pastime. I understand that you're
bored in this wretched little town, so you fall on any paper with writing on it" (405; 313). But words, paradoxically, written, spoken, and
attributed to others, are precisely his instrument. When Peter is first
introduced, the narrator writes:

> His words spill out like big, uniform grains, always choice and always
> ready to be at your service. You like it at first, but later it will become

repulsive, and precisely because of this all too clear enunciation, this string of ever ready words. You somehow begin to imagine that the tongue in his mouth must be of some special form, somehow unusually long and thin, terribly red, and with an extremely sharp, constantly and involuntarily wriggling tip. (180; 144–45)

Peter is doubly connected with diabolical verbal manipulation, both through the description of the serpentine sharp tongue and through the narrator's subtle intoning, "You like it at first." His creative force comes precisely from a sort of ventriloquism, a subtle insinuation of fabrications into the domain of the real and of words into the mouths of others. As we see, he uses the same subtle intoning and pretension to reticence as the narrator to turn his interlocutor-victims into characters and absorbed readers in his narrative. For one, he pretends not to create; indeed, to resist discussion, to resist introducing ideas: "Well, I didn't really come here for discussions" (406; 314). This sentence implies that he is a man of action, but also subtly connects that action to a calculated reticence with respect to communication—a reticence, or apparent reticence, that enables the action. Just as the narrator underscores his prudent distance from the action, so too does Peter distance himself from the action that he in fact orchestrates. And just as the narrator pretends to describe rather than to fabricate, Peter pretends to respond rather than to initiate. To the lame man's "No, sir, perhaps we won't leave the common cause yet! This must be understood," Peter blurts, "What, you mean you'd really join a fivesome if I offered it?" (407; 315). To the lame man's alarm that recruiting is being done "in an unknown company of twenty people," Peter responds, "Gentlemen, I consider it my duty to announce to you that all this is all foolishness and our talk has gone too far [*daleko zashel*]" (409; 317). To that same man's question of why he is being addressed first, Peter declares: "Because you started it all. Kindly don't evade, dodging won't help here" (410; 317).

PETER VERKHOVENSKY AS NARRATOR: POLITICAL AMBITION AND THE BUSINESS OF FICTION

Throughout this discussion, Peter presents himself either as a detached philosopher, a prudent interpreter, or a sensible interlocutor. His comments resemble observations, syntheses of radical ideas presented, rather than introductions of those radical ideas. In fact, though, his interventions have two purposes: introduction of ideas, and postulation of his interlocutor (or an innocent third) as the author of those ideas. Given these methods, we can discern important parallels between narrative invention and political manipulation. The narrator accentuates his hesitations, his shortcomings, even as he starts without warning to narrate incidents that he could not have known—incidents, indeed, that he has just reminded us that he could not have known. While the basis of his authority and his trustworthiness (such as it is) had been his scrupulous restraint, on the strength of that authority, he departs from that very restraint, thus producing the contradictions that have demanded critical interpretation. So it is too with Peter Verkhovensky who, declaring he has nothing to state, proceeds to state much—who, articulating surprise at the direction of the discussion, proceeds to direct that discussion. The narrator and Peter also claim to narrate (or act) under duress, in deference to an outside force. For instance, the narrator, who starts by announcing, "I am forced, by want of skill, to begin somewhat far back," also writes, "I would not have begun speaking in particular about this scoundrel, and he would not be worth dwelling upon, but at that time a certain outrageous incident occurred in which, it was asserted, he also took part" (323; 252). Here the narrator has the same innocent pretense of scrupulous documentation as does Peter when he states, "What, you mean you'd really join a fivesome if I offered it?" "I consider it my duty . . ." "Because you started it all. Kindly don't evade, dodging won't help here." This ventriloquism, this creation of others through rumor and rhetoric, are the bases of Peter's demonic nature and his scandalous action.

Peter does not just place on others responsibility for events that he himself has produced. He also informs those very others that they are responsible, that they are acting of their own volition and, at times, he is believed. Here, we see the narrator's inconsistencies as emblematic of a discursive stratagem, of a way to generate alternate versions of reality. In the instance of Kirillov's suicide, for instance, Peter first describes Kirillov to Lembke as "a maniac, a madman" (355; 276). He then comes to Kirillov: "I've come to remind you of our agreement" (373; 289), though there is no precise antecedent to this reminder (the "agreement" at issue is that Kirillov kill himself and in so doing assume guilt for the murder of Shatov—a murder Peter in fact commits). During the second encounter: "I have always been sure that you would do your duty as an independent and progressive man . . . I mean, you see, you yourself already joined your plan with our actions . . . I understand, it's entirely as you will, and we are nothing, just as long as this entire will of yours gets carried out" (557; 468). In the third encounter: "I didn't think it up for you, you did yourself even before me, and you originally announced it not to me but to the members abroad" (613; 468). And: "If you shoot yourself, you'll become God, is that right?" thus casting the suicide as a supreme act of will. After the murder of Shatov, in which Peter pulls the trigger, he announces, "Gentlemen, we will now disperse. You undoubtedly must feel that free pride which is attendant upon the fulfillment of a free duty. And if, unhappily, you are now too alarmed for such emotions, you will undoubtedly feel it tomorrow, by which time it would be shameful not to feel it" (606; 462). This sentence displaces responsibility ("a free duty") and also articulates a manipulative force of insinuation reminiscent of the narrator's "you like it at first." Like the human-God narrator, he transitions smoothly from description to creation to persuasion. And like the human-God narrator, he produces and then maintains a fiction of realism.

It should of course be said that though grandiose manipulation is Peter's intention, he is not in any genuine sense the author of his interlocutors. Peter Verkhovensky is a master manipulator, a monologic God-Creator of sorts, but the discussion at Virginsky's is a dialogue. Much has been made of the correct translation of Dostoevsky's title, translated as "*The Possessed*" and as "*Demons.*" Robert Jackson writes, "Only Bakhtin among the major critical thinkers, it would seem, has drawn an analogy between Dostoevsky the artist and God. In this comparison, simultaneously aesthetic and theological, Dostoevsky emerges in his novelistic activity as God-Creator, but above all as God in His relation to man, a relation allowing man to reveal himself utterly (in his immanent development)."[11] So too at Virginsky's, where, arguably, the interlocutors are not so much created as pushed into self-revelation—where, perhaps, ironically, desire for autonomy leads them to accept an agency that is not theirs. Important to this reading of the narrator is not the innocence of the interlocutors but the sinister intentions and discursive strategies of the serpentine Peter. This character combines calculated reticence with violent action and, in so doing, posits himself as a scandalous human-God figure and recreates the duplicitous inconsistencies practiced by the narrator.

The similarities between the narrator's inconsistencies and Peter's manipulations function as a dramatic instrument for examining the spiritual problems not just with Peter Verkhovensky, but also with political action in general. Much of the nineteenth-century Russian political struggle, the Slavophile-Westernist debate, was in essence a battle for the ideological high ground as well as for power. But these battles were in some sense fundamentally incompatible. We know, for instance, that the social reforms of the 1860s were frequently couched in the discourse of religious conflicts, wherein the peasants were cast as martyrs. "The massacre of peasants at Bezdna in 1861 . . . was incorporated into radical mythology as a clash between oppressive authority and the authentic, democratic Christianity of the *narod*. . . . Requiem service . . . saluted the 'democratic' Christian prophets who had appeared among the peasants since the 18th century."[12] The revolutionaries in turn were self-cast as divine avengers: "The terrorists looked upon their task as a holy mission. They sacrificed other people's lives for an ideal."[13] Here we are in the realm of messianic delusion, of action that belies the pretense of dedication to an ideal: a disregard for the human-God distinction, as revolutionaries created for themselves the role of divine leaders. Berdyaev described this sort of manipulation as evil creation: "Not all creativity is good. There can be evil creativity. One can create not only in the name of God but in the name of the devil as well. But this is precisely why we should not concede creativity to the devil, to the antichrist. The antichrist has been flaunting his pseudo-creativity [*lzhetvorchestvo*] with a great deal of energy."[14] Arguably, some creation in the name of God can be demonic. Similarly, some action in the name of dedication to justice and public good can be monomaniacal. So it was in the "divine avenger" argument of the revolutionaries, and so it was in *Demons*, whose Peter, pretending reticence, is in fact a sociopath and a murderer and whose narrator, claiming hesitation and incompetence, in fact invents—creates ex nihilo—the entire story.

Vision, Delusion, Liberalism, and the Best of Intentions

Even in cases where the discourse was not as dramatic and the messianic nature of political ambition not as pronounced, the Slavophile-Westernist tension nonetheless meant a clash over (and between) ownership of truth and ownership of power, and as such posed problems of spiritual consistency fundamental to *Demons*. For instance, in a discussion of Dostoevsky's understanding of the West-ernist-Slavophile conflict, Bruce Ward explains the mediatory na-ture of the author's political position:

[Dostoevsky] defends the Slavophil return to the Christianity of the Rus-sian people against the enlightened and cosmopolitan atheism of the Westernists. And he defends the passion for truth and universality of the Westernists against the complacent and inward-looking religious nation-alism of the Slavophils. Dostoevsky never abandoned his mediatory posi-tion between the two movements . . . He was a Slavophil insofar as Slavophilism affirmed the truth of Christianity and the Russian people as bearers of this truth. He was a Westernist insofar as Westernism moved toward the truth of the universal human community.[15]

Remembering the disconnect between humble dedication and po-litical domination, we can read "enlightened and cosmopolitan atheism" and "complacent and inward-looking religious national-ism" as indicative of a world vision that at some crucial moment crosses the line from hesitation into dominance, from dedication into manipulation. This crossing, this subtle transition, is not pecu-liar to Westernists or Slavophiles. Both can practice the inconsisten-cies and transitions of Fitzgerald's narrator, as this practice simply means an implicit casting of oneself in the role of creator.

Ideological contradictions arise when those who pretend to rep-resent justice end up in a quasi-despotic position. Indeed, lesser ver-sions of such a disconnect can stain even admirable political intentions, as desire to see justice done can turn into manipulation of justice. The narrative inconsistencies that Fitzgerald describes, the transition from observation to fabrication, represent a problem-atic political ethos: "Whenever the 'experiencing' perspective is used, it is at the choice of the narrator's 'narrating self,' and is an indication of his ability to control and manipulate the narrative point of view."[16] And: "He first relates a scene or action in which he personally participates, thus remaining within the 'legitimate' framework of his point of view. Then, by using the same descriptive epithets, opinions, and evaluations the narrator 're-creates' isolated private scenes and characters consistent with his earlier observa-tions."[17] Of course, the very notion that the narrator could supple-ment what he sees with what he imagines he could see renders the division between vision and imagination radically unstable and ac-centuates the sense in which observation *is* (re)creation. This equivalence, Dostoevsky understood, stands as an obstacle both to clarity of vision and to social justice. For instance, Bruce Ward wrote of Dostoevsky's return to Christianity during his years in Siberia: "Dostoevsky's liberalism was perhaps primarily responsible for his persistent effort to establish contact with these Russian representatives of oppressed humanity; but it was precisely this liberalism that made contact so problematic. He found it difficult to see and accept the Russian people as they actually were, rather than as he and his fellow Petrashevtsi had imagined them to be."[18] Seeing can turn into—or be from the start—a form of invention, an insinuation of the fabricated into the real. Such an inclination to invention touches nearly every character in *Demons*. As Michael Holquist observed, "The relation of the novel's protagonists to each other is essentially that of an author to the characters he invents."[19] Nancy Anderson describes this sort of invention as everywhere present in *Demons*: in the narrator's description of Varvara Petrovna's relationship to Stepan Trofimovich ("She invented [*vydumala*] him, and was the first to believe in her invention" [15; 16]), and in Fedka and the narrator's comments about Peter: "I tell you, sir, it's very easy for Pyotr Stepanovich to live in the world, because he imagines a man and then lives with him the way he imagined him [*on cheloveka sam predstavit sebe*] (259; 205) [*on cheloveka sam sochinit*] (362; 281)."[20]

This notion of invention constitutes an organic obstacle to disinterested vision. Indeed, with this notion of invention, *Demons* anticipates not just twentieth-century critiques of communism, but also critiques of realism. *Demons* has been called prophetic, and indeed, it anticipates the argument that a principal obstacle to realist representation is political and philosophical prejudice. It notices that political and philosophical interests rely on the fiction of realism; that realism must remain a fiction in order for political interests to be sustained, and that political interests must be sublimated in order for that fiction to remain realistic. The symbiosis between realist conventions and political interest becomes clear in Peter's discourse. On his word, for instance, the lame man "started it," Peter's recruitment plan is "our talk," the "common cause" is a "fivesome." But equally fundamental to his acts of creation is a pretense of innocent inspection: "What?" "Our talk has gone too far." "You started it."

THE NARRATOR AS KARMAZINOV, OR
THE SCANDAL OF SELF-REFERENCE

As we see, the scandal of the split narration can assume various proportions and various levels of seriousness—from a distorted and violent manipulation of incidents to a subtle and at times entirely unconscious delusion with respect to the real. Here, we can leave the political domain for the moment and come to the second narrative scenario: the vision of an author "who drops the narrator to act as an omniscient author when reporting private conversations and scenes at which the chronicler could not have been present." This scenario has as its foundation the same inconsistencies and the same fluctuations in distance as the first scenario, the same sense of a problematically permeable barrier between finite and infinite. But instead of reading the narrator as a human being who sometimes launches into creation, Matlaw reads the narrator as an author, as Dostoevsky or his author figure, who assumes and discards the persona of a human narrator. This scenario involves a different sort of crossing. This narrator, because an author, is omniscient and omnipotent: thus his creation (because a creation, not a chronicle) is reliable. Less genuine in this scenario are the moments when the narrator assumes a humble human form: "I am forced, for want of skill, to begin somewhat far back," "Generally, as far as I can recall," "What our troubled time consisted of, and from what to what our transition was—I do not know," "And what if I myself witnessed it?" "He told it to me himself the next day," "I had no time to go to Liputin."

In this scenario, as in the first, we get the sense of split narrative strands, of a story continuing even when the narrator is not telling it. In this scenario, as in the first, the narrator distances himself at certain moments from the real. The nature of that distancing is different, though, for this narrator does not leave the story in order to supplement or substitute his fabrications for the real. Instead, he leaves the story to concentrate on himself, to demonstrate his self-consciousness, to pause and turn inward.

There are a number of writers and instances of writing represented in the novel. Lebyadkin and Liputin produce the governess poem, Lembke authors a novel, Stepan Trofimovich writes both historical documents and an incomprehensible allegorical drama, Shatov writes poems, Karmazinov writes numerous works of fiction, and Stavrogin, finally, writes his own confession—and, in narrating himself, as I will argue at the end of this chapter, connects the narrative scenarios at issue here. Furthermore, each writer and each instance of writing in the novel is in some sense absurd, ridiculous rather than artistic. First mentioned are Stepan Trofimovich's thesis "on the nearly emerged civic and Hanseatic importance of the German town of Hanau" and his play in which "an altogether inanimate object gets to sing about something" (9–10; 8–9). The governess poem is scandalous, Lembke's novel mediocre, the student poem a bad imitation of Herzen. The most important writer in the novel, though (aside from Stavrogin whom we consider further on), is Karmazinov. This author is described by Varvara Petrovna as a "puffed-up creature!" (60; 50). Writing in this novel, even at its best, is never about a Bakhtinian dialogism nor even about monologism, but rather about a calculated and mediocre self-display.

Early in the novel, the narrator articulates his opinion of Karmazinov's writing:

> He described the wreck of a steamer somewhere on the English coast, of which he himself had been a witness and had seen how the perishing were being saved and the drowned dragged out. The whole article, quite a long and verbose one, was written with the sole purpose of self-display. One could simply read it between the lines: "Pay attention to me, look at how I was in those moments. What do you need the sea, the storm, the rocks, the splintered planks of the ship for? I've described it all well enough for you with my mighty pen. Why look at this drowned woman with her dead baby in her dead arms? Better look at me, at how I could not bear the sight and turned away. Here I am turning my back; here I am horrified and unable to look again; I've shut my eyes—interesting, is it not?" I told Stepan Trofimovich my opinion of Karmazinov's article, and he agreed with me. (85; 70)

Robert Jackson compared Dostoevsky to the God of the New Testament: "The artist-god here is not the monologically oriented personal god of the Old Testament who is always interfering with the destinies of his people . . . but the God of the New Testament who leaves man free to decide for himself, free 'to judge himself, to refute himself' in self-regulating dialogical processes."[21] If Dostoevsky as artist-God frees his characters to discover and disclose themselves, Karmazinov as artist-God maintains such a distance from his characters that he gradually abandons them and decides instead to discover and disclose himself. Dostoevsky, as Bakhtin and Jackson noted, would not encapsulate his characters. Nor would Karmazinov. But in Karmazinov, that refusal to encapsulate, or even to look, is the entire subject of the article. His is not a hesitation that "leaves man free to decide for himself, free to judge himself, to refute himself in self-regulating dialogical processes," but a hesitation that displaces those processes and becomes a spectacle in itself.

THE PERILS OF SELFISHNESS, OR WASTING NARRATIVE TIME

Berdyaev praised creativity and compared it favorably to the "self-obsession" of the humble. In a sort of believer's reprisal of Nietzsche's critique of humility in the *Genealogy of Morals*: "Humility is an inward [or even 'inward-looking' or 'introspective'] (*vnutrennee*) spiritual practice, in which man is concerned with his soul, with self-transcendence, self-perfection, self-salvation. Creativity is a spiritual practice in which man forgets about himself: he renounces himself in the creative act, absorbed by the object [of his act],—[or because it is the object of his act that absorbs him]."[22] Humility in his assessment resembles what Flaubert mocks in Emma Bovary: "Her soul, tortured by pride, at length found rest in Christian humility, and, tasting the joy of weakness, she saw within herself the destruction of her will opening wide the gates for heavenly grace to conquer her [*qui devait faire aux envahissements de la grâce une large entrée*]."[23] In place of this sort of humility, Berdyaev proposes creativity or, more precisely, absorption within the subject. Jung makes a similar point in his discussion of extroverted and introverted creation,[24] as does Jackson when he comments that "in its deeper action artistic cognition approaches religious revelation."[25] Unfortunately, the object of that cognition is in this case one's own delicacy or sensitivity, and Karmazinov represents a vaunting of inner processes rather than of the outside world, a celebration of faith rather than a celebration of God, a closed circle of representation rather than an open road of creativity. This delicate and humble author ends up creating a fiction whose principal character, whose principal focus, is the delicacy and humility of the author.

Entrancement with one's own perceptions and hesitations resonates not just as bad art but as an indication of self-absorption. That criticism, which is as much spiritual as it is artistic, becomes accentuated as Turgenev's "Execution of Tropmann" is transformed in

Demons into an account of a shipwreck. In Turgenev's account, it was the vengeance and violence of the execution (of the person and the social order) that the narrator turned from, but here, it is an act of nature, a simple manifestation of nature's incontrovertible dominance. Turning away from a shipwreck, much more than turning away from an execution, I would propose, reads as a denial of the natural world order—resistance or willful blindness to the outside world and to the power of acts of God.[26]

With Karmazinov's closed eyes in mind, we can recall Bakhtin's notion that "Living an idea is somehow synonymous with unselfishness."[27] Bakhtin had written of Stepan Trofimovich in particular: "He [Stepan Trofimovich] spouts his 'verities' because he lacks a 'dominant idea' which would determine the core of his personality; he possesses separate impersonal verities which because of their impersonality, cease to be completely true, but he lacks a truth of his own."[28] Being the embodiment of a "dominant idea," in this formulation, constitutes the foundation of both self and selflessness. Without such an idea, according to Bakhtin, Dostoevsky's characters are at once empty and closed. Karmazinov, in the shipwreck story, has one dominant idea: his own sensibilities, his delicate constitution, his humble hesitation in the face of nature's force. And yet, these are the sorts of dominant ideas that do not count as dominant ideas—that do not liberate one from selfishness (or, to be more prudent, and to evaluate Karmazinov on narrative rather than on spiritual terms, do not liberate the story from the constraints of the narrator's self-consciousness). What is more, according to Berdyaev's criterion of absorption, this dominant idea does not constitute but rather precludes creativity. It is perhaps because of these constraints, these inversions, that Karmazinov, as seen by Anton Lavrentevich, is an uninteresting narrator and his *fabula* impoverished by the preciosity of his *sjuzet*.[29]

Karmazinov's modesty, according to the narrator, detracts from rather than enriches his stories. So it is in a literal sense with the narrative scenario that Matlaw describes—an omniscient author who sometimes pauses to introduce gratuitous perceptual limitations. As cited earlier: "I am forced, for want of skill, to begin somewhat far back," "Generally, as far as I can recall," "But strangely, did run by to see Darya Pavlovna, where, however, I was not received . . . what I could have said to her, and why I ran by, I do not know." Some of the narrator's disclaimers read as parodies of Karmazinov that is, read as precious, or, worse, as an indication of incomprehen sion of the outside world. For instance: "I find it difficult to give the plot [of Stepan Trofimovich's play], because to tell the truth I understand nothing of it" (10; 9). And: "What our troubled time consisted of, and from what to what our transition was—I do not know." "Certain accompanying ideas also appeared . . . there was no way to adapt and find out just exactly what these ideas meant." These read as much cruder articulations of Karmazinov's humble sentiments: demonstrations not of respect and hesitation before the rich intricacies of life, but rather of flat incomprehension. What seems to be scrupulous modesty is in fact a want of understanding combined with (or perhaps due to) an unwillingness to place the narrative focus outside oneself. As the narrator puts it frankly at the start: "It is not for me to tell of certain things, nor would I be able to" (334; 261). Further on, in a moment that seems to mock Karmazinov directly, Anton declares: "The whole of the night constitutes—for me at least—the most difficult part of my chronicle" (502; 385). "For me at least" seems to imply a thoughtful admission that his point of view is merely one among many, that he can only write from his own particular perspective. And yet, that "for me at least" only underscores the fact that Anton is the narrative's sine qua non. Others may have experienced that night, and found it difficult or not, but the ideas of those others are nowhere in this chronicle. Anton Lavrentevich is the sole narrator and what he finds difficult either to experience or to write, the reader will never see. So it is with the shipwreck in Karmazinov's portrait of sensitivity, for, as we learn, Karmazinov finds much difficult.

The negative aesthetic and ethical evaluation of Karmazinov's verbosity, indicated by the aforementioned examples, is further accentuated by the circumstances and placement of his readings. At Yulia Mikhailovna's evening, for instance, the author takes the stage: "Mr. Karmazinov, mincing and preening, announced that 'he had flatly refused to read at first' (much he needed to announce that!). 'There are lines,' he said, 'which so sing themselves from a man's heart as cannot be told, and such a sacred thing cannot simply be laid before the public' (why was he laying it, then?)" (476; 365). In this episode as in his narration of the shipwreck, he is a distraction, narrating himself rather than the world around him. Because of his concentration, the readers of *Demons* (as well as the guests and ushers at the evening, including the narrator) have access only to him, and not to the world outside him. Later that evening, the town is burning, and Lebyadkin and Marya are murdered. Had Karmazinov not occupied narrative space with his recitation, these incidents could have been more important on the narrative scale, or come earlier in narrative time. Furthermore, one cannot help wondering if, had Karmazinov not occupied the guests' attention, the fire and murder could have been prevented. The superimposition of Karmazinov's reading onto an evening of catastrophe turn the reading into a distraction, which makes the point that self-reference, even (and perhaps especially) humble self-reference, uses up valuable narrative time.

As the narrator comments about the content of "Merci," "who could make out the theme? It was some sort of account of some sort of impressions, some sort of recollections. But of what? But what about?" (477; 366). Emphasis on recollections rather than on what is recollected seems vacuous to the chronicler, who notices that, "He smiles haughtily at Russia, and he likes nothing better than to proclaim Russia's bankruptcy in all respects before the great minds of Europe, but as regards himself—no, sir, he has already risen above these great minds of Europe, they are all only material for his puns" (479; 367). Interestingly, as Karmazinov rises above the great minds of Europe, so the chronicler rises above the mind of Karmazinov. On various planes, then, the act of narration becomes the substance of the narration, a shrinking of scope leads to more shrinking, and vision is placed at a distance, at several degrees remove, from actual representation of or absorption in real-world events.

THE SIN OF PRIDE: REPRODUCING THE MEANS OF (AND NEED FOR) NARRATIVE PRODUCTION

In this novel, focus on the act of narration and on the dominance of the narrator is, I would contend, a particularly Western sin—a sin of pride comparable in nature, if not in scale, to that of the '60s revolutionaries. Henri Peyre wrote that Dostoevsky's own forgiveness "did not extend to those Russian intellectuals who had lost touch with their native soil and traditions."[30] It is true that Karmazinov, like Turgenev, has lived most of his life abroad and at one point in the novel declares himself proud to be German. But what makes Karmazinov a Western narrator is, more than location, his fondness for and his repeated references to his own vision. Our readings of the French novels in this study discovered the self-conscious character of their narrative construction. In each of these novels, the narrator generates an order (or an ironic absence of order, or a disorienting multitude of orders) that underscores the dissolution of master narratives and the transference of force from the hand of God to the hand of the author. The transition to a secular culture thus becomes an occasion for narrative play and dominance. Karmazinov's pretentious concentration on himself does not come near this sort of dominance, but nonetheless constitutes a palpable vaunting of the human authorial voice. When the time comes to recognize something greater than himself, he retreats and refuses to look. This retreat is problematic, *Demons* implies, because it is situated on a long continuum whose other end is political carelessness. Bruce Ward's comments on Dostoevsky's resistance to the "complacent and inward-looking religious nationalism" of the Slavophiles speak to this concern. An "inward-looking" narrator can be problematic in the same sense as an "inward-looking" politician. Both are operating in a closed circle, a circumscribed arena of vision.

Matlaw writes of Dostoevsky's narrator: "The verbal surface reflects and emphasizes a portrait of a disintegrating society and the chronicler plays a leading role in that process" and notices "the deliberate obfuscation Dostoevsky introduces through him, a kind of verbal equivalent of the darkness in which society finds itself."[31] The verbal surface, in this reading, functions as a metaphor for social darkness. Without abandoning this metaphoric value, we can consider that the verbal surface also embodies the convolution of the act of verbalization. The darkness represented is one not just of social distortion but of narrative self-consciousness and the closed circle that results therefrom. With respect to Peter Brooks's connection of nineteenth-century narrative production to the loss or perceived loss of providential plots, it could be said that nineteenth-century narrative production exacerbates, rather than merely responds to, "anxiety at the loss of providential plots."[32] That is, the sense that "one no longer can look to a sacred master plot" can be a result rather than a cause of Western narrative production and, more precisely, of the Westernist form of narration embodied in Karmazinov. In fact, Karmazinov and the narrator's inconsistencies could point to a capitalist theory of narration, or a narratological reading of capitalism, though to take this argument to its fullest conclusions is outside the scope of the present chapter.

Turgenev and Dostoevsky: The Perils of Nuance

Self-absorption in the artistic domain has problematic ethical and political as well as aesthetic consequences. The ramifications of such absorption find expression in an important intertext between *Demons* and Dostoevsky's favorite Turgenev novel, *A Nest of Gentry*. Karmazinov's character comes in a structural sense from Turgenev, his shipwreck at least in part from the "Execution of Tropmann," his physical appearance and comportment, his tone of voice, from those of Turgenev. Dostoevsky had much criticism for this writer. But without extending to Turgenev the comments and criticisms that the narrator levels against Karmazinov, and without assuming that Dostoevsky intends such an extension, we can nonetheless point to this intertext, to Dostoevsky's engagement with a Turgenev critique of Westernism—a dramatic elaboration that connects artistic to political egoism and at the same time connects narrative reticence to political and philosophical carelessness.

A Nest of Gentry contains a subtle condemnation of Westernism, a preference for the fathers over the sons, the hesitant over the precipitous. Vladimir Panshin, a young man who has come to town on government assignment, represents the young and hasty generation. In the political arena, Panshin declares that "clever people must reform everything":[33]

> "Russia has lagged behind Europe; she must catch up with it. People assert, that we're young—that is nonsense; and moreover, that we possess no inventive genius: X . . . himself admits that we have not even invented a mouse-trap . . . The best heads among us,"—he went on,— "*les meilleurs têtes*—have long since become convinced of this; all nations are, essentially, alike; only introduce good institutions, and there's an end of the matter. One may even conform to the existing national life [*narodnomu bytu*]; that is our business, the business of men . . ." (he came near saying: "of statesmen"). (197–98; 243–44)

Westernism in this novel signifies not just an unadmirable political stance but also an unadmirable character. The narrator evaluates Panshin: "In soul he was cold and cunning, and in the midst of the wildest carouse his clever little brown eye was guarding and watching; this bold, this free young man could never forget himself and get completely carried away" (19; 149–50). Panshin is rather shallow and self-conscious, not just in his political ideas, but in his responses to art, music, ideas, people, and the entire world outside him. The moment of interest for the present comparison is Panshin's encounter with Liza's piano teacher, Lemm. Of this poor German immigrant, the narrator writes, "Confirmed, inexorable grief had laid upon the poor musician its ineffaceable seal, had distorted and disfigured his already ill-favored figure; but for any one who knew enough not to stop at first impressions, something unusual was visible in this half-wrecked being" (28; 154). Liza has shown Panshin a cantata composed by Lemm on the condition that Panshin not speak to Lemm about it. Panshin breaks this promise, announcing to Lemm: "It's a very fine thing! Please do not think that I am incapable of appreciating serious music,—quite the contrary: it is sometimes tiresome, but on the other hand, it is very beneficial" (24; 152), and then declares to Liza by way of justification, "What would you have me do, Lizaveta Mikhailovna? From my earliest childhood, I have never been able to endure the sight of a German: something simply impels me to stir him up" (31; 156). When Liza reprimands him for his coldness, Panshin announces, " 'You are right, Lizaveta Mikhailovna. My eternal thoughtlessness is responsible for the whole thing. No, do not say a word; I know myself well. My thoughtlessness has done me many an ill turn. Thanks to it, I have won the reputation of an egoist.' Panshin paused for a moment. No matter how he began a conversation, he habitually wound up by speaking of himself, and he did it in a charming, soft, confidential, almost involuntary way" (32; 156).

When Panshin announces to Lemm that he has seen the cantata, Lemm is embarrassed and disappointed in Liza, but he understands that Panshin does not appreciate music ("He cannot understand anything . . . He is a dilettante" [36; 159]). Indeed, most everyone understands Panshin's carelessness, which, in the end, renders him pathetic rather than dangerous. He is a sort of Karmazinov, interested more in his own reactions and recollections than in the world around him, egocentric but comparatively harmless. As for the quiet Lemm, he dies, with the sympathies of the narrator, the reader, and the more admirable characters.

Both characters, Lemm and Panshin, operate on an understated scale, the encounter between them a subtle brush between vacuousness and substance. But a version of Panshin and Lemm, and of the moment between them, reemerges in *Demons*, in a more sensational form and with more dramatic consequences. In *Demons*, the indelicate Westernist is Peter Verkhovensky, and the German with artistic ambitions but with little success is Lembke. Lembke has tried writing: "In secret from the authorities, he sent a novella to a magazine, but it was not published" (310; 243). In this disappointment he recalls Lemm, whose musical compositions, published by a friend, vanish from stores "as though someone had flung them into the river by night" (29; 154). Lembke then ventures a novel, which he decides to show to Peter. Here, though, *Demons* departs from *A Nest of Gentry* as Lembke, entertaining delusions that Lemm resisted, embraces Peter: "Fancying him to be a fervent young man of poetry, and having long dreamed of a listener, one evening, still in the first days of their acquaintance, he read two chapters to him. He listened with unconcealed boredom, yawned impolitely, uttered not a word of praise, but on leaving asked Andrei Antonovich for the manuscript so as to form an opinion at home at his leisure, and Andrei Antonovich gave it to him" (312; 245).

The contact between Peter and Lembke, particularly in contrast with the comparatively harmless encounter between Panshin and Lemm, functions as a sinister warning about the tendencies sketched in Turgenev's novel. The younger generation has become more dangerous: Peter, in contrast with the passive Panshin, shows a demonic energy, a more acute intellect, and tendency toward violence. The older generation, in turn, has become less discriminating. The transformation of the humble and sentimental Lemm into the insecure Lembke demonstrates a weakening of the older generation, an opening to Westernist caprice. Furthermore, the fact that Lembke is both a writer and governor of his province (Turgenev's Panshin was himself "at the disposal of the regional governor, General Zonnenberg") connects moral contamination in art and in politics. Lemm is uninterested in praise from the dilettante Panshin, but Lembke has no such discernment. His own artistic conceit, reminiscent of Karmazinov's, leads in turn to political corruption, as Peter exploits it to gain an audience.

The rendition of Panshin and Lemm as Peter and Lembke, outsized and dangerous versions of their more pastoral counterparts, comes from an abandonment of narrative reticence in form and scale. Henry James wrote that Turgenev "pricked in his outlines," and in *A Nest of Gentry*, as in *Fathers and Sons*, as in the entire Turgenev corpus, the characters' pride is problematic in an indirect sense, in a sentimental sense, not as a source of pernicious or murderous action. And this restraint, this pastoral nature, comes precisely from a reticence in both form and content. In the description

of Panshin, for instance, the narrator of *Nest* demonstrates a reluctance to condemn: "To his honour it must be said, that he never
bragged of his conquests" (19; 150). There is no reason that this last
sentence "must be said" other than the narrator's desire to mediate
his criticism. *Demons* has no such particular interest in mediation;
indeed, when Anton Lavrentevich declares that something "must be
said," that "something" tends to be more rather than less radical
than what preceded. The dramatic consequences of political pride
are accentuated in *Demons* and the Westernist's "cold cunning," un-
fettered by *Nest*'s gentle attenuation, reaches sociopathic proportions.

Dostoevsky, critical as he was of Turgenev, had recorded this
praise for *A Nest of Gentry*: "I consider this poem as the highest justification of truth and beauty in all Russian literature."[34] In *Demons*,
Dostoevsky goes where the delicate narrator of *Nest* did not. The diabolical force of Peter Verkhovensky, the silliness of Lembke, combined with the narrator's implication that concentration on delicate
sensibilities is a misuse of space, all insinuate that restraint has political as well as artistic resonance and can be evaluated on ethical
grounds.

The connection of artistic egoism to political recklessness, implied through this comparison, is articulated throughout *Demons*.
Ambitious Lembke, inward-looking Karmazinov, and calculating
Peter present a political and social menace founded on artistic
pride. In the case of Lembke, for instance, a desire to disclose his
artistic talents leaves him paradoxically unable to evaluate: he sees
Peter as a "fervent young man of poetry" (Lemm would not have
been so fooled). This tendency to see what he wants to see (which
recalls Holquist's and Anderson's comments about invention) in
turn opens him to political manipulation. As for Karmazinov, friend
to Peter and relative of Lembke, his artistic contemplation translates
into a precipitous dismissal of the entire nation: "Russia is preeminently the place in the whole world where anything you like can happen without the least resistance . . . Russia as she is has no future.
I've become a German and count it as an honor" (370; 287). In this
place where anything is possible, Karmazinov chooses to write about
his own reluctance to describe. In this place where anything can
happen, Karmazinov, like the contemptuous Panshin, sees no future. Not surprisingly, Karmazinov's dismissal of Russia functions as
encouragement for Peter: "Karmazinov is right that there's nothing

to cling to. Karmazinov is very intelligent. Just another ten crews like that all over Russia, and I'm uncatchable" (416; 322).

THE NARRATOR AS STAVROGIN

The Westernist political revolutionaries complement the Westernist artists, just as the first vision of the narrator complements the second. In this sense, the narrator represents the two principal spiritual scandals that permeate *Demons* and also articulates their connection. These scandals, the political manipulativeness of precipitous reformers and the gratuitous humility of Western narrators, compose a moral and ethical Mobius strip of problematic Westernist visions. Here, we can turn to the end of the novel, where the sides of this strip join. The Tikhon episode combines the ethical problems discussed in this chapter as Stavrogin, man of action, manipulation, and diabolical inspiration becomes, or tries to become, a ruminating, introspecting narrator. This episode describes both action and narration as born of a spiritual emptiness—as responses to and, ironically, as perpetuations of that emptiness.

The Tikhon chapter was originally the ninth chapter of part 2, but in most editions it is now placed at the end, as an appendix. This chapter recounts Stavrogin's meeting with Bishop Tikhon. He has gone to the monastery where the bishop has retired and gives him to read, in his presence, an account wherein he describes his seduction (or rape, it is never entirely clear which) of fourteen-year old Matryosha and Matryosha's suicide. The chapter "At Tikhon" opens with a number of narrative inconsistencies to remind the reader of the problematic nature of what Matlaw names the "verbal surface." For instance: "I will add, running ahead of myself, that this last is decidedly nonsense."[35] "Alongside clumpish old furniture stood three or four elegant pieces—all given to him" (683; 11:6). "The library, they say, had also been assembled in a much too varied and contrasting way . . . Nikolai Vsevolodovich was still greatly distracted by some inner anxiety that was oppressing him. It looked as if [*poxhozhe bylo na to, shto*] he had resolved upon something extraordinary and unquestionable but at the same time almost impossible for him. For a minute or so he looked around the study, apparently [*vidimo*] not noticing what he was looking at; he was thinking and, of course, did not know what about" (683; 11:7). Within this one page, the narrator writes as chronicler, documenter of public opinion, province resident, and reader of souls. Within the last sentence alone, "apparently," "it looked as if" and "of course" indicate incompatible and unstable distances from the scene. Before Stavrogin even begins, then, the novel predicates narration as a spectacle in and of itself, a problematic kaleidoscope rather than a transparent screen.

Some further clues in this chapter's introduction to the problematic nature of Stavrogin's narration arise when Tikhon responds to Stavrogin's "Do you know me?" by saying that he had seen Stavrogin four years earlier. Stavrogin denies this and suggests: "Perhaps you simply heard about me and formed some idea, and so you confused that with seeing me" (684; 11:7). If Stavrogin is reliable (and I believe we are invited to think he is), and if he was not there four years ago, then we can conclude that, for Tikhon, hearing about someone is in some sense tantamount to seeing and knowing that someone. This supreme value placed on words and rumor is precisely what Stavrogin wants in an interlocutor and a reader. At the same time, the confounding of words with substance, rumors with direct vision, reproduces a foundational element of the narrator's inconsistencies. Tikhon's vision is as complicated as the "verbal surface" of *Demons*, which combines observation, fabrication, and rumor. On the other hand, it is through the confounding of words with substance that we can read character in "verbal surface" and see the connection of problematic narration to problematic action.[36]

In the episode of the shipwreck, Karmazinov turns from the catastrophe and narrates the difficulty of narration. But because of this restraint, paradoxically, he retains an even greater narrative and moral authority. So meticulous a regard for one's own perceptions and sentiments must, Karmazinov seems to insinuate, indicate rare sensibilities, rare nuances of consciousness. So it is with Stavrogin, a man without ethics or empathic sensibilities who narrates the sensation of that lack. He is also a man without an idea, or rather, a man who does not yet have an idea, or has abandoned his ideas, but who nonetheless narrates the "idea" of that emptiness.

In Stavrogin's narration, we can discern what would happen were Peter to produce a chronicle of his actions, or were Karmazinov to become a sociopath. In a more visible manner than Karmazinov, Stavrogin is narrating a vacuum. But more, he narrates—chronicles— the turning of that vacuum into an action, or a series of actions. His document, like the "abominations" described, like Peter's manipulations, like Karmazinov's narration, indicates and perpetuates the spiritual vacuum that it wants to eliminate: "I intend to tell everything in the firmest words, so that nothing remains hidden any longer. Every extremely shameful, immeasurably humiliating, mean, and, above all, ridiculous position I have happened to get into in my life has always aroused in me, along with boundless wrath, an unbelievable pleasure" (692; 11:14). "If I was stealing something I would feel, while committing the theft, intoxication from the awareness of the depth of my meanness. It was not meanness that I loved (here my reason was completely sound) but I liked the intoxication from the tormenting awareness of my baseness" (693; 11:14). And: "I am setting this down precisely in order to prove the extent of my power over my memories, and how unfeeling for them I had become. I would reject them all in a mass, and the whole mass would obediently disappear each time the moment I wanted it to" (702; 11:21). These comments are reminiscent of the narrator's comment about Karmazinov: "Better look at me . . . Here I am turning my back; here I am horrified and unable to look again; I've shut my eyes—interesting, is it not?"

Stavrogin's narration, intending to disclose seduction, murder, theft, violence, and so on, simultaneously discloses the emptiness that subtended those actions and produced this narration. As Tikhon notices, and to Stavrogin's displeasure, failure to abandon oneself and "live an idea" can only be compounded through narration. The priest comments, "I was horrified at this great idle force being spent deliberately on abomination" (707; 11:25) but his more serious criticism is that "Certain places in your account are stylistically accentuated; as if you admire your own psychology and seize upon every little detail just to astonish the reader with an unfeelingness that is not in you. What is that if not the proud challenge of a guilty man to his judge?" (706; 11:24). John Jones points out that the word "confession" is nowhere in the chapter, and indeed, this document does not so much confess a sin as insist that something has occurred and that the narrator has acted.[37] The penance, then, and indeed the punishment, is not to narrate but to abstain from narration, to stop the pretense of action: "You are in the grip of a desire for martyrdom and self-sacrifice; conquer this desire as well, set aside your pages and your intention—and then you will overcome everything. You will put to shame all your pride and your demon! You will win, you will attain freedom . . ." (712; 11:29).

At the close of the novel, the narrator declares, "Our medical men, after the autopsy, completely and emphatically ruled out insanity."[38] Holquist comments: "The act could be understood by others. The system of medicine can explain even Stavrogin's ultimate gesture of idiosyncrasy. He did not do it alone."[39] The mention of medical men reduces Stavrogin to his embodied presence and to a sane course of action. But the denial of insanity is also in a sense the denial of a force outside one; of a demon, but also of a God. "Cursed psychologist!" accuses Stavrogin, for reduction to the human domain means that even in suicide, Stavrogin cannot transcend, and cannot be open to the intrusion of a force outside him, cannot be more than what he is. Denied expression, he is equally denied the drama of possession and madness.

THE SCANDAL OF THE UNCERTAIN ARCHITECT, OR THE NARRATOR AS A HESITANT GOD

Both narrative scenarios discussed in this chapter are in essence forms of role-playing: the first describes a human author who writes as a man pretending to be God, and the second describes an author who writes as God pretending to be a man. These scenarios, I have argued, raise fundamental questions about human pretension to incarnate or represent God. Still another understanding of these narrative scenarios becomes possible when we read the narrator as commenting on the nature of divinity. Matlaw writes of Anton Lavrentevich: "The clumsy prose resulting from his eagerness to justify and qualify is aggravated by his attempt to convey his urbanity and conviviality through a bantering tone and irony that quickly proclaim him a far less genial person than he would like to appear."[40] If we consider this same narrator as the God of this particular narration—and he does encourage this consideration—then his eccentricities and disclaimers become near-blasphemous satires of divine force. Numerous moments resonate as parodic comments on the relationship of a master author to the course of the world and of individual lives, especially since the plot of this novel is drawn from actual historical incidents. For instance: "I was sure as two times two that he would not get out of there without a catastrophe"[41]; "Somehow almost without intending to (what on earth possessed me?) I went up to him as well"; "To this day I do not understand and marvel myself at how I could have shouted that to him then. But I had guessed perfectly: it had all happened almost exactly the way I said, as turned out afterwards"; "But strangely, I did run by to see Darya Pavlovna, where, however, I was not received . . . what I could have said to her, and why I ran by, I do not know." These instances raise doubts about God's sense of direction. "Why did I do that?" is perhaps a strange question for a God figure to ask, but it is one by which Dostoevsky, whose own narrative almost came to a precipitous and rather arbitrary end in Siberia, might not be surprised. Dostoevsky, as has been amply demonstrated, is much more interested in protecting God from the hand of humans than he is in protecting humans from the hand of God, even a demonic God. Nonetheless, some questioning about the nature of divinity can be discerned in this novel. Perhaps that questioning is not so sinister, for the same narrator who is so filled with self-doubt confronts Peter: "Here I suddenly got beside all patience and shouted furiously at Pyotr Stepanovich: 'You set it up, you scoundrel!'" (500; 384).

GOD-MAN AND MAN-GOD: THE NARRATOR AS PALE IMITATION OF CHRIST

Each reading of the narrator represents a particular narrative ethos that corresponds to real-world inconsistencies and transgressions. In other words, this narrative construction contains a narratological social criticism—a rich and elsewhere unarticulated series of responses to Westernist political and narrative strategies. But to go one step further, I would venture that intended here, aside from a criticism of human transgressions, is a celebration of one being who can cross, or transcend, the human-God line: Christ. When we read the narrator not as an incarnation of inconsistencies but as a compendium of multiple natures, we can discern in him a composite of God and human, Father and Son, creator and consoler. Indeed Dostoevsky's Christianity was founded in a love of Christ, represented as the only being who can both know God and incarnate God, as the only being whose crossing of the human-God line is no scandalous. As Jesus says to Thomas in John 14:6–15:

> Jesus said to Thomas, "I am the way, and the truth, and the life. No one comes to the Father except through me. If you know me, you will know my Father also. From now on you do know him and have seen him." Philip said to him, "Lord, show us the Father, and we will be satisfied." Jesus said to him, "Have I been with you all this time, Philip, and you still do not know me? Whoever has seen me has seen the Father. How can you say, 'Show us the Father'? Do you not believe that I am in the

Father and the Father is in me? The words that I say to you I do not speak on my own; but the Father who dwells in me does his works."[42]

These words articulate separation and incarnation simultaneously. On the one hand, Christ points to a God and a truth that are separate from him. But Christ also incarnates that same God and truth, and bears them within him into the world. To put this multiple nature in narrative terms, he is a narrator who bears the author within him as he points outside himself to that author: who bears the truth within him as he points outside himself to that truth. This double spiritual role, this combination of the human and the infinite, the incarnation and the creation, was enormously appealing to Dostoevsky. As the author famously said, "To believe that there is nothing more beautiful, more profound, more sympathetic, more reasonable, more manly and more perfect than Christ. And not only is there nothing but I tell myself with jealous love that there can be nothing. Besides, if anyone proved to me that Christ was outside the truth and it really was so that the truth was outside Christ, then I would prefer to remain with Christ, than with the truth."[43] And as Shatov said to Stavrogin: "But wasn't it you who told me that if someone proved to you mathematically that the truth is outside Christ, you would better agree to stay with Christ than with the truth? Did you say that? Did you?" (249; 198).

Christ in this formulation means both adoration of God and embodiment of God: adoration of truth and embodiment of truth, incarnation of humankind and understanding of humankind. Only Christ, according to this representation, can know truth and incarnate truth at the same time. No person can do it; the narrator, as demonstrated by his numerous inconsistencies and blunders, cannot do it. The flounderings that arise in his narration underscore those human incapacities and, by extension, or by contrast, vaunt the inimitable spiritual force and wisdom of the Christ figure.

Conclusion

SECULARISM AS LIVED IN THESE NOVELS IS NEITHER A HISTORICAL EVENT nor even particularly a historical process. Rather, it stands as an idea and an impression: as a way of looking at the world and of asking questions about the forces that act upon us. J. Hillis Miller described the secular world as "broken" while Lukács, connecting the novel to the "beginning of the time when the Christian God began to forsake the world," called the problems of the novel form "the mirror-image of a world gone out of joint."[1] These images of fragmentation call up a sense of mourning or despair, or at least of some sort of negative. But in fact, worlds go out of joint in radically different ways for different people and cultures at different times, to different effects. The idea of the "broken world" inspires a vast range of reactions, from enthusiasm (Julien Sorel) to depression (Emma), indifference (Rodolphe), denial (Liza and Lavretsky), righteous outrage (the aristocrats of L'Ensorcelée), or megalomania (Peter Verkhovensky). One person's world out of joint is another's playground; one person's desolate landscape is another's open door to self-determination. In *Le rouge et le noir*, Julien Sorel is prepared to frolic in the open space that God has abandoned (for him, secularism means open season for the autonomous individual), while the narrator inscribes him in a vaster order, or series of orders. And yet, that narrator is in turn inscribed, denied omniscience, because the elimination of God does not mean the elimination of outside forces, nor a wholesale turning over of power to the individual; it simply means an elimination of universal consensus about what that order might be. In *Madame Bovary*, the absence of God from Emma's life means the absence not of order or comprehension, but of hope: of all the emotional and sentimental benevolence associated with spiritual connection. For the narrator, on the other hand, that absence is both the punch line and the foundational circumstance for the enormous joke he is perpetrating. In *L'Ensorcelée*, secularism is represented as grim for everyone: it means a dismantling of world order and a decline into darkness and depression for individuals and for

170

society. But while the characters mourn the fact that the secular world does not revere God, what they seem really to mind is that the secular world does not revere the individual who represents God—does not revere the aristocrat. The fantasy of a return to religious order means a reinstatement not just of order or meaning or spiritual connection, but also of the grandeur that accompanies religious association. The Russian authors, in contrast, see secularism in a different light. In *A Nest of Gentry,* as in *Madame Bovary,* secularism is a cruel joke that is just beginning to dawn on the Russian population. But whereas Flaubert's narrator sat happily in God's vacant chair, Turgenev's narrator ultimately refused, as his better characters refused, to wield the hand of God. The very idea of God's absence is a specter raised and then denied, suppressed with an almost superstitious insistence. *Demons'* narrator, like Barbey's narrator, has a dim view of secularism. Or rather, he has a dim view of those characters that embrace the idea of secularism either implicitly or explicitly—those characters, in other words, that act as if there were no God, no system of reward and punishment, and no system of ideals. But whereas Barbey's narrator ultimately took up and ran with the abandoned scepter of God, the abandoned grandness of God, Dostoevsky's narrator condemned that sort of appropriation.

In each of these five novels, the idea of secularism functions as a litmus test for the narrator's and the characters' understanding of the outside world. I have argued that the narrators' action upon the characters, combined with the characters' responses to that action, represents a series of ideas or fantasies about what it means to live with and without the intrusion (or comfort) of a supreme power. As we see, those ideas—and the narrator-character relationship that embodies them—vary with cultural and individual circumstances. The dissolution of master narratives enables the French narrator to generate an order to which the characters have no access. The transition to a secular culture becomes an occasion for narrative play—for the intrusion of chance, simultaneous narrative strands, and for the ironic use of the discourse of sacred order. The Russian narrator, on the other hand, resists this transition—true whether or not he is a believer—utilizing hesitation, disclaimer, and inconsistency to both embrace and lament his freedom. In the French novels, what is perilous about the move to secularism is first and foremost the possibility that some residue of supernatural outside order might curb individual freedom. In the Russian novels, though, the primacy of the individual—the movement of the individual into the place of God—is in itself the perilous scenario.

In this study, perceptions of secularism have generally divided down national lines. But it cannot be said simply that French narrators are "for" secularism while the Russians are not. On the one hand, what is problematic about secularism in the French novels is its incompleteness, but just as troublesome is the possibility that the power relations from cultural-political models based on divine authority might not transfer adequately. God must recede enough to leave space to the individual, but not so definitively that the God function becomes meaningless. In the Russian novels, the decision to see the world with faith instead of cynicism testifies to a resistance to secular consciousness. And yet, even the devout are aware that the embracing of faith *is* a decision: a narrative act, as it were, in and of itself.

J. Hillis Miller described secularism as a blankness to be mourned, but the novels examined here testify to the wide range of emotion and conduct that emerges in the imagined absence of God. When determinism is dismantled and the promises of redemption and retribution eliminated, the result is a series of extremes of boldness, fantasy, fear, political machinations, or narrative production—a reenvisioning or reconstruction or renegotiation of world order. But what is striking in these novels is that the reenvisioned secular order is in essence a reassembled religious order. The same questions are posed, and the same answers given—simply with different names inserted. In each of these novels, the qualities and powers associated with the departed God (or departed idea of God, or idea of a departed God) are not dissolved, but are rather transposed onto the outside world, onto individuals, onto whatever forces the characters see as dominant. Julien Sorel, who views God (and fate and chance) as an impediment to his plans and desires, comes at the rest of the world (institutions, friends, lovers, employers, garden furniture) with the same preemptive paranoia. Emma Bovary, who imagines God as a combination Santa Claus and dramatic screenwriter, accords these same characteristics to the men she meets. Liza and Lavretsky are no more willing to rail against Panshin and Varvara and the forces of chance than they are to rail against the injustice of God. Croix-Jugan, who senses God not so much outside in the world as within his own mind and memories, ends up venerating himself and the Chouans. The fivesome participants in *Demons* who both believe in God and long for individual power end up revering the man–God Peter Verkhovensky. The view that was held of God becomes the view of the outside world; the fantasy of God becomes transposed onto whatever force one perceives as prevailing. A world without God, in these cases, does not mean a world without inscrutable forces. Or, put another way, a world without God is not really a world without God—it is simply a world with God transposed into other places and given other names.

I have argued in this study that the idea of secularism informs our understandings of narrative construction. I have also argued that narrative construction, thus informed, constitutes a particularly productive avenue for exploring questions of individual power and voice. Spiritual authority has always been both a metaphor for and an important practical component of sociopolitical dominance both direct and indirect. And spiritual authority is inextricably connected to narrative, the medium through which that authority is recounted and its justifications maintained. For much of the twentieth century, spiritual authority has been more metaphor for, than practical component of, political power, but political discord in the twenty-first century is becoming increasingly connected with conflict over spiritual clout. The answers to the question of what constitutes a viable relationship to the idea of God bear importantly upon modern political and social realities, as much, arguably, in a world become secular as in a world that has maintained a religious consciousness. In this study, I have tried to examine these questions (and answers) in their relation to such a world, and to find in the novel form a model for the idea and the experience of a world without God.

Notes

INTRODUCTION

The epigraphs at the beginning of the introduction are from George Lukács, *The Theory of the Novel*, 88, and James Wood, *The Broken Estate*, xvi.

1. J. Hillis Miller, *The Disappearance of God*, 2.

2. As Peter Brooks has written: "The enormous narrative production of the nineteenth century may suggest an anxiety at the loss of providential plots: the plotting of the individual or social or institutional life story takes on new urgency when one no longer can look to a sacred masterplot that organizes and explains the world" (Brooks, *Reading for the Plot*, 6). Carol Mossman goes further than this and proposes that the masterplot is itself (and always has been) such a production: "Confronted with the expanses of time undifferentiated, the human mind has, through religion and myth, reached out towards time's end, that is, toward an Apocalypse. And, in so doing, man has wrought himself a cosmic plot" (Mossman, *The Narrative Matrix*, 23).

3. Jameson, *A Singular Modernity*, 40.

4. Lyotard, *The Postmodern Condition*, 22.

5. Ibid., xxiv.

6. While there are numerous points of overlap between the idea of secularism and historico-philosophical visions of modernity, they are not identical. Social and political systems ascribed to modernity (the rise of the bourgeoisie or the coming of the industrial age, for instance) and philosophical theories associated with modernity (Hegel's theories of knowledge) are not reducible to secularism, but neither is the idea of secularism reducible to them. A full discussion of the connections between secularism and modernity is outside the scope of this study. Literary studies linking the novel form to secular culture and modernity include Ricoeur (*Time and Narrative*), Moretti (*The Modern Epic* and *Atlas of the European Novel*), Auerbach (*Mimesis*), James Wood (*The Broken Estate* and *Book Against God*), Virginia Woolf, René Girard, Alice Jardine, and Rey Chow, among many others. Tom Rockmore's *On Hegel's Epistemology and Contemporary Philosophy* provides a good discussion of, and a diverse bibliography on, philosophical theories of modernity and the (nineteenth-century) epistemological modes associated with modernity.

7. Bakhtin, *The Dialogic Imagination*.

8. "The art of storytelling is reaching its end because the epic side of truth, wisdom, is dying out. This, however, is a process that has been going on for a long time. . . . It is, rather, only a concomitant symptom of the secular productive forces of history, a concomitant that has quite gradually removed narrative from the realm of living speech and at the same time is making it possible to see a new beauty in what is vanishing. The earliest symptom of a process whose end is the decline of

storytelling is the rise of the novel at the beginning of modern times" (Benjamin, "The Storyteller," in *Illuminations*, 87).

9. Ricoeur, *Time and Narrative*, vol. 1:3. Further on: "The Augustinian analysis gives a representation of time in which discordance never ceases to belie the desire for that concordance that forms the very essence of the *animus*" (4).

10. The history of modern Western (Christian) thought is in some sense the history of ambivalence between the desire to be cared for by a supreme power and the desire to stand in the place of that supreme power. This ambivalence is particularly dominant in contemporary American thought. Whether or not we believe in God, we are sometimes willing to credit the "parking gods" with the space we find (right in front!) on a busy street. This sort of mundane credence permeates human existence. And this credence, I would further argue, is not just about arbitrariness versus order, but about the absence or presence of an active force that sees us and actually *wants* (the element of desire is crucial) to inscribe us in a coherent narrative. It is not enough to be an electron in an ordered universe: there seems to be an element of human nature that desires interaction with an animated force that is greater than the individual. And yet, another impulse is equally potent: the desire to dominate, to master the world without recourse to the idea or to the hand of God. If we cast this ambivalence about secularism in narrative terms, we immediately perceive both the desire to be an author, and the desire to be authored by a loving hand.

11. Wood, *The Broken Estate*, xv.

12. "If, in the course of narrating his story, the historian provides it with the plot structure of a Tragedy, he has 'explained' it one way; if he has structured it as a Comedy, he has 'explained' it in another way. Emplotment is the way by which a sequence of events fashioned into a story is gradually revealed to be a story of a particular kind" (White, *Metahistory: The Historical Imagination in Nineteenth-Century Europe*, 7). See also Ricoeur's discussion of emplotment in *Time and Narrative*.

13. Richard Wortman's 1995 two-volume study, *Scenarios of Power: Myth and Ceremony in Russian Monarchy*, examines the "supernatural character" of power in tsarist Russia.

14. "Whether or not one accepts God, theology, in some loose sense, provides a language and a framework for such issues (of narrative and temporal coherence). It is in this sense, at least, that Bakhtin's works on time and freedom are also theological" (Morson, *Narrative and Freedom*, 86).

15. The vocabulary of modernism did not, of course, burst fully formed from the French revolution, but has antecedents as early as the seventeenth century—and earlier: it has been said that the tragic hero began to die with Euripides.

16. Another distinction between secularism and modernity is that the latter is a much more particularly Western (as well as particularly theoretical and aesthetic) notion.

17. Cf. Watt, *The Rise of the Novel*, and Lukács, *The Theory of the Novel*.

18. "After Buddha was dead, his shadow was still shown for centuries in a cave—a tremendous, gruesome shadow. God is dead; but given the way of men, there may still be caves for thousands of years in which his shadow will be shown. —And we—we still have to vanquish his shadow, too" (Nietzsche, *The Gay Science*, 167).

19. Eighteenth-century Enlightenment philosophies, by contrast, neither repu-

diate God nor bring an active assault on transcendence as an idea. Instead, they subtly work around that idea, constructing a mode of reasoning that presents God as an explanatory principle whose utility is on the wane. These philosophies, in other words, did not arise in response to a perceived spiritual or philosophical vacuum. That vacuum—or, more precisely, that idea of a vacuum—arose only in the nineteenth century, when the idea of secularism metamorphosed. It was here that the idea of secularism took another turn. The removal of God from explanatory narratives was no longer essentially an economic decision or a theoretical side effect of enlightenment but a philosophical and spiritual *event*, a displacement in the human condition. Secularism, in other words, was transposed into the domain of content: more than simply a surface characteristic of the *discours*, it became the substance, the nucleus of the *histoire* (Genette, *Narrative Discourse*). By the twentieth century, the idea that there is no God had become largely absorbed into European literature; there was much less need to flaunt it or wrestle with it as such. While Camus' absurd, Sartre's existentialism, and Kharms's negation are concerned with meaning in a world without God, "without God" in the twentieth century is less an emerging problem than a given circumstance.

CHAPTER 1. NAVIGATING THE SECULAR WORLD

1. In 1814 came an order to close restaurants and stores during services, and another dictating that those living on church parade routes must raise certain banners when the procession passed. In 1825, Charles X insisted on a *cérémonie du sacre*, but as René Rémond writes, this ceremony "inspires more derision than fervor, and its failure underlines the irremediably archaic character of Restoration pretenses" (Rémond, *Religion et société en Europe: Essai sur la secularisation aux XIXe et XXe siècles*, 13). Translations mine, when not otherwise attributed.

2. Taylor, *Hegel*, 9.

3. D. A. Miller points out: "The world of *Le Rouge et le Noir* is defined by little else than an incessant play of conspiratorial forces. Yet Julien's adaptation is strikingly dysfunctional. The paranoia is nearly always misplaced, and the progress from Verrières to Besançon to Paris depends less on Julien's actual schemes of advancement than on lateral, unforeseen developments" (Miller, *Narrative and its Discontents*, 196).

4. Stendhal, *Red and Black*, 81; in the French edition, *Le rouge et le noir*, 102. Further references to both editions will be cited in the text by page number with the English listed first, followed by the French.

5. Bell, *Circumstance: Chance in the Literary Text*, 59.

6. Ibid., 79.

7. Lukács, *The Theory of the Novel*, 98.

8. Ibid., 103.

9. Ibid., 117.

10. Ibid, 17.

11. Holzman, *Lukács's Road to God: The Early Criticism against its Pre-Marxist Background*, 126–27. Holzman also explicates the opening lines of Lukács's book ("Blessed are those Ages when the starry sky is the map of all possible paths . . .") (29), describing them as "something of an incantation" (119). And then: "We

should not find it unusual that the genesis of *The Theory of the Novel* was an ethical situation, not a literary question. The beginning of *The Theory of the Novel* shows that the book's proper end is not the understanding of a few novels, or even of the nature of literary creation as such, but rather how one might best approach the ethical problems of living in an 'age of absolute sinfulness'" (130).

12. Ibid., 129.

13. Bourgeois, *L'ironie romantique: Spectacle et jeu de Mme de Staël à Gérard de Nerval*, 107. For Lukács, "Irony gives form to the malicious satisfaction of God the creator at the failure of man's weak rebellions against his mighty, yet worthless creation and, at the same time, to the inexpressible suffering of God the redeemer at his inability to re-enter that world. Irony, the self-surmounting of a subjectivity that has gone as far as it was possible to go, is the highest freedom that can be achieved in a world without God" (93).

14. Cf. Sandy Petrey, *Realism and Revolution*.

15. Kierkegaard, *Either/Or*, 121.

16. Here and elsewhere, the abbreviation "tm"—translation modified—indicates my alterations of the English version.

17. Joseph de Maistre, *Soirées de Saint Petersbourg, Considérations sur la France*, and so on.

18. Taylor, *Hegel*, 79.

19. Thielicke, *Nihilism*, 58.

20. Petrey, *Realism and Revolution*, 135.

21. One example of this performative weaving can be found in Charles X's aforementioned insistence on a *cérémonie du sacre* in 1825, to ennoble both himself and the Church. This gesture, essentially a ceremonial replacement of *hasard* with *Providence*, did not so much resuscitate as devalue the sacred. Another such ceremonial conversion was found in the 1814 ordinances cited earlier. These ordinances seemed not to be an expression of divine order, but rather a clumsy and random fabrication of it—a misguided desire to turn *hasard* into *Providence*.

22. Brombert, *Stendhal: Fiction and the Themes of Freedom*, 68.

23. Felman, *La "folie" dans l'oeuvre romanesque de Stendhal*, 146.

24. Crouzet, *Le rouge et le noir: Essai sur le romanesque Stendhalien*, 63.

25. Brombert, *Stendhal: Fiction and the Themes of Freedom*, 95.

26. Mossman, *The Narrative Matrix*, 25.

27. D. A. Miller, *Narrative and its Discontents*, 219.

28. Cf. Felman, *La "folie" dans l'oeuvre romanesque de Stendhal*, and Crouzet, "Julien Sorel et le Sublime."

29. Ellenberger, *The Discovery of the Unconscious*, 208.

30. Quoted in Ellenberger, 207.

31. Ibid., 210.

32. Ibid., 273.

33. Darwin, *The Expression of the Emotions in Man and Animals*, 66.

34. Ellenberger, *The Discovery of the Unconscious*, 313.

35. Ibid., 354.

36. Freud, *Beyond the Pleasure Principle*, 34–36.

37. Ibid., 44.

38. Groddeck, *The Book of the It*, 16.

39. Felman, *La "folie" dans l'oeuvre romanesque de Stendhal*, 33.

40. Ibid., 88.
41. Crouzet, "Julien Sorel et le Sublime," 91.
42. Ibid., 105.
43. D. A. Miller, *Narrative and its Discontents*, 196
44. Brombert, *Stendhal: Fiction and the Themes of Freedom*, 99.
45. I thank Jared Stark.
46. Ginsburg, "On Not 'Yielding a Return': Plot and the Concept of Freedom in *The Red and the Black*," 99.
47. Talbot, *Stendhal Revisited*, 51.
48. La Fontaine, *The Complete Fables*, trans. Norman Spector, 453–54 (in the French, *Fables contes et nouvelles*, 225–26):

Un bloc de marbre était si beau, / Qu'un Statuaire en fit l'emplette. / "Qu'en fera, dit-il, mon ciseau? / Sera-t-il dieu, table ou cuvette?

Il sera dieu; même je veux / Qu'il ait en sa main un tonnerre. / Tremblez, humains! faites des voeux: / Voilà le maître de la terre!"

L'artisan exprima si bien / Le caractère de l'idole, / Qu'on trouva qu'il ne manquoit rien / A Jupiter que la parole.

Même l'on dit que l'ouvrier / Eut à peine achevé l'image, / Qu'on le vit frémir le premier, / Et redouter son propre ouvrage.

A la foiblesse du sculpteur / Le poète autrefois n'en dut guère, / Des dieux dont il fut l'inventeur / Craignant la haine et la colère.

Il étoit enfant en ceci; / Les enfants n'ont l'âme occupée. / Que du continuel souci / Qu'on ne fâche point leur poupée.

Le coeur suit aisément l'esprit : / De cette source est descendue / L'erreur païenne, qui se vit, / Chez tant de peuples répandue.

Ils embrassoient violemment / Les intérêts de leur chimère: / Pygmalion devint amant / De la Vénus dont il fut père.

Chacun tourne en réalités, / Autant qu'il peut, ses propres songes: / L'homme est de glace aux vérités; / Il est de feu pour les mensonges.

49. Brooks, *Reading for the Plot*, 84.
50. Ibid., 75.
51. Mossman, *The Narrative Matrix*, and Lukacher, "*The Red and the Black*: Transforming the Maternal Myth."
52. When Julien stops in at Verrières in the end of part 1, bound for Paris, his mind on his future at the Hôtel de La Mole, there are once more three children.

Chapter 2. Flaubert's Superior Joke

1. Flaubert, *Correspondance*, vol. 2, 154 (letter of April 1853).
2. Ibid., 37 (letter of October 1852).

3. Ibid., 62 (letter of December 1852).

4. Bourdieu, *The Field of Cultural Production*, 211.

5. Culler, *Flaubert: The Uses of Uncertainty*, 79.

6. Flaubert, *Madame Bovary*, trans. Paul de Man, 28; in the French edition (1971), 41. Further references to both editions will be cited in the text by page number with the English listed first, followed by the French.

7. Poulet, *The Metamorphoses of the Circle*, 264.

8. Richard, *Littérature et sensation*, 158–59.

9. Lukács, *The Theory of the Novel*, 117.

10. Ibid., 117.

11. The temptation is to use the word "author" in lieu of "narrator": indeed, the concealment of the narrator as such is integral to what Culler calls Flaubert's "thoroughly demoralizing effect." And yet, the opening sentence of the novel establishes a narrative persona: a persona whose subsequent erasure leaves a trace, and leads not so much to an unproblematic transfer of attention to the author as to an awareness of an emptiness at the point of narrative creation.

12. Wing, *The Limits of Narrative*, 72. See also Leo Bersani, "The Hazards of Literary Fusion": "Nothing is meant by these words [*félicité, passion ivresse*] in life; they 'mean' only verbally, and especially in books . . . The gap between an excessively signifying imagination and an insignificant world occasionally produces attacks of acute anxiety in Emma" (33).

13. Chambers, *The Writing of Melancholy*, 176.

14. Terdiman, *Discourse/Counter-Discourse*, 210.

15. For a rich discussion of such an interpretation, see Avital Ronell's reading of Emma in *Crack Wars*.

16. Wing, *The Limits of Narrative*, 49.

17. Thibaudet, *Gustave Flaubert*, 110.

18. René Girard includes a discussion of zoology in *Des choses cachées depuis la fondation du monde*. He notes that scientists are content to observe and document behavior without recourse to psychological explanations—that the oedipal complex, for example, is not invoked to explain the behavior of gorillas.

19. Owens, "Address to the British Association," 51 and 90, cited in Darwin, *The Origin of Species*, xvii.

20. Claude Bernard, *Philosophie*, 82.

21. Quoted in the preface to Darwin's *The Origin of Species*, xix–xxi: "Naudin, a distinguished botanist . . . in an admirable paper on the Origin of Species (*Revue Horticole*, p. 102; since partly republished in the *Nouvelles Archives du Muséum*, tom. i. p. 171) . . ."

22. Barnes, *Flaubert's Parrot*, 213.

23. Bakhtin, *Problems of Dostoevsky's Poetics*, 71.

24. Ibid., 79.

25. Thibaudet, *Gustave Flaubert*, 121.

26. Cf. Don Cupitt, *Taking Leave of God*: "[Theological realists] declare their unshakable allegiance to a vanished world in which the prevailing cultural conditions made it possible really to believe in objective theism. We do not have that particular mode of consciousness any longer because we do not live in that world any more. Theological realism can only actually be true for a heteronomous consciousness such as no normal person ought now to have" (12).

27. Schopenhauer, *Religion: A Dialogue*, 16.

28. Fredric Jameson, contrasting nineteenth-century approaches to religious symbolism, writes: "Any doctrine of figurality must necessarily be ambiguous: a symbolic expression of a truth is also, at the same time, a distorted and disguised expression, and a theory of figural expression is also a theory of mystification or false consciousness. Religion is thus here the distorted or symbolic coming to consciousness of itself, of the human community, and the critic's distance from religious figures will vary depending on whether, as is the case with Feuerbach (and with Hegel), stress is laid on its symbolic and alienating function, or whether, as in Durkheim's far more retrospective and anthropological account, its vocation as the locus of group identity is foregrounded" (Jameson, *The Political Unconscious*, 70). In *Madame Bovary*, it is precisely the equivalence of "symbolic" with "alienating" that the narrator moves to establish.

29. Brombert, *The Novels of Flaubert*, 18.

30. Bourdieu, *The Field of Cultural Production*, 157.

CHAPTER 3. FAITH IN REALISM

1. *A Nest of Gentry* is the usual rendition of *Dvoryanskoe Gnezdo*, and it is this translation that I use here. The Hapgood translation, however, uses *A Nobleman's Nest*.

2. Turgenev, *A Nobleman's Nest*, 207–8; in the Russian, *Dvoryanskoe Gnezdo*, 250. Further references to both editions will be cited in the text by page number with the English listed first, followed by the Russian.

3. Flaubert, *Correspondance*, 61.

4. Gerald Prince's *Dictionary of Narratology* defines *discours*, after Benveniste and Genette, as "the EXPRESSION plane of NARRATIVE as opposed to its CONTENT plane or STORY: the 'how' of a narrative as opposed to its 'what'" (21). *Histoire*, on the other hand, is "the CONTENT plane of NARRATIVE as opposed to its EXPRESSION plane or DISCOURSE: the 'what' of a narrative as opposed to its 'how'" (91).

5. Woodward, *Metaphysical Conflict: A Study of the Major Novels of Ivan Turgenev*, 66–67.

6. Elena is the heroine of Turgenev's novel *On the Eve*.

7. Woolf, "The Novels of Turgenev," 143.

8. Freeborn, *Turgenev: The Novelist's Novelist*, 62.

9. Gregg, "The Wimp, the Maiden and the Mensch: Turgenev's Bermuda Triangle," 60.

10. Tolstoy, *War and Peace*, trans. Louise and Aylmer Maude, 603; in the Russian, *Voina I Mir*, 8:3.

11. Allen, *Beyond Realism: Turgenev's Poetics of Secular Salvation*, 19.

12. Ibid., 43.

13. Vogüé, *Le roman russe*, 45.

14. Woodward, "Determinism in the Novels of Turgenev," 20.

15. Ibid., 27.

16. Nietzsche, *The Will to Power*, 451–52.

17. Vine, *The Chimney Sweeper's Boy*, 15.

18. Dostoevsky, *Demons*, 476; in the Russian, *Besy*, 365.

19. James, *The Future of the Novel*, 228.

20. Dostoevsky, *Demons*, 370; in the Russian, *Besy*, 287.

CHAPTER 4. THE JOY OF MYSTIFICATION

1. Barbey d'Aurevilly, *Bewitched*, trans. Louise Collier Willcox, 2; in the French, *L'Ensorcelée*, 556. Further references to both editions will be cited in the text by page number with the English listed first, followed by the French. While Stendhal used the *lande* as a metaphor for monotony ("No doubt the reader shares all Julien's boredom at this life without interest that he was forced to lead. These are the flat-lands of our journey [*les landes de notre voyage*]" [334]), Barbey embraces it as a locus of creation.

2. I call *L'Ensorcelée* a "story" rather than a "novel" because the narrator insists on this distinction. Further on, we will examine this distinction as it relates to the narrator's purported restraint.

3. "La Revue combat depuis son premier jour contre le dragon à plusieurs têtes du rationalisme moderne" (*Revue du Monde Catholique*, 1848, 160). In *L'Ensorcelée*, the figure of the monster *à plusieurs têtes* is used to represent the revolutionaries, murderers of La Clotte: "This crowd, this legion, this enormous multiple animal with many heads and many arms, lost some of its fleece or outer rank of men in the thickets along the road" (226; 708).

4. Norbert Dodille describes "the marvelous and the psychological" as a "ques-tion of codes, that the Narrator puts forth with such insistence only to underline its futility" (Dodille, "*L'Ensorcelée*: Les sources de l'histoire ou l'origine du mal," [165]. Alain Toumayan writes, "Structurally and rhetorically, the text attests to an epistemological effort and failure in the face of this tragic story" (Toumayan, *La littérature et la hantise du mal*, 28). Susanne Rossbach comments that this epistemo-logical failure is repeated at the lexical level, in expressions such as "amoureuse-ment cruelle" or "bleu d'enfer" that derail the search for meaning (Rossbach, "Dandyism in the Literary Works of Barbey d'Aurevilly: Ideology, Gender, and Nar-ration," 99). For Claudie Bernard, the story's epistemological complications repre-sent the historical obscurity that surrounds the Chouans (Bernard, *Le Chouan romanesque*).

5. F. Lecaplain writes, "[Barbey d'Aurevilly] succeeds bit by bit in nudging real-ity closer to the supernatural, or rather in infusing reality with the supernatural, which seems more and more to be an integral part of reality; it seems only a hidden aspect of reality, like a golden thread that, skillfully hidden, woven into a fabric, makes it shine" (Lecaplain, "Realité et surnaturel dans *l'ensorcelée* et *les diaboliques*," 65).

6. Leburruyer, "Les landes, paysage d'angoisse," 45.

7. Bloch-Dano and Zorla, *L'Ensorcelée, Barbey d'Aurevilly: Des repères pour situer l'auteur*, 62.

8. Ellenberger, *The Discovery of the Unconscious*, 208, 207, 615, 651; Groddeck, *The Book of the It*, 16; Freud, *Beyond the Pleasure Principle*, 44, 66.

9. Lévi-Strauss, *La pensée sauvage*, 326. Claudie Bernard, in *Le Chouan roman-esque*, describes science as a mechanism not of dissolution, but of reconstruction:

"Natural sciences today show themselves to be what indeed they have been for centuries: (re)creators of their object" (13).

10. Culler, *Structuralist Poetics*, 28. Twentieth-century trauma theories return to this notion of the fragmented mind. For instance, Jonathan Cohen writes, "Unmodified primal repressions are common to all psychopathology, where they operate like 'holes' in a person's mind. In these holes, structure is absent, in that there are no representations of need-satisfying interactions that provide the basis for symbolic interaction with the world and for goal-directed behavior. If there is mind in this region, there is only the crudest protosymbolic functioning, in which everything is capable of representing or becoming everything else" (Cohen, "Trauma and Repression," 180–81). And as Cathy Caruth (*Trauma: Explorations in Memory, Unclaimed Experience*), Shoshana Felman and Dori Laub (*Testimony: Crises of Witnessing in Literature, Psychoanalysis, and History*), and others have commented, "holes" in the mind become holes in the narrative.

11. As the narrator elsewhere declares: "Thank God, all this psychology is useless" (153, 659). And Michel Crouzet, who had commented on the flattening force of psychoanalysis in the context of *Le rouge*, writes of psychoanalysis: "What an enormous mill of oxymorons!" and declares that critics who "want to find [in psychoanalysis] a key to understanding Barbey, seem just to repeat him" (Crouzet, "Barbey d'Aurevilly et l'oxymore: Ou la rhetorique du diable," 83). Barbey would no doubt extend this warning to the modern sciences in general, indicating that to "explain" the world through the discourse of science is, in the end, to perpetuate and reproduce its disorder.

12. Mickel, "Barbey's 'Poetic' Technique in *L'Ensorcelée*," 419.

13. Djourachkovitch, *L'Ensorcelée*, 106.

14. Hirschi, "Barbey 'Conteur,'" 24.

15. Toumayan, *La littérature et la hantise du mal*, 113.

16. Djourachkovitch, *L'Ensorcelée*, 84.

17. Tranouez, *Fascination et narration dans l'œuvre romanesque de Barbey d'Aurevilly (La Croix-Jugan et la Grace Accordée)*, 253.

18. In the introduction of Jeanne Le Hardouey, the narrator describes her husband: "[Thomas Le Hardouey] had bought up government lands [*avait acquis des biens nationaux*], an active, industrious man, of the kind who springs up amid the ruins made by revolutions like gillyflowers, though less pure, in the crevices of crumbled walls [*comme les giroflées (mais un peu moins purs) dans les crevasses d'un mur croulé*]" (64; 599). Thomas sprouts from the financial and structural ruins of the dismantled church. The distribution of properties through the secular state is thus analogous to the proliferation of wild weeds, the residue, the fall-out from the deterioration of religion.

19. The catastrophe brought on by Marie Hecquet's improvised Angelus ("But what ought to save us sometimes brings ruin. This sign of the cross was her misfortune"), for instance, begs the question: if the *foudroiement social* is a divine punishment for the faltering faith of the people—that is, if the unbelieving have brought divine retribution upon themselves—why does this retribution fall on those who want, as Marie Hecquet does, to maintain their former religious practice? And, with respect to the narrator's earlier statement that "[the peasants] accept as an immutable fact, whose law is founded on their faith, the simultaneity which the Church has established between the festivals of its rituals and the movements of the sea-

sons": if absence of faith brought the *foudroiement*, why would the presence of faith not mitigate it? When this "simultaneity" breaks down, when the peasants' faith is shown to be ineffective as an enforcer of laws, "faith" becomes a sort of blindness, leading the faithful to disaster (Marie Hecquet) or disappointment (the peasants).

20. Ellenberger, *The Discovery of the Unconscious*, 313.

21. Dodille, "*L'Ensorcelée*: Les sources de l'histoire ou l'origine du mal," 165.

22. Rossbach, "Dandyism in the Literary Works of Barbey d'Aurevilly: Ideology, Gender, and Narration," 100.

23. Benjamin, *Illuminations*, 87.

24. Flaubert, *Madame Bovary*, trans. Paul de Man, 25–26; in the French edition, 37.

25. Ibid., 28; 41.

26. Seltzer, "Wound Culture," 3.

27. Ibid., 4. See also Richard Burton, *Blood in the City*, and Lynn Hunt, ed., *Eroticism and the Body Politic*.

28. Also in Seltzer's "Wound Culture" is a discussion of cartographies of wound culture, landscapes that represent the "pathological public sphere." Among these landscapes is a photograph by Richard Misrach entitled *Dead Animals #284* (Seltzer, 14). This photograph, though, is not of dead animals, but of a vast open terrain crossed by bulldozer tracks. These tracks, reminiscent of the gullies in the *lande*, constitute for Seltzer a scene of trauma, a landscape of pain. In *L'Ensorcelée*, that pain, the impoverishment of secularism, is centered in and on the body, in the crevices in Croix-Jugan's head: the narrative's foundational landscape.

29. There is also something theatrical in *L'Ensorcelée's* religious rituals and church services, reminiscent of the bishop of Agde practicing his benedictions in *Le rouge*. As in the case of Emma Bovary rushing to pray in the Rouen cathedral as Leon looks on or decorating her room with the accoutrements of a saint, of Varvara Pavlovna sinking onto her knees while Lavretsky looks on, of political leaders being repeatedly photographed in prayer, the narrator of *L'Ensorcelée* turns faith into something more or other than what it is, endows it with another element, a dramatic side, a contestation, and thus increases its value. When the church becomes the scene of murder (twice), and when the narrator writes that "all the pews in the church were occupied by the families who rent them by the year" (249; 724), the congregants become season ticket holders to the serial drama that *is* participation in religion.

30. This consciousness, this subtle self-admiration, is for the narrator of *Demons* a particularly unadmirable characteristic of Western narrators. It is also so for Turgenev, whose Varvara Pavlovna and Panshin are forever pausing to comment—not with contemplation but with indulgence—on their own reactions and feelings. Panshin announces at one point, " 'You're right. It's my eternal thoughtlessness that's to blame. So much damage has been done to me because of this thoughtlessness. As a result of it, I'm considered an egotist.' Panshin paused. Whatever subject he began a conversation with, he usually ended up talking about himself, changing the subject so easily, so smoothly, so sincerely, that it seemed unintentional" (343). The same critique of self-centeredness is present in Tolstoy, whose Hélène (*War and Peace*) has similar mannerisms to Varvara Pavlovna.

CHAPTER 5. THE NARRATOR WHO KNEW TOO MUCH

1. Likhachev, "Letopisnoe vremya u Dostoevskogo," 360.

2. Zundelovich, *Romany Dostoevskogo: Stat'i*, 110.

3. Matlaw, "The Chronicler of *The Possessed*: Character and Function," 37.

4. Fitzgerald, "Anton Lavrent'evic G–v: The Narrator as Re-Creator in Dostoevskij's *The Possessed*," 122–23.

5. Matlaw, "The Chronicler of *The Possessed*: Character and Function," 40–41.

6. Dostoevsky, *Demons*, trans. Richard Pevear and Larissa Volokhonsky, 7; in the Russian, *Besy*, vol. 10, p. 7 (hereafter, unless otherwise noted, all references to *Besy* are from vol. 10). Further references to both editions are given by page number in the text with the English first, followed by the Russian.

7. Matlaw, "The Chronicler of *The Possessed*: Character and Function," 44.

8. Cerny, *Dostoevsky and his Devils*, 50–51.

9. Gerald Prince's *Dictionary of Narratology* defines *fabula* as "the set of narrated situations and events in their chronological sequence; the basic STORY material (as opposed to PLOT or SJUZET), in Russian Formalist terminology" (30). *Sjuzet*, on the other hand, is defined thus: "In Russian Formalist terminology, the set of narrated situations and events in the order of their presentation to the receiver (as opposed to FABULA); the arrangement of incidents; MYTHOS; PLOT" (87).

10. Fitzgerald, "Anton Lavrent'evic G–v: The Narrator as Re-Creator in Dostoevskij's *The Possessed*," 124.

11. Jackson, *Dialogues with Dostoevsky: The Overwhelming Questions*, 279.

12. Zelnik, "'To the Unaccustomed Eye': Religion and Irreligion in the Experience of St. Petersburg Workers in the 1870s," 50.

13. Foxcroft, "The Spirit of an Age as Reflected in *Fathers and Sons* and *The Possessed*," 14.

14. Berdyaev, *Philosofiya, Tvorchestvo*, trans. Penny Burt, 362.

15. Ward, *Dostoyevsky's Critique of the West: The Quest for the Earthly Paradise*, 33.

16. Fitzgerald, "Anton Lavrent'evic G–v: The Narrator as Re-Creator in Dostoevskij's *The Possessed*," 124.

17. Ibid., 128.

18. Ward, *Dostoyevsky's Critique of the West : The Quest for the Earthly Paradise*, 31.

19. Holquist, *Dostoevsky and the Novel*, 135.

20. See, also, Anderson, *The Perverted Ideal in Dostoevsky's "The Devils."*

21. Jackson, *Dialogues with Dostoevsky: The Overwhelming Questions*, 279.

22. Berdyaev, *Philosofiya, Tvorchestvo*, trans. Penny Burt, 361.

23. *Madame Bovary*, trans. Paul de Man, 154; in the French edition, 219.

24. Jung, "On the Relation of Analytical Psychology to Poetry."

25. Jackson, *Dostoevsky's Quest for Form*, 81.

26. The shipwreck episode is reminiscent also of Herzen ("Oceano Nox," in *My Past and Thoughts*).

27. Bakhtin, *Problems of Dostoevsky's Poetics*, 71.

28. Ibid., 79. Radoyce discerned shades of Turgenev not in Karmazinov, but rather in Stepan Trofimovich.

29. André Gide, upholding Dostoevsky to a French audience, finds the characters' embodiment of ideas an antidote to abstraction and remove: "I am bound at once to add that he never approaches a question from the abstract, ideas never exist for him but as functions of his characters, wherein lies their perpetual relativity and source of power. . . . In conclusion I have only one comment to offer: though pregnant with thought, Dostoevsky's novels are never abstract, indeed, of all the books I know, they are the most palpitating with life." Gide, *Dostoevsky*, 16.

30. Peyre, "The French Face of Dostoevski," 122.
31. Matlaw, "The Chronicler of the *Possessed*: Character and Function," 45, 47.
32. Brooks, *Reading for the Plot*, 6.
33. Turgenev, *A Nobleman's Nest*, 199; in the Russian, *Dvoryanskoe Gnezdo*, 245. Hereafter page numbers from both editions will be cited in the text with the English translation first, followed by the Russian.
34. Dostoevsky, *PSS.*, vol. 28:190, trans. Penny Burt.
35. *Demons*, 683; *Besy*, vol. 11:6. Page numbers in the Russian edition from here on are from vol. 11 until otherwise indicated.
36. As Russell Valentino argues: "One of the symptoms of Stavrogin's disease, and by extension the sickness of radical thought in Dostoevsky's estimation, is an inability to understand figurative speech as such: . . . the figure always stands for potential fact" (Valentino, "The Word Made Flesh in Dostoevskii's *Possessed*," 42). And: "The fundamental confusion of the men of the forties lay in their idealization of reality; their offspring of the sixties merely invert the paradigm by an attempted realization of the ideal" (45).
37. Jones, *Dostoevsky*, 263.
38. *Demons*, 678; *Besy*, vol. 10:516. Page numbers in *Besy* from this point on are from vol. 10.
39. Holquist, *Dostoevsky and the Novel*, 147.
40. Matlaw, "The Chronicler of *The Possessed*: Character and Function," 39.
41. *Demons*, 483; *Besy*, vol. 10:370.
42. *The Holy Bible*. New York: Hawthorn Books, 1958. Eastern Orthodoxy is much rooted in Johannine scripture. Writes Sergei Bulgakov: "Eastern Christianity considers as its first apostle the Beloved Disciple whom Christ from the Cross gave as son to His Mother, the Apostle of love. Western Christianity is especially filled with the spirit of the two princes of the Apostles: Peter (Catholicism) and Paul (Protestantism). John wished to rest on the Master's breast, while Peter asked if two swords were enough and concerned himself with the organization of the Church. This explains the contemplative character of monastic life in the East. Here monasticism does not show the variety and the shades of difference evident in Catholic religious orders. Contemplation in the West is proper only to certain orders; in the East it is the characteristic trait of all monastic life" (Bulgakov, *The Orthodox Church*, 176). Cf. *Dostoevsky's New Testament*.
43. Dostoevsky, *PSS*, vol. 28:176, trans. Penny Burt.

CONCLUSION

1. Lukács, *The Theory of the Novel*, 103, 17.

Bibliography

Allen, Elizabeth. *Beyond Realism: Turgenev's Poetics of Secular Salvation.* Palo Alto, CA: Stanford University Press, 1992.

Anderson, Nancy K. *The Perverted Ideal in Dostoevsky's "The Devils."* New York: Peter Lang, 1997.

Bakhtin, Mikhail. *Problems of Dostoevsky's Poetics.* Edited and translated by Caryl Emerson. Minneapolis: University of Minnesota Press, 1984.

Barbey d'Aurevilly, Jules. *L'Ensorcelée.* Translated by Louise Collier Willcox. New York: Harper & Brothers, 1928.

———. *Œuvres romanesques complètes.* Vol. 1, *L'Ensorcelée.* Paris: Bibiliothèque de la Pléiade / Editions Gallimard, 1964.

———. Revue du Monde Catholique (1848): 160.

Barnes, Julien. *Flaubert's Parrot.* New York: Knopf, 1984.

Bell, David. *Circumstance: Chance in the Literary Text.* Lincoln: University of Nebraska Press, 1993.

Benjamin, Walter. *Illuminations.* Edited by Hannah Arendt. Translated by Harry Zohn. New York: Schocken Books, 1969.

Berdyaev, Nicholas. *Philosofiya, Tvorchestvo, Kultury I Iskusstva.* Vol. 1, *Salvation and Creativity,* translated by Penny Burt. Moscow: Izdatelstvo "Iskusstvo," 1994.

Bernard, Claud. *Philosophie.* Paris: Hatier-Boivin, 1954.

Bernard, Claudie. *Le Chouan Romanesque: Balzac, Barbey d'Aurevilly, Hugo.* Paris: Presses Universitaires de France, 1989.

Bersani, Leo. "Flaubert and Emma Bovary: The Hazards of Literary Fusion." In *Flaubert's Madame Bovary,* edited by Harold Bloom. New York: Chelsea House, 1988.

Blin, Georges. *Stendhal et les problèmes du roman.* Paris: Librarie José Corti, 1954.

Bloch-Dano, Evelyn, and Jacqueline Zorla. *L'Ensorcelée, Barbey d'Aurevilly: Des repères pour situer l'auteur.* Paris: Nathan, 1994.

Bourdieu, Pierre. *The Field of Cultural Production: Essays on Art and Literature.* New York: Columbia University Press, 1993.

Bourgois, René. *L'ironie romantique: Spectacle et jeu de Mme de Staël à Gérard de Nerval.* Grenoble, France: Presses Universitaires de Grenoble, 1974.

Brombert, Victor. *The Novels of Flaubert: A Study of Themes and Techniques.* Princeton, NJ: Princeton University Press, 1966.

———. *Stendhal: Fiction and the Themes of Freedom.* New York: Random House, 1968.

Brooks, Peter. *Reading for the Plot: Design and Intention in Narrative*. New York: Knopf, 1984.

Bulgakov, Sergius. *The Orthodox Church*. Translated by Elizabeth Cram. New York: Morehouse Publishing Company, 1944.

Burton, Richard. *Blood in the City: Violence and Revelation in Paris, 1789–1945*. Ithaca, NY: Cornell University Press, 2001.

Caruth, Cathy. *Trauma: Explorations in Memory*. Baltimore: Johns Hopkins University Press, 1995.

———. *Unclaimed Experience: Trauma, Narrative, and History*. Baltimore: Johns Hopkins University Press, 1996.

Cerny, Václav. *Dostoevsky and his "Devils."* Translated by F. W. Galan. Ann Arbor, MI: Ardis, 1975.

Chambers, Ross. *The Writing of Melancholy: Modes of Opposition in Early French Modernism*. Translated by Mary Seidman Trouille. Chicago: University of Chicago Press, 1993.

Chevreul, Michel-Eugène. *De la baguette diniatoire, du pendule explorateur, des tables tournantes, au point de vue de l'histoire, de la critique et de la méthode éxpérimentale*. Paris: Mallet-Bachelier, 1854.

Cohen, Jonathan. "Trauma and Repression." *Psychoanalytic Inquiry* 5 (1985): 163–89.

Crouzet, Michel. "Barbey d'Aurevilly et l'oxymore: Ou la rhetorique du diable." In *L'Ensorcelée et les diaboliques: La chose sans nom*, edited by Philippe Berthier, 83–98. Paris: Sedes, 1988.

———. "Julien Sorel et le sublime." *Revue d'Histoire Littéraire de la France* 86, no. 1 (1986): 86–108.

———. *Le rouge et le noir: Essai sur le romanesque Stendhalien*. Paris: Presses Universitaires de France, 1995.

Culler, Jonathan. *Flaubert: The Uses of Uncertainty*. Ithaca, NY: Cornell University Press, 1974.

———. *Structuralist Poetics: Structuralism, Linguistics and the Study of Literature*. Ithaca, NY: Cornell University Press, 1975.

Cupitt, Don. *Taking Leave of God*. New York: Crossroad, 1981.

Darwin, Charles. *The Expression of the Emotions in Man and Animals*. New York: Greenwood Press, 1955.

———. *The Origin of Species*. New York: Heritage, 1963.

Derrida, Jacques. *Of Grammatology*. Translated by Gayatri Spivak. Baltimore: Johns Hopkins University Press, 1975.

Djourachkovitch, Amélie. *L'Ensorcelée*. Paris: Presses Universitaires de France, 1998.

Dodille, Norbert. "*L'Ensorcelée*: Les sources de l'histoire ou l'origine du mal." In *Représentations de l'origine*, edited by Jean-Michel Racault, 157–66. Paris: Didier-Erudition, 1987.

Dostoevsky, Fyodor. *Demons*. Translated by Richard Pevear and Larissa Volokhonsky. New York: Vintage, 1994.

———. *Polnoe Sobranie Sochineniy* (*PSS*). Vol. 10–11, *Besy*. Leningrad: Nauka, 1974.

———. *Polnoe Sobranie Sochineniy* (*PSS*). Vol. 22. Leningrad: Nauka, 1974.

————. *Polnoe Sobranie Sochineniy (PSS)*. Vol. 28, *Letters, 1832–1859*. Leningrad: Nauka, 1974.

Ellenberger, Henri. *The Discovery of the Unconscious*. New York: Basic Books, 1970.

Felman, Shoshana. *La "folie" dans l'oeuvre romanesque de Stendhal*. Paris: Librairie José Corti, 1971.

Fitzgerald, Gene D. "Anton Lavrent'evic G–v: The Narrator as Re-Creator in Dostoevskij's *The Possessed*." In *New Perspectives on Nineteenth-Century Russian Prose*, edited by George Gutsche and Lauren Leighton, 121–34. Columbus, OH: Slavica, 1982.

Flaubert, Gustave. *Correspondance*. Paris: Conard, 1926–33.

————. *Madame Bovary*. Paris: Editions Garnier Frères, 1971.

————. *Madame Bovary*. Translated by Paul de Man. New York: W.W. Norton and Company, 1965.

Ford, Ford Madox. "Turgenev, the Beautiful Genius." In *Ivan Turgenev and Britain*, edited by Patrick Waddington, 1949–62. Oxford: Berg Publishers Limited, 1995.

Foxcroft, E. "The Spirit of an Age as Reflected in *Fathers and Sons* and *The Possessed*." *Unisa English Studies: Journal of the Department of English* 19, no. 2 (1981): 11–16.

Freeborn, Richard. *Turgenev: The Novelist's Novelist*. Oxford: Oxford University Press, 1960.

Freud, Sigmund. *Beyond the Pleasure Principle. Standard Edition 18*. London: Hogarth Press, 1955.

Genette, Gérard. *Narrative Discourse: An Essay in Method*. Translated by Jane E. Lewin. Ithaca, NY: Cornell University Press, 1980.

Gide, André. *Dostoevsky*. Translated by Arnold Bennett. Norfolk, CT: New Directions Books, 1949.

Ginsburg, Michal Peled. "On Not 'Yielding a Return': Plot and the Concept of Freedom in *The Red and the Black*." In *Approaches to Teaching Stendhal's "The Red and the Black,"* edited by Dean de la Motte and Stirling Haig, 96–103. New York: Modern Language Association of America, 1999.

Girard, René. *Des choses cachées depuis la fondation du monde*. Paris: B. Grasset, 1978.

Gregg, Richard. "The Wimp, the Maiden and the Mensch: Turgenev's Bermuda Triangle." *Russian Literature* 38 (1995): 51–82.

Groddeck, Georg. *The Book of the It*. Translated by V. M. E. Collins. London: Lund Humphries, 1950.

Herzen, Aleksandr. *My Past and Thoughts*. Translated by Constance Garnett. New York: Knopf, 1924.

Hirschi, Andrée. "Barbey 'Conteur.'" *La Revue des Lettres Modernes: Histoire des Idées des Littératures* 199–202 (1969): 7–30.

Holquist, Michael. *Dostoevsky and the Novel*. Princeton, NJ: Princeton University Press, 1977.

Holzman, Michael. *Lukács's Road to God: The Early Criticism against its Pre-Marxist Background*. Washington, DC: Center for Advanced Research in Phenomenology, 1985.

Hunt, Lynn. *Eroticism and the Body Politic*. Baltimore: Johns Hopkins University Press, 1991.

Jackson, Robert Louis. *Dialogues with Dostoevsky: The Overwhelming Questions.* Stanford, CA: Stanford University Press, 1993.

———. *Dostoevsky's Quest for Form.* New Haven, CT: Yale University Press, 1966.

James, Henry. *The Future of the Novel: Essays on the Art of Fiction.* New York: Vintage Books, 1956.

Jameson, Fredric. *The Political Unconscious: Narrative as a Socially Symbolic Act.* Ithaca: Cornell, 1981.

———. *A Singular Modernity: Essay on the Ontology of the Present.* London: Verso, 2002.

Janet, Pierre. *L'automatisme psychologique.* Paris: Alcan, 1889.

Jones, John. *Dostoevsky.* New York: Oxford University Press, 1983.

Jones, Malcolm. *Dostoevsky: The Novel of Discord.* New York: Barnes & Noble, 1976. 236.

Jung, Carl. *The Collected Works.* Edited by Herbert Read, Michael Fordham, Gerhard Adler. Translated by R. F. C. Hull. Vol 15, *On the Relation of Analytical Psychology to Poetry.* New York: Pantheon Books, 1983.

Kierkegaard, Søren. *Either/Or.* Translated by David Swenson and Lillian Marvin Swenson. Princeton, NJ: Princeton University Press, 1941, 1944.

La Fontaine, Jean. *The Complete Fables.* Translated by Norman Spector. Evanston, IL: Northwestern University Press, 1988.

———. *Fables.* Paris: Editions Garnier Frères, 1960.

Laub, Dori, and Shoshana Felman. *Testimony: Crises of Witnessing in Literature, Psychoanalysis, and History.* New York: Routledge, 1992.

Leburruyer, Pierre. "Les landes, paysage d'angoisse." *La Revue des Lettres Modernes: Histoire des Idées des Littératures* 137–40 (1966): 35–50.

Lecaplain, F. "Realité et surnaturel dans *L'Ensorcelée et les diaboloques*." In *L'Ensorcelée et les diaboliques: La chose sans nom,* edited by Philippe Berthier, 49–69. Paris: Sedes, 1988.

Lévi-Strauss, Claude. *La pensée sauvage.* Paris: Plon, 1962.

Likachev, D. S. "Letopisnoe vremya u Dostoevskogo." In *Poetica Drevnorusskoy Literaturi.* 2nd edition. Leningrad, 1971. Cited in Fitzgerald, 122.

Lukacher, Maryline. "*The Red and the Black:* Transforming the Maternal Myth." In *Approaches to Teaching Stendhal's "The Red and the Black,"* edited by Dean de la Motte and Stirling Haig, 148–54. New York: Modern Language Association of America, 1999.

Lukács, Georg. *The Theory of the Novel.* Translated by Anna Bostock. Cambridge, MA: MIT Press, 1971.

Lyotard, François. *The Postmodern Condition: A Report on Knowledge.* Translated by Geoff Bennington and Brian Massumi. Minneapolis: University of Minnesota Press, 1984.

Matlaw, Ralph, "The Chronicler of *The Possessed:* Character and Function." *Doestoevsky Studies: Journal of the International Dostoevsky Society* 5 (1984): 37–47.

Mickel, Emanuel. "Barbey's 'Poetic' Technique in *L'Ensorcelée*." *Romance Quarterly* 35, no. 4 (1988): 415–34.

Miller, D. A. *Narrative and its Discontents: Problems of Closure in the Traditional Novel.* Princeton, NJ: Princeton University Press, 1981.

Miller, J. Hillis. *The Disappearance of God: Five Nineteenth-Century Writers.* Cambridge, MA: Harvard University Press, 1963.

Morson, Gary Saul. *Narrative and Freedom: The Shadows of Time.* New Haven, CT: Yale University Press, 1994.

Mossman, Carol. *The Narrative Matrix: Stendhal's "Le Rouge et le Noir."* Lexington, KY: French Forum Publishers, 1984.

Naudin. "Revue Horticole." Cited in Darwin, *The Origin of Species.*

Nietzsche, Friedrich. *The Gay Science.* Translated by Walter Kaufmann. New York: Vintage Books, 1974.

———. *The Will to Power.* Translated by Walter Kaufmann and R. J. Hollingdale. New York: Random House, 1967.

Owens. "Address to the British Association." Cited in Darwin, *The Origin of Species.*

Pervushin, N. C. "Dostoevsky and Turgenev: A New Element in Their Relationship." *Dostoevsky Studies: Journal of the International Dostoevsky Society* 3 (1982): 191–92.

Petrey, Sandey. *Realism and Revolution: Balzac, Stendhal, Zola, and the Performances of History.* Ithaca, NY: Cornell University Press, 1988.

Peyre, Henri. "The French Face of Dostoevski." In *Dostoevski and the Human Condition after a Century,* edited by Alexej Ugrinsky, Alexej and Valija Ozolins. 115–30. New York: Greenwood Press, 1986.

Poulet, Georges. *Les Métamorphoses du Cercle.* Paris: Plon, 1961.

———. *The Metamorphoses of the Circle.* Translated by Carley Dawson and Elliott Coleman. Baltimore: Johns Hopkins Press, 1966.

Prince, Gerald. *The Dictionary of Narratology.* Lincoln: University of Nebraska Press, 1987.

Radoyce, Lubomir, "L'Idee de 'Realite' dans *Les Demons." Dostoevsky Studies: Journal of the International Dostoevsky Society* 5 (1984): 129–39.

Rémond, René. *Religion et société en Europe: Essai sur la secularisation aux XIXe et XXe siècles.* Paris: Seuil, 1998.

Richard, Jean-Pierre. *Littérature et sensation.* Paris: Editions du Seuil, 1954.

Ricoeur, Paul. *Time and Narrative.* 3 vols. Chicago: University of Chicago Press, 1984.

Ronell, Avital. *Crack Wars: Literarture Addiction Mania.* Lincoln: University of Nebraska Press, 1992.

Rossbach, Susanne. "Dandyism in the Literary Works of Barbey d'Aurevilly: Ideology, Gender, and Narration." *Modern Language Studies* 29, no. 1 (1999): 81–100.

Schopenhauer, Arthur. *Religion: A Dialogue.* Translated by T. Bailey Saunders. London: Swan Sonnenschein, 1899.

Seltzer, Mark. "Wound Culture: Trauma in the Pathological Public Sphere." *October* 80 (Spring 1997): 3–26.

Stendhal. *Red and Black.* Edited and translated by Robert Adams. New York: W. W. Norton, 1969.

———. *Le rouge et le noir.* Paris: Editions Garnier Frères, 1950.

Talbot, Emile. *Stendhal Revisited.* New York: Twayne Publishers, 1993.

Taylor, Charles. *Hegel.* Cambridge: Cambridge University Press, 1975.

Terdiman, Richard. *Discourse/Counter-Discourse: The Theory and Practice of Symbolic Resistance in Nineteenth-Century France.* Ithaca: NY: Cornell University Press, 1985.

Thibaudet, Albert. *Gustave Flaubert.* Paris: Editions Gallimard, 1935.

Thielicke, Helmut. *Nihilism: Its Origin and Nature—with a Christian Answer.* Translated by John Doberstein. Westport, CT: Greenwood Press, 1981.

Todorov, Tzvetan. *Poétique de la prose.* Paris: Éditions du Seuil, 1971.

Tolstoy, Leo. *Voina i mir.* Moscow: Khudozh Lit, 1978.

———. *War and Peace.* Translated by Louise and Aylmer Maude. New York: Simon and Schuster, 1942.

Toumayan, Alain. *La littérature et la hantise du mal.* Lexington, KY: French Forum, 1987.

Tranouez, Pierre. *Fascination et narration dans l'oeuvre romanesque de Barbey d'Aurevilly (La Croix-Jugan et la Grace Accordée).* Paris: Lettres Modernes, 1987.

Tunimanov, Vladimir. *Tvorchestvo Dostoevskogo.* Leningrad: Nauka, 1980.

Turgenev. *The Novels and Stories of Ivan Turgénieff.* Translated by Isabel Hapgood. Vol. 4, *A Nobleman's Nest.* New York: Charles Scribner's Sons, 1922.

———. *Sobranie Sochineniy.* Vol. 2, *Dvoryanskoe Gnezdo.* Moscow: Gosudarsvennoe Izdatelstvo, 1954.

Valentino, Russell. "The Word Made Flesh in Dostoevski"'s *Possessed.*" *Slavic Review: American Quarterly of Russian, Eurasian and East European Studies* 56, no. 1 (Spring 1997): 37–49.

Vine, Barbara. *The Chimney Sweeper's Boy.* New York: Harmony Books, 1998.

Vogüé, E. M. *Le roman russe.* Paris: Editions l'Age d'Homme, 1886.

Ward, Bruce. *Dostoyevsky's Critique of the West: The Quest for the Earthly Paradise.* Waterloo, ON: Wilfrid Laurier University Press, 1986.

Watt, Ian. *The Rise of the Novel: Studies in Defoe, Richardson, and Fielding.* London: Chatto & Windus, 1960.

White, Hayden. *Metahistory: The Historical Imagination in Nineteenth-Century Europe.* Baltimore: Johns Hopkins University Press, 1973.

Wing, Nathaniel. *The Limits of Narrative: Essays on Baudelaire, Flaubert, Rimbaud, and Mallarme.* Cambridge: Cambridge University Press, 1986.

Wood, James. *The Broken Estate: Essays on Literature and Belief.* New York: Random House, 1999.

Woodward, James. "Determinism in the Novels of Turgenev." *Scando-Slavico* 34 (1988): 17–27.

———. *Metaphysical Conflict: A Study of the Major Novels of Ivan Turgenev.* Munich: Varlag Otto Sagner, 1990.

Woolf, Virginia. "The Novels of Turgenev." In *Ivan Turgenev and Britain,* edited by Patrick Waddington, 143–48. Oxford, UK: Berg Publishers, 1995.

Wortman, Richard. *Scenarios of Power: Myth and Ceremony in Russian Monarchy.* Princeton, NJ: Princeton University Press, 1995.

Zelnik, Reginald. " 'To the Unaccustomed Eye': Religion and Irreligion in the Experience of St. Petersburg Workers in the 1870s." In *Christianity and the Eastern Slavs*. Vol. 2, *Russian Culture in Modern Times,* edited by Robert P. Hughes and Irina Paperno, 49–82. Berkeley: University of California Press, 1994.

Zundelovich, J. *Romany Dostoevskogo: Stat'i.* Tashkent: Srednajaja i vyssaja skola USSR.

Index

(Continued from front flap)

Especially in nineteenth-century Europe, secularism was an idea in motion, formed, disseminated, and received both with bursts of creativity and with gloom. It was seen as a code for intellectual clarity and spiritual emptiness, sometimes for both at once. It was also considered as a philosophical condition, a view of a world in need of, or open to, a different narrative. European literary criticism of that century generally reads secularism as a condition of absence or loss. Despite such critical assessments secularism is not a random spiritual disaster, not a cosmic accident, but a human creation. There was not a single morning when the world woke up, sensed a curious absence, and understood that God had departed. Instead, secularism developed as an idea that was introduced and absorbed into modern thought because it held considerable attraction. The elimination of God from master narratives—indeed, the elimination of master narratives entirely—constitutes not simply a menace but also a significant series of opportunities. Secularism and attendant philosophies such as capitalism promise a way to be exceptional—to expand the boundaries and indeed the very quality and volume of self.

The transition to a world without God generates major questions about individual power and voice, order and justice. And as the foundational discourse for a modern conception of self, history, and social relations, narrative is crucial to our attempts to answer these questions—questions that have particular currency today. *A World Abandoned by God* uses the lens of narrative construction to analyze modern political structures and ideologies and to understand one of the momentous conceptual metamorphoses in history: the elimination of God from the modern landscape.

LC 2005012254
ISBN 0-8387-5609-3
Printed in the U.S.A.

Jacket design and original artwork by Brian Pope